SHAKESPEARE
New Evidence

A. D. WRAIGHT

ADAM HART (Publishers) Ltd.
LONDON U.K.

Other books by A. D. Wraight

In Search of Christopher Marlowe
with Virginia F. Stern
First published 1965, London and NY
Reissued paperback, February 1993

Christopher Marlowe and Edward Alleyn
First published 1993

The Story That the Sonnets Tell
First published 1994

First Published in 1996 by
ADAM HART (Publishers) Ltd.
London, England

Cover design by Peter Cordeaux

A Catalogue Record of this title
is held in the British Library.

Hardback   ISBN 1 897763 08 5
Paperback   ISBN 1 897763 09 3

Printed and bound by THE CROMWELL PRESS
Broughton Gifford, Melksham, Wiltshire, England

*To Alexandre Solzhenitsyn
and all who suffer persecution
for conscience sake*

SHAKESPEARE
NEW EVIDENCE

CONTENTS

PART THREE
THE EVIDENCE REVIEWED

ILLUSTRATIONS

APPENDICES

SHAKESPEARE
NEW EVIDENCE

FOREWORD

In the archives of Lambeth Palace Library three astonishing sets of documents have been discovered. They are a group of letters, a remarkable list of books constituting a personal library, and a catalogue of intelligence reports all relating to the same secret agent. They are filed in four MS volumes dated 1595 and 1596. These documents may well eventually prove to be among the most significant finds ever made in the world of literature, since together they provide us with the final piece in that highly contentious jigsaw puzzle entitled, "Who was the real Shakespeare?"

Whilst any one of them on its own would raise serious questions and open up new avenues of research on an exciting scale, it is the combination of all three items, that all mutually reinforce each other, that makes their discovery of such outstanding importance.

This totally new documentary evidence is the crowning corollary of the research presented in my recently published thesis, *The Story That the Sonnets Tell* (Feb 1995), which I have dedicated to the memory of J. Leslie Hotson, the great Sherlock Holmes of the Elizabethan era as I have called him, on whose unique researches in *Shakespeare's Sonnets Dated* (1949), *The First Night of Twelfth Night* (1954), and *Mr. W.H.* (1964) I have built my thesis. In my recent book I had suggested areas of new research requiring thorough investigation, particularly by decoding the ciphered letters in the Anthony Bacon Papers, where I believed evidence might yet be found. Peter Farey offered his computer expertise to decode these, which was the first step in this investigation. What emerged, however, was entirely unexpected. Surprising new evidence presented itself almost unasked, which amazingly corroborates what I had so far established from other sources, and even more surprising is where this evidence was discovered. Not, as I had expected, in those pages all written in an Elizabethan numerical cipher, which, being decoded, revealed only information relating to intelligence gathered in Spain that turned out to be from the agent Anthony Rolston, over his code signature 'iio'. This was a false trail. The evidence was simply lying there in the open manuscripts waiting to be discovered in these neglected archives of potentially vitally important documentation.

These newly discovered documents are presented in the second half of this paper. The first half is primarily devoted to a recapitulation of my thesis on the Sonnets, as this is the basis of the evidence defining the life of the great dramatist we know as Shakespeare, whose true identity has long been suspect. In taking my orientation from Leslie Hotson's highly original research referred to above, I have fundamentally realigned its focus, which in Hotson's works was aimed at relating all his findings to the person of William Shakespeare of Stratford-upon-Avon, in which he encountered considerable difficulties. Effectually to bring in William Shakespeare, Hotson had necessarily forced his evidence into a straitjacket to fit the preconceived author of the plays and the Sonnets as the Warwickshire actor, presenting an unconvincing association. This was uncomfortable to orthodox Stratfordian tradition and Hotson's idiosyncratic conclusions have not won wide support, in particular because he challenged the long accepted identification of Henry Wriothesley, 3rd Earl of Southampton, as Shakespeare's patron, improbably addressed as 'Mr. W.H.' although his initials are H.W., and an earl may not be addressed as plain Mr., be he H.W. or W.H.

'Mr. W.H.' aside, there is the even more important problem that the content of the Sonnets has been widely acclaimed as **autobiographical** by a major consensus of authoritative and informed scholarly opinion embracing: W.H. Auden, Sir Stephen Spender, C. L. Barber, J. Dover Wilson, G. B. Harrison, A. W. Schlegel, G. P. V. Akrigg, F. S. Boas, Walter Raleigh, Leslie A. Fielder, F. J. Furnivall, A. C. Bradley, J. Leslie Hotson, William Wordsworth, and Edmund Malone, who first mooted this opinion – the list of eminent scholars and poets who hold this opinion, often with passionate conviction, could be extended almost indefinitely. In more recent academic fashion there has been a reaction expressing cynical doubts that these 154 beautiful poems really represent Shakespeare's autobiographical legacy to posterity, his "poetic diary"; but, as James Winny has observed, "the notion that the Sonnets are to be read as a journal of their author's private affairs becomes very difficult to discredit".[1] Such critics as Kenneth Muir, who have tried to discount their autobiographical nature, end up "in a muddle".[2]

The problem is that we have here an inherent paradox. The Sonnets are autobiographical according to general consensus, yet the intensively researched evidence of the life of William Shakespeare cannot be related to a single event, or person, in the sonnet-story, in which many of the poems are written as verse-letters to his dear friend and patron. Nothing seems to fit. This has given rise to the epithet, **The Riddle of the Sonnets**, a mystery so dense and inscrutable that we have been warned against entering the "Wandering Wood" and "Error's Den" of "the Serbonian Sonnet-bog in which whole armies have been sunk".[3] This dire admonition comes from the defeated Logan Pearsall Smith. More recently, another frustrated scholar has come up with the extraordinary idea that T. T. (Thomas Thorpe) was really dedicating the book of the Sonnets to their author William Shakespeare himself, and that 'Mr. W.H.' is merely a printer's error for 'Mr. W.SH.'.[4] Such a total retreat from research begs the question and closes the door with a derisory slam.

Repeated failure to resolve the Sonnet riddle left the challenge wide open, until, girding his loins, it was taken up in his penultimate work by the redoubtable Leslie Hotson in Shakespeare's quatercentenary year, 1964. This remarkably innovative thinker, by applying his deep knowledge of all things Elizabethan, has finally cracked the conundrum of 'Mr. W.H.'. This represents a giant step forward. Even so, it is only half the solution of the Riddle of the Sonnets. This paper presents the other half in a retrospect of what has already been published, plus the exciting, recently discovered new evidence.

In following in Hotson's footsteps I have asked the questions he left unasked. The first of these is: **Why is it that the evidence of William Shakespeare's life does not**

---

[1] James Winny: *The Master-Mistress: A Study of Shakespeare's Sonnets* (1968) London, p.1
[2] Donald W. Foster: 'Master W.H., R.I.P.': *PMLA Vol. 102, No.1, Jan 1987*, p.51
[3] Logan Pearsall Smith: *On Reading Shakespeare* (1939) p.29
[4] Donald W. Foster: *op. cit.* pp.42-52

correspond in any way with what the Sonnets tell us about the author whose autobiographical poems these are? This is answered in precise detail as the main argument presented here.

The second question is: **Why did Thomas Thorpe decide to publish this beautiful sonnet-sequence by the most praised poet of the day in a *cryptic* edition, with a cryptic dedication to a mysterious 'Mr. W.H.'?** The only possible reason for a cryptic publication must be that there was something important to conceal. This poses both a challenge and a clue.

The mysterious 'Mr. W.H.' is, moreover, also sexually involved with the poet's mistress, the equally mysterious Dark Lady. Hotson alone finally discovered the clues and tracked down the identities of both 'Mr. W.H.' and the Dark Lady. This achievement is his monument.

Hotson's brilliant double identification is the basis of my thesis, though with a different slant.

I submit, in conclusion, that if we are genuinely concerned to find the historical truth about Shakespeare, rather than in promulgating more myths about him, research must be extended, despite failures, by asking the relevant questions with an open mind, not subject to academic politics. A courageous stand needs to be taken in pursuing research in the controversial, grey areas surrounding Shakespeare which have been evaded, recognizing the cryptic element, and the involvement with symbolism inherent in Elizabethan culture.

The pioneering research of Dame Frances Yates, whose work has been too little heeded, has pointed us in this direction. Her illuminating research has revealed the historical context in which the study of Shakespeare must be rooted, if we are ever really to understand this genius and his amazing life.

Acknowledgements

I wish to express my sincere thanks to the staff of Lambeth Palace Library, and especially to Miss Melanie Barber, Deputy Librarian and Archivist, for her generous assistance in obtaining the photographs of the manuscripts we have been allowed to reproduce from this treasure trove of archival documents. It has been a privilege to work in this delightful, secluded oasis of learning. In researching the Anthony Bacon Papers my debt to Peter Farey is especially gratefully acknowledged for his help in meeting the time-scale set for publication of this new evidence. He came forward initially offering to decode the ciphered letters and pursued his research from three sets of microfilm reels I gave him to enable him to work near home without travelling to London, whilst I pursued my research at Lambeth Palace Library. Subsequently he took upon himself, unsolicited, the time-consuming task of analyzing the amazing library of fifty-six books belonging to the intelligence agent whose identity every piece of data seemed to confirm as the quarry I was seeking, and his considerable industry forms the basis of Part Two of this book.

My warm appreciation herewith to Mme Lucie Bouchon for her invaluable help in translating the sixteenth century French texts of the many letters and documents from the Anthony Bacon Papers with such enthusiasm, making our collaboration a memorable pleasure. I am also grateful to Roger Smithson for his helpful editorial criticisms with the suggestion that readers would appreciate having transcripts of the important letters by Le Doux provided in the Appendix, and then making these with meticulous accuracy, and also suggesting the inclusion of a map.

Finally, my thanks to all my ever supportive family and friends, including many in The Marlowe Society who have given me loyal support and constant help in many ways, most especially to: Frieda and Peter Barker, our President Colin Niven, June Everett, George Metcalfe, Geraldine Hanning, Irene and Ken Pickering. Their enthusiasm for my work has meant a great deal. And also to many who have helped in the production of this book: to Georgie Robins for her endless patience in word processing this book through all its vicissitudes with such care; to Rico Gusman for his artistic and computer skills, and to Peter Cordeaux for allowing me to use his cover design from the King's School Brochure for the 1993 King's Week Quatercentenary Commemoration of Marlowe's tragedy at Deptford; but, above all, most gratefully for invaluable intellectual and material support, to my dear friends Virginia Stern and Wolfgang Deninger, and to Steve Pae and Brendon Glover and Borrie Hyman, who recognized the importance of this research and helped to make it possible for me to bring this work to a state of completion for publication, although information from these voluminous papers is, I believe, not yet exhausted. I hope this book will inspire other scholars to enter this exciting field of research.

A. D. Wraight
August 1996

PART ONE

THE STORY THAT THE SONNETS TELL

A. D. Wraight

*"When a man's verses cannot be understood, nor a man's good
wit seconded with the forward child understanding, it strikes a
man more dead than a great reckoning in a little room."*

Touchstone. *As You Like It*, III, iii 9-13

As introduction to the presentation of new evidence in this paper, I give a review of my research published in *The Story That the Sonnets Tell* which has added a new dimension to Hotson's findings by following up the foregoing two important questions posed in the Foreword.

First, however, it is necessary to state briefly the reasons for rejecting the Stratfordian orthodox case accepting William Shakespeare as the author of the great works, including the Sonnets, which are indeed autobiographical and will lead us unerringly to the real author – the pseudonymous Shakespeare.

He is the supposedly murdered, deeply misunderstood and unjustly maligned Canterbury-born genius, Christopher Marlowe, who was already England's premier poet-dramatist at the time of his faked death at Deptford on 30th May 1593, when he was aged twenty-nine. This event is the dire secret that the cryptic publication of his autobiographical sonnets was concealing, whilst at the same time leaving clues for its discovery. That is the conclusion to which the evidence, as it unfolds, will inevitably lead.

William Shakespeare of Stratford-upon-Avon

The case against William Shakespeare has been best stated by Sir George Greenwood whose books remain classics in the field. This eminent barrister-at-law and Parliamentarian caused a furore in the first quarter of the twentieth century with *The Shakespeare Problem Restated* (1908), *Is There a Shakespeare Problem?* (1916) and *Ben Jonson and Shakespeare* (1921), but orthodoxy finally doused the flames and has been able to ignore the arguments by united academic determination in the absence of any convincing alternative candidate. Greenwood confined himself to the presentation of the negative evidence for the Stratfordian case, which is, in fact, unanswerable. His conclusion sums it up.

> "My last comment on the life of William Shakespeare of Stratford shall be this.
> Meagre as our knowledge of it is, it is yet too much. [5]Mr. Lee's claim that we
> have a 'mass of biographical detail which far exceeds that of any poet

---

[5]   This is Sir Sidney Lee, the great Shakespearean scholar.

contemporary with Shakespeare' is indeed sufficiently ridiculous, but it would be far better for the Stratfordian theory if we had no biographical detail at all. If we knew nothing we might imagine anything. What we do know is fatal to the case. It gives rise to the strongest possible presumption against the identity of Shakespeare the player with Shakespeare the poet."[6]

This negative evidence is the fertile ground from which has sprung the sheer number of Shakespearean authorship candidates, which has discredited the whole authorship question by the wide variety of discrepant theories, that are readily written off as the quasi-historical hobby of the multi-national dabblers who have dredged some sixty-four putative Shakespeares from the pool of their invention. What other author has ever been subjected to such doubts challenging his authorship? Only by stoutly protecting Shakespeare as a national icon, and arguing back from the marvellous plays to imbue the unremarkable actor's character with all those qualities of genius that are revealed in the poems and plays, is it possible to maintain the myth of his authorship. By this argument *in circulo* the negative evidence is conveniently circumvented, and the "divine William" remains on his pedestal awaiting the arrival of the true candidate to take his rightful place, all conditions fulfilled.

The first self-evident reason for doubting William Shakespeare's authorship of the works published in his name is the fact of his limited education. He lived in an age when books were expensive and not easily obtained in such a provincial backwater as Stratford-upon-Avon, so that self-education was not an option for him as is erroneously assumed and hotly argued by critics in his defence. The potential of genius was recognized early in his exact contemporary, the shoemaker's son Christopher Marlowe, who was awarded a scholarship to the King's School, Canterbury, and thence a scholarship to Cambridge. Had such genius existed in the glover's son of Stratford it is inconceivable that no glimmer would have been noticed by his grammar school master. Most significantly, *this* is what is reflected in his entire adult life.

William Shakespeare's lack of any hint of the intellectual qualities that are so amply evident in the plays is borne out by his working life spent in the company of the actors of the Lord Chamberlain's company, from which he never moved except to visit his home town where he purchased property. His careful and detailed will mentions not a single book or manuscript of a playscript or poem, and no literary or intellectual friends. Not even a mention of Ben Jonson who is supposed to have been his bosom friend. Shakespeare left money to purchase memorial rings to his fellow actors, Burbage, Heminge and Condell, and presumably they attended his funeral when he was quietly interred by his family. Yet this was the greatest poet-dramatist of his day!

It was unheard of for even a minor poet to die without some honour being paid by his fellow poets and writers. When Edmund Spenser died his funeral expenses were borne by the Earl of Essex and he was laid to rest in all honour in Westminster Abbey. When Shakespeare died, his patron, the Earl of Southampton, *took not the slightest notice*!

---

[6] George Greenwood: *The Shakespeare Problem Restated* (1908, Athenaeum Press, London ed. 1937) pp.50-1.
See A. D. Wraight: *The Story That the Sonnets Tell* (1995) Chap. IV 'The Broken Link' and Chap.V 'The Shakespeare Mythos'.

When Francis Beaumont died in the same year as Shakespeare, he too was buried in Westminster Abbey, mourned in verse by his fellow poets. When Ben Jonson died, his fellow writers poured forth such a spate of elegiac verses that they were collected in a book, and he was also buried with general mourning in Westminster Abbey. George Chapman's monument in the parish church of St Giles-in-the-Fields was designed by Inigo Jones and poets and intellectual friends mourned his passing. All Shakespeare's contemporary poets and dramatists were similarly honoured. Even the murdered and disgraced Marlowe was mourned in 1593 by George Peele in his poem 'The Honour of the Garter' with the accolade, "Unhappy in thine end, Marlowe the Muses darling", and Henry Petowe wrote: "But Marlowe, still admir'd Marlowe's gone/ To live with beauty in Elysium". Only Shakespeare, the greatest of them all, was totally ignored.

Not until some seven years later was acknowledgement of his greatness made in handsome amends with the appearance of the First Folio, containing memorial verses which hardly explain why he had died seven years before in obscurity, but some of which are certainly cryptic. Pointed reference is made by Leonard Digges to the monument, which suggests that this had been only recently erected. As my research in the Masonic archives reveals, this was erected by the Freemasons, and the great book of the First Folio was a Masonic publication in which the memorial verses and, in particular, Ben Jonson's Ode "To the memory of my beloved, the AUTHOR", have a cryptic purpose. Ben Jonson's contradictory statements about Shakespeare are part of this enigma. These mysteries are dealt with elsewhere, for this research is too extensive to *précis* here.[7]

What is of some significance for the present paper is the complete lack of any valid evidence to show that Shakespeare lived anywhere other than in Stratford-upon-Avon until 1593, when he was aged twenty-nine. In June 1593 his name appeared for the first time in the publication of *Venus and Adonis* by his friend, the printer Richard Field, who hailed from Stratford and had been apprenticed to the Huguenot printer Thomas Vautrollier and at his death inherited his Black Letter press, and later married his widow. Vautrollier had been in trouble with the reactionary Court of Star Chamber for printing unauthorized books, such as the sermons of Martin Luther, and Field continued his policy of publishing quality books that would have been of interest to such questioning intellectuals as Marlowe.

What brought William Shakespeare to London in early 1593? It was probably the severe economic depression in Stratford-upon-Avon where poverty and unemployment were rife that drove him to seek employment elsewhere. We know that Shakespeare's father was in debt.[8] There may also have been some truth in the traditional tale of William Shakespeare's persecution for poaching deer from the lands of Sir Thomas Lucy that encouraged his flight from his native town. In London his old friend Richard Field would probably be the first person he would turn to for lodging and help in gaining employment. This is conjecture. What is certain is that *Venus and Adonis* was in print by 12th June, thirteen days after the murder of Christopher Marlowe at Deptford, launching the hitherto unknown name of a new poet, William Shakespeare, claiming this long narrative poem as "the first heir of my invention" in its dedication to the Earl of

---

[7] See my forthcoming book: *The Legend of Hiram: Shakespeare & the Freemasons*.

[8] Samuel Schoenbaum: *William Shakespeare: A Compact Documentary Life* (1977, OUP, London & NY. Paperback 1978), p.42.

Southampton. It also bore a Latin motto culled from Ovid's *Amores*. One has to ask oneself, is this the Stratford-bred man of an impoverished family with little education? Where had he got hold of Ovid's *Amores*? However, we suspend disbelief in favour of impartiality, but it is certainly an audacious quotation, as is the choice of the dedicatee who is an earl, no less.

Vilia miretur vulgus: mihi flavus Apollo
Pocula Castalia plena ministret aqua

This, in Marlowe's translation of Ovid's *Amores*, is rendered in italics below, but note its conclusion.

Let base conceited wits admire vile things,
Fair Phoebus lead me to the Muses' springs.
About my head be quivering myrtle wound,
And in sad lovers' heads let me be found.
The living, not the dead, can envy bite,
For after death all men receive their right.
Then though death rakes my bones in funeral fire,
I'll live, and as he pulls me down mount higher.

This chosen quotation is in the style of an *impresa* or cryptic motto in which the clue is this: only those who know the rest of the quote will understand it fully and perceive the message. What is so striking about this quote from Ovid is that it precisely reflects Marlowe's situation when he was launching his chosen pseudonym, William Shakespeare, the name of the friend of Richard Field from Stratford-upon-Avon who had fortuitously come to London at just this time. Here I have plunged straight into the hypothesis that Marlowe escaped from the net of the Court of Star Chamber that was closing in on him, using a plot staging his faked death, and that he is the pseudonymous Shakespeare.

Field had registered the poem **Venus and Adonis** on 18th April 1593 without any mention of the author, as was common practice. One month later the poem would have been ready for the press when Marlowe (freed on bail) could have called on Field about his poem, and by strange coincidence met one William Shakespeare (who was likewise in trouble) at Field's print shop. A coincidence? There is much in this history that is stranger than fiction.

A deal with the help of Field, the sympathetic advanced-thinking printer, could have been struck then and there to arrange for a pseudonym for his new poem. If so, the impoverished man from Stratford would have received assurance of payment for his name, his silence, and his entry as a shareholder in a players' company who, in 1594, after the prohibition of playing in London on account of the plague, would have been delighted to welcome a shareholder with money and the promise of quality plays for which he would act as their playbroker. It is Greenwood who suggested that the role of William Shakespeare of Stratford was as playbroker, a role that fits his character to perfection, a good reliable man, discreet and having a sound business sense.[9]

---

9   Greenwood: *Ben Jonson and Shakespeare* (1921), pp.26-7.

In the quotation from Ovid the reference to "sad lovers' heads" perfectly fits the description of *Hero and Leander* which Marlowe was then writing, but which he did not have time to finish before his tragedy overtook him. *Venus and Adonis* was an earlier poem, and inferior to his exquisite *Hero and Leander*, probably written with Southampton in mind when in 1590 he wrote seventeen sonnets to him on a commission from the Earl's legal guardian, Lord Burghley, as will be explained later.

This appraisement fits the chronology of the known events in 1593 precisely. It has the ring of truth and casts credible light on the vexed relationship between Marlowe, the established, famous dramatist, then in dire trouble, and the man from Stratford who became his playbroker.

This is further borne out by my research correcting the long-held, erroneous assumption that Shakespeare is identifiable as the conceited great actor described by the envious dramatist Robert Greene, as he lay dying of dropsy and the pox in September 1592, as "an upstart Crow, beautified with our feathers, that with his *Tygers hart wrapt in a Players hyde* supposes he is as well able to bombast out a blanke verse as the best of you: and beeing an absolute *Iohannes fac totum*, is in his owne conceit the onely Shake-scene in a countrey".[10]

Superficially this looks as though it might be a reference to Shakespeare, but two features of the text weaken this argument. The words "Crow" and "Shake-scene" are used as common nouns denoting an actor and neither is italicized, but only capitalized, as was common practice by Elizabethan printers who always italicized *proper nouns*. The name Greene has chosen for the great actor he is lampooning is *"Iohannes fac totum"* not "Shake-scene", which is not intended as homophonously naming a man whose name is Shakespeare, Shakeshaft or Shake-anything, any more than "Crow" is intended for a man named Mr. Crowe. Secondly, the deliberately altered line taken from a current play is from the Pembroke play, *The True Tragedy of Richard Duke of York*. This play is an early quarto of *3 Henry VI*, attributed to Marlowe by Bakeless, Tucker Brooke and Allison Gaw as chief of the scholars who have expressed this opinion, based on their definitive researches not matched by anyone else. That is, until the recent work in the different field of computerized analysis of style that is the result of an interesting collaborative study by T. V. N. Merriam and Robert A. J. Matthews, whose findings support the attribution of *2 and 3 Henry VI* to Marlowe's authorship.[11] These are all orthodox Shakespearean scholars whose findings are in no way influenced by my thesis presenting Marlowe as the pseudonymous Shakespeare. Gaw also rejects as untenable the long-held hypothesis that Shakespeare could have been "Shake-scene", which has become the linchpin of the Stratfordian case because it argues that he was in London by 1592 already writing plays. Not until 1594 is he first recorded as an actor with the Lord Chamberlain's Men, and the first performance of a Shakespeare play, *Titus Andronicus*, is recorded in January 1594. This play has a significant history.[12]

---

[10] See A. D. Wraight: *Christopher Marlowe and Edward Alleyn* (1993), pp.132-5.

[11] T. V. N. Merriam and Robert A. J. Matthews: 'Neural Computation in Stylometry II: An Application to the Works of Shakespeare and Marlowe', *Literary and Linguistic Computing, Vol.9, No.1, 1994*, OUP.

[12] See Wraight: *The Story That the Sonnets Tell*, pp.359-62.

The conclusive argument for dismissing the identification of Shakespeare as "Shake-scene" is the existence of irrefutable evidence that he was Edward Alleyn, against whom Greene was pitiably railing because he had refused to succour him with yet another loan when he was down-and-out, and a very sick man. Greene had a long-standing business relationship with Alleyn, for whom he wrote his plays, and who acted as unofficial banker to the impecunious dramatists when they needed advance payments on the plays they were writing for his company, the Lord Admiral's Men. Greene was dependent on Alleyn, which he resented, and was deeply envious of his affluence, derived not only from his outstanding histrionic gifts, but from the many strings to his bow, including the writing of plays for his own company to perform. Greene poured scorn on Alleyn's playwriting activity which imitated his "betters" in being couched in blank verse, but showed a sometimes strange use of a "Dogberry"-like use of English words. Alleyn revered learning but was self-educated. He often purchased books and left a respectable small library in his will, unlike Shakespeare. The evidence that Alleyn is both the "Player" lampooned in Greene's *Groatsworth of Wit* semi-autobiographical allegory, and the *"Iohannes fac totum"* of the extremely bitter *Groatsworth* Letter is flawless.[13]

The research reconstructing the mighty quarrel between Greene and Alleyn, which caused a lively scandal in London's theatrical world in the autumn of 1592, has been presented at length in my study of Edward Alleyn, together with a critical review of the orthodox case for Shakespeare-"Shake-scene" offered for comparison[14], so that the reader can make up his or her own mind.

This fallacy has bedevilled Shakespearean study and skewed our understanding of what was really taking place in an episode of some historical importance because of the repercussions it had on the misfortunes of Marlowe. It was Greene, motivated by envy, who sounded the first knell of the doom that was to overwhelm the "famous gracer of Tragedians" six months later in the spring of 1593.

Christopher Marlowe was then the acknowledged leading poet-dramatist of the London stage, virtually without rival. He was also a well trusted government secret agent working in the career to which he had been recruited while still completing his studies at Cambridge, probably after gaining his BA in 1584 when he was aged twenty.

Lord Burghley, as Chancellor of the University of Cambridge, used it as his recruiting ground to seek out intelligent young men to work in the espionage service assiduously developed by Sir Francis Walsingham who, as Secretary of State in charge of foreign affairs, needed an efficient intelligence service; and, most importantly, its function was to protect the Queen's life from the constant assassination plots fomented by her Catholic enemies. In this Marlowe had performed signal service even whilst at Cambridge. He had thus been weaned from his ordained path to enter the Anglican church, and had gained highly placed friends at the Court. These were now to stand him in good stead in the turning of the wheel of Fate which was about to bring his downfall.

---

[13] Wraight: *Christopher Marlowe and Edward Alleyn*, pp.160-4 and pp.274-80.
[14] *Ibid*: Chap. VI, 'The Case for "Shake-Scene" Presented by the New Orthodoxy'.
See D. Allen Carroll: 'Greene's "Vpstart Crow" Passage: A Survey of Commentary', *Research Opportunities in Renaissance Drama XXVIII* (1985) Univ. of Kansas, ed. David M. Bergerson.

MARLOWE'S TRAGEDY

The events now run to a swift conclusion. The story is nothing if not dramatic. It is also extraordinary: full of anomalies and unanswered queries.

The background is the early months of 1593 with London in the grip of rising plague. Riots had broken out against the influx of immigrants from the Netherlands, whose rivalry in trade threatened the livelihoods of the City tradesmen and their apprentices. March and April rumbled with sporadic outbursts of discontent. On 5th May a "lewd and malicious libel" in doggerel verse was pinned onto the wall of the Dutch churchyard openly inciting violence against the foreigners. Officers of the Star Chamber Court, which had responsibility for quelling riots, were ordered to search the rooms of the playwrights who had recently collaborated in writing a play, dramatizing the life of Sir Thomas More, involving scenes of riots. One of these was a friend of Marlowe's, Thomas Kyd.

A search of Kyd's room revealed nothing to connect him with the libellous verses, but something far more incriminating was found amongst his papers. Namely, a copy of an heretical treatise, which was immediately seized upon as evidence of 'atheism'. This serious crime still carried the punishment of burning at the stake. Kyd was charged and dragged off to Bridewell prison to be stretched on the rack for his confession. Under torture he stuck to his denial of the charge, and claimed that the paper was not his but belonged to Christopher Marlowe, who had been writing in the same room with him and, unbeknown to him, the sheets had become "shuffled" with his papers.

A warrant for Marlowe's arrest was signed on 18th May and on 20th May he was arrested, having been traced to the home of his patron, Thomas Walsingham, the moated manor house called Scadbury at Chislehurst in Kent, whither he had gone to escape the plague, as other poets who were fortunate to have patrons with country homes had done. As this was a Sunday and the law courts were closed, he accompanied the warrant officer to the court at Nonsuch Palace to present himself to members of the Privy Council, who doubled as lords of the Star Chamber. He was fortunate not to be sent to prison to be racked, but was granted bail on condition that he "give his daily attendance on their Lordships until he shall be licensed to the contrary".[15] An informer was meanwhile set on his tracks to assemble an indictment as a basis for his trial.

In the circumstances, Marlowe knew well that he was not out of danger. On the charge of atheism it would be easy for an informer to draw up a highly incriminating indictment from fearful witnesses. The list of blasphemies and obscenities in the informer Richard Baines' report testify to this. At a trial based on these, proof of Marlowe's innocence would stand no chance, and it was usual to extract confession of guilt by torture in the proceedings of this dread higher court; the only court empowered to use torture, whose constitution, "vague as it was powerful", mirrored the Holy Roman Inquisition and operated in complete contrast to the English common law.

Marlowe was therefore, although nominally a free man on bail, in very deep trouble. The nine days' freedom granted him would end as the informer's virulent indictment

---

[15] P.R.O. *PC 2/20 P.374.*

11

landed on Lord Burghley's desk, prior to being delivered to the Queen's hand. The date of delivery was before the murder at Deptford, but the copy destined for the Queen has the curious note written across the paper deleting the original heading, which was: "A note contayninge the opinion of one Christopher Marlye concernynge his damnable opinion and Iudgment of Religioun and scorne of Gods worde", and substituting:

> "A Note deliuered on Whitson eve last of the most horrible blasphemes vtteryd by Cristofer Marley who within iii days after cam to a suden & fearful end of his life".[16]

Since Whitsun eve that year fell on 2nd June, this is stating that the date of his death three days later was on 5th June. The actual date was 30th May, and the inquest on the body took place on Friday 1st June, followed by its swift burial in an unmarked grave in Deptford's parish churchyard, so that by 5th June he had been buried four days! The first of several strange anomalies in this most curious case.

The recorded facts surrounding the event at Deptford, all of them curious, are as follows:

- On Wednesday, 30th May 1593, a meeting took place at the house of **Dame Eleanor Bull** in Deptford, a widow of modest social standing for she was a "cousin" of the Queen's beloved, late Chief Gentlewoman, her 'nanny', Blanche Parry, who was herself a "cousin" of Lord Burghley.[17] Dame Bull provided a room and meals on that day, but the meeting was evidently of a private nature, and there is no mention of any other 'guests' in the house.

- The four men who spent all day at Dame Bull's house, from ten o'clock in the morning until six o'clock in the evening, passing the time "in quiet sort together", and sometimes walking in the garden, were:

  * **Christopher Marlowe**, who was on bail on a serious charge of 'atheism', soon to be brought to trial so that his case was now urgent.

  * **Robert Poley**, a highly experienced and trusted espionage agent. He had just arrived at Deptford from The Hague whither he had been carrying her Majesty's letters of "speciall and secret affayres of great importaunce".[18] Curiously he is recorded as being "in her Majesty's service" all this time including his attendance at Deptford when he gave witness at the inquest on the body two days later.

  * **Nicholas Skeres**, another espionage agent of minor status, and the second witness at the inquest. He was an expert in the Elizabethan game of 'conney-catching' (fleecing naive persons of their money by double dealing) and the intimate friend and partner of the fourth man –

---

[16] *B. L. Harleian MS 6853 ff.307-8.*
This copy of Baines's Note has several items scored through.

[17] *B. L. Lansdowne MS 62 f.123.*
Burghley's draft of Blanche Parry's Will discovered by Jane Apple.

[18] Eugenie de Kalb: 'Robert Poley's Movements as a Messenger of the Court, 1588 to 1601': *R.E.S. 9: 13-18 January 1933.*

* **Ingram Frizer**, the servant and agent of Marlowe's patron, Thomas Walsingham, at whose home Marlowe had been arrested nine days earlier. Frizer was a skilful con-man and, like Poley and Skeres, he was an adept liar. That evening after supper, Frizer murdered Christopher Marlowe.

- The connecting link between all four men was **Thomas Walsingham**, who was Marlowe's patron and, as spy-master, had a long association professionally with Poley and Skeres in the espionage service run by his cousin Sir Francis Walsingham (now deceased) and is described as Frizer's "then Maister".[19]

- **Deptford**, the venue chosen for this meeting at Dame Bull's house, had two significant aspects: (a) it was a naval dockyard and a busy port for the traffic of the ships called hoys sailing regularly to and from the Continent; (b) it was situated at this time "within the verge", namely, a twelve miles radius of the Queen's presence, the court being then at Nonsuch in Surrey, which meant that the local coroner would be superseded by the Queen's own coroner in the event of a capital crime occurring at Deptford.

- The **Murder** occurred after supper when a quarrel broke out between Frizer, who was sitting on a bench wedged between Poley and Skeres "so that he could not in any wise get away" and "with the front part of his body towards the table", and Marlowe, who was lying on a bed behind the men – their bench being *"nere the bed"* (this point being emphasised in the coroner's report). Frizer and Marlowe could not agree about "the sum of pence, that is, *le recknynge*" for their day's entertainment in which Marlowe became "moved with anger" when "divers malicious words" were "spoken between them" and "maliciously drew the dagger of the said Ingram which was at his back" and gave him two wounds on his head "of the length of two inches & of the depth of a quarter of an inch; whereupon the said Ingram ... in fear of being slain, & for the saving of his life, then & there struggled with the said Christopher Morley to get back from him his dagger ... and so it befell in that affray that the said Ingram, in defence of his life, with the dagger aforesaid to the value of *12d*, gave the said Christopher then & there a mortal wound over his right eye to the depth of two inches & of the width of one inch, of which mortal wound the aforesaid Christopher Morley then & there instantly died".[20]

- **William Danby**, Coroner of the Royal Household, presided at the inquest two days later, on Friday 1st June, with sixteen good men and true, tradesmen and tenement holders from Deptford and district, and passed the verdict that Frizer had slain Marlowe in self defence. The shadow of the gallows thus removed, according to Elizabethan law, Frizer returned to prison to sojourn there while awaiting the Queen's pardon for disturbing her peace.

- On 1st June, the same day as the inquest, the burial of the body was recorded in the burial register of St Nicholas's Church, Deptford.

---

[19] P.R.O. *LC 4/192 P.267.*

[20] Coroner's Inquisition: P.R.O. *Chancery Miscellanea 64, File 8 No.241b p.294*
J. L. Hotson: *The Death of Christopher Marlowe* (Cambridge Massachusetts, 1925)
Hotson's translation of the Inquisition.

- On 15th June the Queen wrote to "our well beloved William Danby" wishing to see the writ of *certiorari* "concerning the death of Christopher Morley", together with everything touching it, and commanding him "to send the tenor of the indictment ... to us in our Chancery under your seal distinctly & openly without delay".[21]

- On 28th June Frizer received his pardon from the Queen after the amazingly short time of twenty-eight days – the shortest on record.

- On 29th June, the day after his release, Frizer is recorded back in his master's employ, engaged, in fact, in a 'conney-catching' court hearing together with his friend Skeres, which netted them 200 pounds – of which, it seems that Walsingham himself also gained benefit for the bond was in his name![22]

- There was not the slightest hint of adverse repercussion to Frizer for slaying his master's poet and dear friend, the most brilliant poet-dramatist of the day. He remained in the service of Thomas Walsingham until the end of his days living near to the Scadbury estate at Eltham in Kent.

- On 12th June, thirteen days *after* the murder of Marlowe, there is the first record of a purchase of a copy of the newly-published **Venus and Adonis** launching the name of a **new poet, William Shakespeare**, naming this poem "the first heir of my invention", which this totally unknown poet dedicates to the Earl of Southampton.[23]

These are the facts. Several scholars have posited that the dubious and uniquely curious aspects they present are suggestive of a plot. The question is: What kind of plot?

Was it a plot to get rid of Marlowe intentionally? This notion has been put forward by some scholars quite seriously. Namely, that Thomas Walsingham plotted to murder his dear friend, the brilliant poet-dramatist and fellow free-thinker, acting on secret government instructions to get rid of him. But why? For what dire reason? No one can answer this. Vague claims that Marlowe knew too much about hypothetical political intrigues are tossed around, but there is not a shred of evidence to support the claim that his murder was politically motivated. Charles Nicholl in his book *The Reckoning: The Murder of Christopher Marlowe* (1992) attempts to link the murder with the Earl of Essex as a plot about political in-fighting at court against Raleigh, but his investigation has drawn a complete blank. Nicholl's research ignores the fact that Essex was married to Frances Walsingham, widow of Sir Philip Sidney and daughter of Sir Francis Walsingham, so he was now a member of the Walsingham family circle, and that Raleigh was already out of Essex's way as a rival, having been banished the court in disgrace for his clandestine marriage to Elizabeth Throckmorton. So why murder Marlowe? The notion is ridiculous.

---

[21] P.R.O. *Chancery Miscellanea Bundle 64, File 8 No.241a*
     Hotson: *op. cit.* p.27.

[22] Hotson: *op. cit.* p.48
     See J. Bakeless: *The Tragicall History of Christopher Marlowe* (Harvard Univ. Press, 1942) Vol.I, p.168.

[23] *Folger Shakespeare Library MS V. 460, f.9.* The Stonley Diary Account Book, 1593.
     S. Schoenbaum: *William Shakespeare: A Compact Documentary Life* (OUP paperback edition 1978) p.178.

The alternative, that Marlowe was murdered to pre-empt his trial by the Court of Star Chamber, in case he might reveal evidence to incriminate his fellow free-thinkers as 'atheists' or heretics under torture, also lacks all credibility when precisely the same could be achieved by the third alternative, which the evidence itself presents.

Drawing together all the implications of the event at Deptford, it is strikingly evident that here we have all the ingredients for a plot to stage a faked murder, enabling Marlowe to escape persecution under the cloak of his 'death'. Only a faked murder answers all the anomalies of this scenario. It was the perfect and obvious solution to Marlowe's dilemma.[24]

The reader may well ask, Is there anything, beyond the above facts, to support such a revolutionary conclusion?

To answer this we present the following evidence: literary, historical and documentary, beginning with the evidence of Shakespeare's autobiographical Sonnets.

---

[24]   The case for a faked murder has been presented in definitive detail, critically examining every aspect, in Chapter X of my book, *The Story That the Sonnets Tell*.

"With this key Shakespeare unlocked his heart"
William Wordsworth

Thomas Thorpe's cryptic title page using the hyphenated form of the name SHAKE-SPEARE which denotes that this is a pseudonym.

SHAKE-SPEARES

SONNETS.

Neuer before Imprinted.

AT LONDON
By G. Eld for T. T. and are
to be solde by william Aspley.
1609.

TO.THE.ONLIE.BEGETTER.OF.
THESE.INSVING.SONNETS.
Mr.W.H. ALL.HAPPINESSE.
AND.THAT.ETERNITIE.
PROMISED.

BY.

OVR.EVER-LIVING.POET.

WISHETH.

THE.WELL-WISHING.
ADVENTVRER.IN.
SETTING.
FORTH.

T. T.

The cryptic dedication to 'Mr. W.H.' that has defied solution for 355 years, until Hotson's publication of *Mr. W.H.* in 1964.

THE EVIDENCE OF THE SONNETS

The story that the Sonnets tell is a unique tragedy of a genius who was struck down and eclipsed just as he was burgeoning into glorious maturity in his art. He was driven underground into obscurity to live only in his pseudonym, like a disembodied ghost. Inherent parallels exist with the pseudonymous life of Voltaire, who was also driven into exile because he satirized church and state, exposing social injustice and championing religious tolerance and free thought. These Marlowe also championed.

A pseudonym tends to take on a life of its own, and we forget that Voltaire was really the obscure Monsieur François-Marie Arouet, who once attended a public burning of his own books. In the case of the pseudonymous Shakespeare, even his actual identity has disappeared, deliberately hidden for the purpose of *total* protection, leaving us only with the famous pseudonym without an identity. Into this lacuna, which had to be filled to prevent endless unwelcome speculation and investigation, was snugly fitted the Stratford actor, a safe, uncontentious image, whose shortcomings in intellectual quality and education have been glossed over by the simple expedient of investing him with all the attributes of genius exhibited in the plays published in his name. It has proved a fail-safe formula, successfully marketed all over the world.

The weak link in all this solid story is the legacy of the autobiographical poems left by the author, the genius who stands in the shadows behind William Shakespeare of Stratford-upon-Avon. No one before has ever been able satisfactorily, cogently, coherently to answer **The Riddle of the Sonnets**. The key has now been found.

This is a unique case in historical mysteries. The one obvious clue that has been left to us, has been recognized as a clue to the identity of the patron only, the mysterious 'Mr. W.H.'. What is less obvious is the clue to the identity of the poet. 'Mr. W.H.''s name in initials is presented as a challenge inviting us to discover him. Of course a challenge for such a prize is too intriguing to be ignored.

To succeed, the first requirement must be an open-minded, totally unprejudiced reading of the sonnets themselves. For almost all these poems only a *literal* reading will suffice. What are these autobiographical sonnets telling us? That is the question that must be asked, and answered in the historical context of the lives of both the patron and the poet.

Of all who have tried their hand at solving the conundrum of Thomas Thorpe's cryptic dedication of the book he published under the title SHAKE-SPEARES SONNETS, only Hotson has convincingly resolved the hidden identity of 'Mr. W.H.'. Recognizing the curiously printed dedication – which employs full stops between every word and is set in a careful tabulated format of two triangles of text – as indicative of an Elizabethan cryptogram, Hotson set about 'squaring' the text as the first step in decoding according to the strict rules which govern such cryptograms. These are also subject to a numerical equation, and this proved to be the number 7 and its components $3 + 4 = 7$.

Taking his cue from the only blank space or 'white' in this text after the name 'Mr. W.H.', which appears on line 3, Hotson began his decoding from this point after 'squaring' the text. The important words and letters all fall on lines 3 and 4 and 7, to produce a *seven-letter name* – W.HATLIV.

Hotson numbered off the text for decoding as follows:

```
              1 2 3 4 5 6 7 8 9 10.11 12 13 14 15 16 17 18 19 20 21 22
Line No.3     M r . W . H . A L L . H A P P I N E S S E .
     No.4     A N D . T H A T . E T E R N I T I E .
     No.5     P R O M I S E D .
     No.6     B Y .
     No.7     O V R . E V E R-L I V I N G . P O E T .
```
[25]

This is precisely how an Elizabethan cryptogram must work out responding to the following of the clues governed by numbers. The name of 'Mr. W.H.' is thus revealed as W.HATLIV. What is particularly curious about the wording of this text is the use of "EVER-LIVING" to describe the Poet, not the Patron as would be normal in such dedications designed to flatter the dedicatee. As we shall see, this has a special significance in this subtle and extremely clever piece of Thorpean cryptography designed with more layers of concealment and revelation than has been realized. We are only at the first layer.

Hotson's skilful decoding yielded the unknown name W.Hatliv. Who could this be? In his reading of the Sonnets, Hotson had been struck by the recurring imagery of royalty, which led him to conclude that the patron who was so ardently hymned by the sonneteer was in some way a 'royal' personage. Seeking someone who was both 'royal' and a plain Mr., his Sherlock Holmesian instinct told him to search in the records of the two rival Inns of Court, Gray's Inn and the Middle Temple, who each had their own 'Christmas Prince' who might be elected to rule over a mock court for the Twelve Days of Christmas. These were enormously lavish festivities involving great expense to furnish their mock court with all the trappings of royalty: liveried servants, trumpeters and musicians, court officials played by the students, mock ceremonials, banquets, dramatic entertainments, dances and, of course, a poet to immortalize the 'Prince' in verse. It was a delightful scenario, a great occasion, which was only rarely played out when an ideal candidate appeared among the law students who must be young, wealthy, extremely beautiful and personable in every way, and well born of an armorial family of sufficient standing in the landed gentry class.

Because of the rarity of these Christmas Princes, Hotson's search was brief. He found that Gray's Inn had, in the relevant period, elected a Prince of Purpoole to rule over their court of Graya only in 1587 and 1594, whereas the Middle Temple did not produce a Prince d'Amour at all until 1614 and in 1635. To Hotson's immense joy the Gray's Inn

---

[25] Leslie Hotson: *Mr. W.H.* (1964) London, pp.154-6

record for 1587 revealed that one Master **William Hatcliffe**, aged nineteen years, of an armorial Lincolnshire family related to the Earl of Lincoln, became their Prince of Purpoole for the Christmas season of 1587/88. W.Hatliv – Hatliffe – Hatcliffe – the Elizabethan way with names was characteristically variable – and undoubtedly this *was* his 'Mr. W.H.'. Found at last!

But what of William Shakespeare, the sonneteer for this Prince of Purpoole? Where was he in 1587? There is not the slightest evidence that he was in London at this time, nor is there any evidence of his relationship with Master William Hatcliffe at any time in their lives, a relationship which Hotson's thesis envisages as having been on-going in both patronage and dear friendship to the end of their days. I confess that I, too, had been on the point of discarding Will Hatcliffe as not fitting this story, which for me must have the ring of truth to be valid. But then, being recently immersed in the study of Christopher Marlowe after completing my biography as a tribute to the quatercentenary[26] of his birth in 1964, which he shared with William Shakespeare, I turned the spotlight onto Marlowe. At once the whole picture blazed into light presenting a brilliant historical scenario.

Marlowe and Hatcliffe had been at Cambridge for four years contemporaneously. Marlowe had arrived at Corpus Christi College just before Christmas 1580, aged almost seventeen, on a scholarship from Archbishop Matthew Parker which seems to have been especially created with him in mind as the next step from the scholarship he held at the King's School to prepare him as a future divine of the Anglican church, which was Parker's darling scheme. In 1582 the fourteen year-old William Hatcliffe arrived to matriculate at the nearby Jesus College, a young man whose stunning looks, if we are to judge by his later election as Prince of Purpoole and the eulogy of the sonnets describing his beauty, must have made him noticeable even at Cambridge.

In 1586, Hatcliffe, aged eighteen, left Cambridge without taking a degree to come to London's 'Third University' of the Inns of Court and entered Gray's Inn. Marlowe arrived in London in the summer of 1587, now graced with his Master of Arts degree, and bringing with him the completed playscript of his first masterpiece, *Tamburlaine the Great*, which was on the boards by the autumn of that year. It was an immediate and resounding success, bringing forth a spate of imitations from the pens of the contemporary playwrights, including Robert Greene whose envious lampoons have identified this play for us as from Marlowe's pen, for when it was published in 1590 it was, as was common practice, printed without any name of the author.

The law students loved to see a play in the afternoon, and we cannot doubt that Will Hatcliffe would have gone to see *Tamburlaine the Great* and then and there probably renewed his acquaintance with his erstwhile fellow student at Cambridge, who had suddenly become the talk of the theatre-loving Londoners with this epoch-making play. *Tamburlaine the Great* represents the birth of Shakespearean blank verse drama. Of that there is no question. As Harry Levin has remarked: "Marlowe was a born playwright".[27]

---

[26] A. D. Wraight & Virginia F. Stern: *In Search of Christopher Marlowe* (1965, London and NY; reprinted 1993 in paperback).

[27] Harry Levin: *The Overreacher* (1954), p.24

1587 was a most significant year for both Marlowe and Hatcliffe. Marlowe had 'arrived' as the 'new dramatist', enthusiastically acclaimed as the genius of the stage for which the Elizabethan age was waiting. He had spent his time at Cambridge in conscious preparation for his destiny, employed in self-set tasks translating Lucan's *De Bello Civili* into English blank verse, and Ovid's *Amores* into rhyming couplets. The Sonnets are redolent of Ovid. Marlowe developed early as a poet, but he had still much to learn as an innovative young dramatist breaking the mould of the Three Unities which dominated the drama of the courtly makers, and establishing the new form of Shakespearean drama.

That year Hatcliffe, whose genius was in his looks, was elected to the high honour of becoming the Grayans' Prince of Purpoole, to reign in splendour for the Twelve Days of Christmas from 26th December 1587 until 6th January 1588 (new style). Nothing would have been more natural than that he should invite Marlowe to become his 'official' court sonneteer for this rare festive season, offering him also his patronage. The tenor of the sonnets written in praise of the beautiful young 'Prince' makes it clear that he was now the poet's patron. *Sonnet 53* specifically refers to his "*bounty*".

> Speak of the spring and foizon of the year,
> The one doth shadow of your beauty show,
> The other as your bounty doth appear,
> And you in every blessed shape we know.

Note the plural pronoun *we* indicating that this sonnet speaks for the entire court. 1587 was the year of the inception of the sonnet-sequence, which opens with one of the loveliest of them all, *Sonnet 18*:

> Shall I compare thee to a summer's day?
> Thou art more lovely and more temperate:
> Rough winds do shake the darling buds of May,
> And summer's lease hath all too short a date.
> Sometime too hot the eye of heaven shines,
> And often is his gold complexion dimm'd,
> And every fair from fair sometime declines,
> By chance, or Nature's changing course untrimm'd:
> But thy eternal summer shall not fade,
> Nor lose possession of that fair thou ow'st,
> Nor shall Death brag thou wander'st in his shade,
> When in eternal lines to time thou grow'st.
> > So long as men can breathe or eyes can see,
> > So long lives this, and this gives life to thee.

Here, in the bleakness of mid-winter comparing his 'royal' patron to the loveliness of a summer's day, the young poet immediately found his voice in the adoption of the fourteen-line English sonnet, which he made very much his own. He continued to use the sonnet-form all his life to express his thoughts and feelings, his joys and his anguish when life dealt him some of "the slings and arrows of outrageous fortune". In this year as the Armada threat rumbled closer, 'Prince' and poet were riding high on the flood-tide of fortune: Marlowe, London's new poet-dramatist, and Will Hatcliffe as the Prince of

Purpoole, whose flamboyant progresses through the City with his trumpeters and retinue would have raised admiring crowds.

This delightful picture of the 'Prince' and his poet emerges from Hotson's decipherment of Thorpe's conundrum, decoded according to the rules governing Elizabethan cryptograms. In yielding its secret, identifying 'Mr. W.H.' as W.Hatliv or Hatcliffe, Thorpe's dedication presents us with a 'royal' personage who is also a plain 'Mr.' removing at a stroke the vexed problem of wrongly addressing the patron that besets the identification of the Earl of Southampton. On this count alone, Hotson's identification takes precedence over all other 'Mr. W.H.'s. But the importance of Will Hatcliffe in this autobiographical history goes far beyond this and derives from an error – a very important error to which all students of the Sonnets, including Hotson himself, have subscribed. This is the erroneous assumption that 'Mr. W.H.', named as the 'ONLIE BEGETTER' of the Sonnets, is their sole patron. This is how Thorpe presents him, but it is a 'red herring' slipped into the dedication to mislead us.

The word 'Begetter' is used in flattery to the patron denoting him as the 'father' or 'begetter' of the works of poetry and literature that are begotten under the *aegis* of his patronage, implying also that the patron inspires his poet to write. *Sonnet 38* addresses the patron clearly expressing this Renaissance concept:

> Be thou the Tenth Muse, ten times more worth
> Than those old nine which rhymers invocate,
> And he that calls on thee, let him bring forth
> Eternal numbers to out-live long date.

This same concept of the patron as 'father' is seen in Edward Blount's dedication of Marlowe's **Hero and Leander** posthumously in 1598 to his patron, Sir Thomas Walsingham, describing Marlowe's poems as his "children":

> "I cannot but see so far into the will of him dead, that whatsoever issue of his brain should chance to come abroad, that the first breath it should take might be the gentle air of your liking; for, since his self had been accustomed thereunto, it would prove more agreeable and thriving to his right children than any other foster countenance whatsoever."[28]

In this sense 'Mr. W.H.' is rightly described as the 'ONLIE BEGETTER' for the sonnet-sequence was begotten under his patronage as the Prince of Purpoole, that is, its inception was thus *begotten*. However, in attributing the whole of the sonnets to 'Mr. W.H.' as their sole patron, scholars have fallen into Thorpe's crafty trap – and this has created its own problem of identification that has been perceived by those who have studied the sonnets with insight, notably Sir Stephen Spender.[29] He comments on the apparently unstable and self-contradictory character of 'Mr. W.H.', who is praised with unalloyed admiration for his beauty and his virtuous nature, and yet is *also* severely

---

[28] *Hero and Leander*, Quarto ed. by Adam Islip, Folger Shakespeare Library. The only surviving copy of Blount's publication in 1598.

[29] Stephen Spender: 'The Alike and the Other': *The Riddle of the Sonnets* (1962) N.Y., p.112

criticized for his bad character which is anything but virtuous. This "*beauteous Youth*" proves to be a false friend, and is "*lascivious*" and given to vices. How to reconcile the apparently self-contradictory character of 'Mr. W.H.' as revealed in the Sonnets?

Blinded by Thorpe's presentation of the 'Onlie Begetter' no one had perceived that the schizophrenic character of the patron indicates that here we have not one patron – but *two totally different men*! One is the "*lovely Boy*", 'Mr. W.H.', who was at first uncritically praised for both his beauty *and* his virtue, until this proved to be false. The other is the True Patron to whom the bulk of the sonnets are written, whom Marlowe found later and who remained his loyal and loving friend throughout his life.

We have the interesting picture of 'Mr. W.H.' as the original 'Begetter' and the inspiration of the Sonnets – but he is not their sole patron. At first, taken in by the exquisite beauty of the youthful 'Prince', and attributing to him all the virtues associated with royalty, the sonneteer wrote fifteen delightful sonnets in his praise; but soon he became disillusioned with the character of this paragon which patently did not match his outward beauty. The group of increasingly critical sonnets follows, numbering thirteen poems in all, until with *Sonnet 126* the poet finally severs his relationship with his first youthful patron, who did not live up to the high standards of his poet's ideal of what a patron should be. It was a brave break for a poet of humble origin to make on principle in this age when assured patronage was the very life-line of the poet, who was dependent on his patron to gain acceptance. Marlowe was not afraid to speak his mind, or to act upon his principles, which brought him eventually to his ruin; and here, early in his career when he had fallen on his feet in finding the patronage of a wealthy young man of excellent family connections, he did not hesitate to demonstrate this singlemindedness in his critical sonnets admonishing his erring young patron.

> How sweet and lovely dost thou make the shame,
> Which like a canker in the fragrant rose,
> Doth spot the beauty of thy budding name!
> Oh in what sweets dost thou thy sins enclose!
> That tongue that tells the story of thy days,
> Making lascivious comments on thy sport,
> Cannot dispraise, but in a kind of praise;
> Naming thy name, blesses an ill report.
> Oh what a mansion have those vices got
> Which for their habitation chose out thee,
> Where beauty's veil doth cover every blot,
> And all things turn to fair that eyes can see!
>   Take heed (dear heart) of this large privilege:
>   The hardest knife ill us'd doth lose its edge.

Sonnet 95

One wonders whether these critical sonnets were ever shown to his 'Prince'. Certainly, they would not have been shown to the 'courtiers' as those delightful sonnets praising their Prince of Purpoole would have been, probably being read aloud to the admiring court in public poetry readings.

The Dark Lady

For the present, we will stay with 'Mr. W.H.' accepting Hotson's premise that he is the patron. Who then was the Dark Lady? She is closely associated with 'Mr. W.H.' and is ultimately the cause of the rift between poet and 'Prince'. The first fifteen sonnets dating from Christmas 1587-88, but deliberately scattered through the sequence to confuse the reader, *(Nos. 18, 19, 20, 21, 22, 53, 54, 55, 59, 62, 63, 64, 65, 105, 106)* all ardently praising 'Prince' Will, show that a true friendship was developing between the young men. True friendship inherently involves true loyalty. And there's the rub. Our sonneteer finds that his friendship is betrayed by his 'Prince', who steals the sonneteer's mistress *(Sonnets 40, 41, 42)*. At first he forgives him making an excuse of his beauty and youth. However, increasingly he perceives that this outward beauty covers an inner nature that is spoilt, selfish, false and *"lascivious"*; character faults that are borne out by the history of the real Master William Hatcliffe, as is established by Hotson's research tracing the decline of his fortune, which he evidently squandered leaving his family impoverished.[30]

'Prince' Will repeats the trespass, this time causing his poet genuine anguish by stealing the woman he passionately loves, his adored mistress the Dark Lady. This time the poet is not inclined to forgive his rival in love, and he turns also to upbraid his raven-eyed mistress who has easily been won to prefer the glamorous, fair, young 'Prince' to her poor poet. She is Hotson's Dark Lady, **Luce Morgan**, the one-time gentlewoman of Queen Elizabeth who was banished the court, presumably because she became a fallen woman through an affair with one of the courtiers whose game it was to seduce these court beauties and break their maidenheads. Perhaps in revenge for her lost virginity, for this was an age when chastity was most highly valued, she set up her love-nest in Clerkenwell.

Beginning, it would seem as a high-class courtezan with some private clients from the court, she eventually became notorious as 'Black Luce' – the term 'black' referring not to any ethnic aspect of this Dark Lady, but to her profession as a harlot. Harlotry in Elizabethan terminology was 'black', and although this seductive siren's most striking feature was her black eyes, she was evidently of Welsh origin. Black eyes are found in Wales quite often, perhaps deriving from ancient Celtic blood. The Welsh are also a musical nation and Luce Morgan played the virginals to enchant her poet lover *(Sonnet 128)*.

Sonnet 131 is explicit on this use of the term 'black'.[31]

> Thou art as tyranous, so as thou art,
> As those whose beauties proudly make them cruel,
> For well thou know'st to my dear doting heart
> Thou art the fairest and most precious jewel.
> Yet, in good faith, some say that thee behold,
> Thy face hath not the power to make love groan;

---

[30] Hotson: *op. cit.*, pp.291-300
[31] *Ibid.* Chap. XI, 'Black Eyes'. The interested student should consult this chapter.

To say they err, I dare not be so bold,
Although I swear it to myself alone.
And to be sure that is not false I swear,
A thousand groans but thinking on thy face,
One on another's neck do witness bear
Thy black is fairest in my judgement's place.
    In nothing art thou black save in thy deeds,
    And thence this slander, as I think, proceeds.

There is much subtle play with the word 'black' throughout these sonnets, often anguished, sometimes bitter and satirical for he longed to have her for himself alone, but whilst abhorring her harlotry he could not tear himself away from her. Hotson's research recording her career, as of his reading of the clues to her name with which the sonnets to her are littered, have identified Luce Morgan unequivocally as the Dark Lady of the Sonnets.[32]

This identification is impeccably confirmed by the 'Gesta Grayorum' in John Nichols' Progresses of Queen Elizabeth for 1594 describing what was obviously a re-enactment of the rituals and ceremonials of the 1587 Grayan court of 'Prince' Will Hatcliffe. At Christmas 1594 Queen Elizabeth herself visited the mock court of Graya during the brief reign of 'Prince' Henry Helmes, and accordingly we are fortunate in having the fascinating detailed report in Nichol's Progresses of Queen Elizabeth for that year describing the manner in which these mock 'royal' courts were conducted, the Inns of Court each having their own traditions to which they would doubtless adhere each time these festivities were revived under a new Christmas Prince.

The eligible young Henry Helmes being Prince of Purpoole in 1594, we learn of the stunning arrival at this mock court of a lady "homager" who comes to present her tribute to the 'Prince' at his enthronement. On this occasion he received the homage due to him from those who held "Tenures" and owed "Services" thereto belonging. Much of this ceremonial is laced with innuendo that must have convulsed the court in delighted laughter. The "Solicitor" reading from an ancient "book of Doomsday" which was preserved in "the 50th and 500th chest" of the 'Prince's' Exchequer, proclaimed the "homagers and vassals" by name, who each advanced, announced by trumpets, to the Prince's footstool to kiss his hand. They included such eminent personages as "Mariotto Marquarillo de Holborn" and "Amarillo de Paddington", and "Baldwine de Islington". The latter "holdeth the town of **Islington**, of the Prince of **Purpoole**, by grand-serjeantry; and rendering, at the coronation of his Honour, for every maid in Islington, continuing a virgin after the age of fourteen years, one hundred thousand million sterling".[33]

The sums of money cited are ridiculously huge! Both these inordinately large numbers and the sexual innuendo are reflected in the sonnets to the Prince of Purpoole which praise him to the skies, and were obviously written for public presentation at the Grayan Court. (Sonnet 20 presents innuendo; Sonnet 53 speaks of "millions of strange shadows"

---

[32]   Ibid. pp.241-2.
        Wraight: The Story That the Sonnets Tell, pp.222-4
[33]   John Nichols: Progresses of Queen Elizabeth & c. (1788 - 1821) 'Gesta Grayorum' Vol. II, p.809

that *"on you tend"* – namely the students acting as his courtiers. The actors are *"shadows"* – millions of them!)

We can imagine the scene in the throne room with the assembled court and the liveried retainers, trumpeters and courtiers revelling in their play-acting. According to Nichols it was following the *"homage"* rendered by *"Marquarillo de Holborn"* that the only lady come to pay her homage in this ceremony was announced. One can sense the murmur of expectation and excitement. Enter the Dark Lady!

> *"Lucy Negro*, abbess de *Clerkenwell*, holdeth the nunnery of *Clerkenwell*, with the lands and privileges thereunto belonging, of the Prince of *Purpoole* by night-service in *Cauda*, and to find a choir of nuns with burning lamps to chant *Placebo* to the gentlemen of the Prince's privy-chamber, on the day of his Excellency's coronation."[34]

What a sensation! 'Negro' derives from the Italian for 'black' and has no ethnic connotation but identifies her as 'Black Luce' the harlot. Hotson reckons she must have been aged about twenty-eight in 1587 when, her black eyes flashing their message to the admiring courtiers as she came forward to kneel at the 'Prince's' throne to kiss his hands, she completely captivated the twenty-three-year-old Marlowe who fell head over heels in love with her. *Sonnets 23* and *24* placed immediately after the introduction of 'Mr. W.H.' as patron and 'Prince', admired and beloved by his court, record the poet's falling in love with Luce Morgan, whose name is featured in the word-play in these two sonnets in the repetition of *"eyes"* connoting her name *Luce*, as Hotson has amply demonstrated, and the triple repetition of *"more"* indicating *Morgan*.[35] As I have shown in my full analysis of the sonnets,[36] the sensation of being tongue-tied by the overwhelming experience of falling in love is typical of Marlowe. The specific placement of these two sonnets here associates Luce Morgan with the 'Prince' and the court of Graya in a strongly autobiographical context as an event in his life that was of importance to the young poet.

In the evidence of Nichols' *Progresses* we have confirmation of Hotson's Dark Lady in this historical record revealing Luce Morgan, the harlot beloved of the youthful Marlowe in 1587, in a situation that would inevitably lead to a sexual liaison between the 'Prince' and the harlot. If Nichols' record represents a repeat performance by popular request of her sensational appearance at the previous court of Graya when, at the age of twenty-eight, she was, according to her poet, very beautiful, this marvellously corroborates the sonnet-story of the Dark Lady, giving a depth of insight into this episode in the poet's life and shedding light onto his character and his emotional experiences.

Of all the Dark Ladies that have been presented, only Luce Morgan rings true in relation to every nuance in the sonnets to her, *and in the historical context* of the 'Mr. W.H.' as 'Prince' Will Hatcliffe with his poet, the Cambridge M.A. Christopher Marlowe at the Christmas of 1587-88. There is no forcing of evidence or sophistical argument involved.

---

[34]   *Ibid*

[35]   Hotson: *op. cit.* Chap.XI

[36]   Wraight: *op. cit.* pp.452-3, 'The Sonnets of First Love'.

Hotson's identification of the Dark Lady as Luce Morgan stands on the firm basis of his expert reading of the sonnets to her which reveal her name in the witty usage of Elizabethan semantics. There is repeated word-play on her name, Luce or Lucy, which connotes "*eyes*" and "*brightness*", and in the references to her profession as a harlot in the repetition of the word "*black*". The word "*eyes*" or "*eye*" is repeated twenty-four times in the twenty-five sonnets of the Dark Lady, frequently supported by "*sight*", "*looks*", "*blind*" and "*blindness*", which reflect the legends associated with Saint Lucy, as also "*brightness*". So insistent and so clearly deliberate is this word-play by the sophisticated poet of the Sonnets that only a stubborn blindness on the part of scholars has prevented recognition of the clue to her identity. This has been hampered by prejudice against Will Hatcliffe as 'Mr. W.H.' displacing the favourite of so many decades, the Earl of Southampton. With Marlowe in the picture the whole focus has changed to one of credibility and her association historically with the Prince of Purpoole presents an undeniably telling conjunction and a perfect Photofit for this Dark Lady, 'Black Luce'.[37]

The raven-eyed courtezan preferred her glamorous 'Prince', but it seems he soon tired of her. She sulked at first, but finally her poet-lover won her back in an on-going affair that may have lasted some years, for it resulted in his contracting the less serious and curable venereal disease, gonorrhoea. This, too, is frankly described *(Sonnets 147, 153, 154)*. His jealousy and anguish at losing her are described in the sonnets playing on the name of his rival *"Will"*, being also the Elizabethan term *will* denoting sexual desire. Even when strong emotions are being expressed, the sonnets remain wonderfully witty in their sophisticated use of language.

> Whoever hath her wish, thou hast thy *Will*
> And *Will* to boot, and *Will* in over-plus,
> More than enough am I that vex thee still,
> To thy sweet will making addition thus.
> Wilt thou, whose will is large and spacious,
> Not once vouchsafe to hide my will in thine?
> Shall will in others seem right gracious,
> And in my will no fair acceptance shine?
> The sea, all water, yet receives rain still,
> And in abundance addeth to his store,
> So thou being rich in *Will*, add to thy *Will*
> One will of mine to make thy large *Will* more.
>   Let no unkind, no fair beseechers kill,
>   Think all but one, and me in that one *Will*.

Sonnet 135

The capitalization and italicization of the name *Will* follows Thorpe's printing of a name according to Elizabethan printing practice, and is clearly intentional. In this extremely witty and subtle poem he has also woven in a reference to her name Morgan, which Hotson has identified as deriving from the Welsh for sea, which is *Mor*, so that the imagery of the sea combines again with the introduction of the word *"more"* to point out

---

[37]   Hotson: *op. cit.* pp.244-55

26

his mistress as Luce Morgan, the harlot.[38] There is never mention of a professional relationship with her poet in terms of money and payment for her services, so that one is left with the impression that theirs was in fact a relationship as lovers; but she seems to have gained satisfaction from exerting her power to torment him knowing that his love for her was genuine and passionate, not merely the sexual lust of a client.

The companion sonnet has a problematic ending.

> If thy soul check thee that I come so near,
> Swear to thy blind soul that I was thy *Will*,
> And will, thy soul knows, is admitted there:
> Thus far for love, my love-suit sweet fulfil.
> *Will*, will fulfil the treasure of thy love,
> Ay, fill it full with wills, and my will one.
> In things of great receipt with ease we prove,
> Among a number one is reckon'd none.
> Then in the number let me pass untold,
> Though in thy store's account I one must be;
> For nothing hold me, so it please thee hold,
> That nothing me, a something sweet to thee.
> > Make but my name thy love, and love that still,
> > And then thou lov'st me for my name is *Will*.

Sonnet 136

This sonnet is frequently cited as firm evidence that the Sonnets are indeed the autobiographical poems of Will Shakespeare; and so they are, for in 1609 the concealed poet *was* the pseudonymous William Shakespeare. These sonnets, however, date from 1587-88. In that case a minor alteration to the rhyming couplet at the end would have been added to bring in a neat touch of obscurity to the identification of the concealed poet once he had decided to risk publishing his sonnet-sequence.

In seeking him within the context of the passionate sexual relationship of the Dark Lady episode, the author is clearly heterosexual. I have demonstrated that the theme of the Sonnets is essentially a celebration of Beauty and Love (see Chapter XIV, *The Story that the Sonnets Tell*), the two qualities most highly valued by the poet who is here declaring his credo of Platonic love between men as the highest form of human relationship, the concept of True Love in a Platonic Friendship, as advocated by the great Renaissance Neo-Platonist, Marsilio Ficino, whose books had such a powerful inspirational influence on the circle of Free-thinkers to which Marlowe belonged; that band of rare spirits with "aspiring minds" who were bound together in their pursuit of knowledge that was proscribed by the reactionary authority of the ecclesiastical and state power vested in the Court of Star Chamber, which exercised strict control over all university education and the printing presses. The latter were in the firing line, subject to censorship and fines and seizure of forbidden texts, or worse punishment if considered dangerous. One of the books burned by edicts of Archbishop Whitgift and the Bishop of London in 1599 was

---

[38] *Ibid*, pp.250-2

Marlowe's translation of Ovid's *Amores*, which he had been working on surreptitiously at Cambridge. This is not an exercise that a young man with homosexual interests would have chosen as his self-set task. These erotic poems are among the most heterosexual literature to come out of the ancient writers who so influenced the Renaissance poets.

Marlowe's lost play, *The History of George Scanderbeg*, probably written when he was only seventeen or eighteen as his first essay in full-length drama based on history, is another reliable indicator of his sexuality as heterosexual. Scanderbeg was seemingly his adolescent hero-figure. Gabriel Harvey, who probably knew the young poet-dramatist well at this time hoping to take him under his wing, as he had Edmund Spenser, refers to Marlowe in his cryptic poem on his death in 1593, *Gorgon or the Wonderfull Yeare*, by the names of both Scanderbeg and Tamburlaine, the two great warriors who each successfully fought the Turks. Scanderbeg was a most virtuous Christian prince of Albania, or Epirro as it was then called, who freed his country from the Turkish domination, and led his soldiers to follow him with high moral precepts, forbidding them to rape women, and especially abhorring the sin of the "*Citie of* **Gomorra**".[39] We have to ask ourselves, would a young homosexual have chosen to write his first important dramatic opus about the life of a character like Scanderbeg? He was a heroic figure both in his physical prowess as an invincible warrior and in his moral stature, whose strange life was marked with almost miraculous success. There is a suggestion in Harvey's obscure poem that Marlowe in some sense identified himself with Scanderbeg as a freedom fighter.[40]

In assessing these autobiographical poems it would be easy to fall into the trap of misunderstanding them completely because of our modern ignorance of the Elizabethan usage of the words 'love' and 'lover', which appear throughout the sonnets addressing his male friend and patron. In this context they refer to the sacred bond of true friendship with a beloved friend in a chaste Platonic relationship which was regarded as the most desirable and life-enhancing possible to mankind. The word 'lover' is used in this sense in *Julius Caesar* when Brutus refers to Caesar as "my best lover". He addresses the assembled crowd over Caesar's murdered body as "Romans, countrymen and lovers!" In *Coriolanus*, his friend Menenius calls him "my lover". Elizabethan literature, letters and life supply ample examples of the wholly different connotation of these words. This applies equally to relationships between women, with no hint of a Lesbian relationship. Rosalind and Celia in *As You Like It* spring immediately to mind. Elizabethans shared beds, which were often capacious, and the term 'bedfellow' commonly refers to this without implying a sexual relationship. In Webster's *The Duchess of Malfi*, when the Duchess is visited in her bedroom by her secretly-married husband, Antonio, demanding "a night's lodging" there is much merry badinage in which her lady's maid Cariola joins, saying she knows the Duchess to be "the sprawling'st bedfellow".[41] The twentieth century does not easily understand the Elizabethans.

---

[39] John Shute: *Two Very Notable Commentaries* (1562) bound with Cambine's *Turkish affares* and *A Commentarie of the Warres of the Turcks made against George Scanderbeg, prince of Epirro*, Sig. U iii

[40] Wraight: *op. cit.* Chap. XI 'Gorgon or the Wonderfull Yeare', gives an analysis of Harvey's archaic, obscure poem that makes sense for the first time. On Harvey's relationship with Marlowe, see pp.132-3.

[41] John Webster: *The Duchess of Malfi* Act III, Sc.2, l.14

Patronage was a dominant factor in Elizabethan life, around which social intercourse revolved, with the Queen at its apex representing the ideal of virginity in an age when chastity was a prized virtue. Yet the passionate love-language of patronage employed the sexual imagery demanded by the elaborate charade of the court in which every courtier was, by definition, in love with the unattainable Virgin Queen. This imagery represented a kind of sublimation of sex. The ardent flattery of the patron was the style of the time. It is present throughout the poetry and literature of the Renaissance, nowhere more ardently than in Shakespeare's Sonnets.

In employing the love-language of patronage redolent with its sexual imagery, Marlowe is worshipping at the shrine of Beauty, *"Mother of the Muses"*. It would not be an exaggeration to say that he was in love with Beauty, the source of his inspiration. To the modern reader his descriptions of the beauty of his patron suggest a homosexual element in their relationship; but a better informed reading shows that he is writing as an Elizabethan and a Ficinian Platonist celebrating his love of Beauty. Marlowe hated 'lasciviousness', and, above all, he hated hypocrisy. He would not have betrayed his principles. By the same token, he was not a prude. For the Elizabethans, exhortation to sexual continence went alongside their relish of ribaldry. Marlowe came of a family who revelled in the bawdy tales of Canterbury life as has now been well established from the records of the City archives.[42] Shakespearean comedy richly bears this out.

There is no hint of prudery in the sonnets to the Dark Lady. They are among the most explicit of Elizabethan writings in describing sexual experience, as are his translations of Ovid's *Amores*, from which Marlowe probably imbibed his sexual education. The same attitude of frankness, depicting the human condition truthfully without shying away from what is difficult, is seen in his dramatization of *Edward II* – a courageous choice presenting the real tragedy of a homosexual king, which is, however, certainly not the work of a homosexual, for no homosexual could have written this play. Jarman had totally to rewrite it to fit his own sexuality, and made a travesty of Marlowe's masterpiece. Much has been made of Marlowe's inclusion of a minor scene in his *Dido Queen of Carthage* depicting Jove in his traditional character dallying with Ganymede, which necessarily provides the dramatic reason for Juno's jealousy that underlies the tragedy of Dido's love for Aeneas. Similarly the inclusion of Neptune's disappointed overture of love to Leander as he swims the Hellespont is part of the artistic concept of his narrative poem *Hero and Leander* which Marlowe would have shown as Neptune's revenge, had he completed the tragedy, bringing Leander to his watery grave.

Let it be noted that the informer attributes to Marlowe the opinion: 'That all they that love not Tobacco & Boys were fools'; which is tantamount to paederasty. The most formidable weapon in the informer's arsenal was the accusation of sexual depravity, which he reserved for his most important victims. This practice was unchanged since mediaeval times. The fashionable, modern presentation of Marlowe as a homosexual has no warranty beyond the informer's libellous report, which sets out to victimize him in the knowledge that in Tudor law it was a capital offence that would ensure the desired verdict at his trial, which was pre-empted by his Deptford eclipse.

---

42 William Urry: *Christopher Marlowe and Canterbury* ed. Andrew Butcher (1988), Faber & Faber, London; Introduction, pp.xxxii - xxxv

Pandora's Box

I have posed the question: Why did Thomas Thorpe publish Shakespeare's 154 beautiful sonnets in a cryptic publication? The answer can only be that there was something important to hide in this autobiographical legacy.

Pondering on this I decided to take the entire sonnet-sequence apart, and to reassemble the poems under their theme-groups of subject matter by the most careful reading and repeated rereadings of each sonnet, phrase, word in its *literal* sense – a *modus operandi* which Hotson had used to discover the meaning of three obscure and 'difficult' sonnets, numbers *107, 123* and *124*, which had defied all previous attempts to elucidate their meaning. By contrast, the use at times of poetic imagery in a way not intended to be read literally, or of hyperbole in flattering his patron, can readily be recognized the more one becomes familiar with these poems and one draws closer to the mind and heart of the poet. At the same time, of prime importance was the setting of each autobiographical sonnet into a precisely fitting historical context.

As this checking and assessing progressed, it became possible with increasing confidence to establish the separate theme-groups and the different persons to whom the poems are addressed. It was only then that the revelation of their true autobiographical story emerged in its chronological order. And what a revelation it was! Rather like opening Pandora's box. Now there was no going back. The secret was out.

What emerged were fourteen distinct, but often related, theme-groups, and not one, but three different patrons beside the Dark Lady. These three patrons are 'Mr. W.H.' who is certainly **Master William Hatcliffe**; the young **Earl of Southampton**, to whom the first group of seventeen sonnets are addressed; and the man I have called the True Patron, **Thomas Walsingham**, to whom the sonnets are mainly addressed, many of them as verse-letters written from the poet's exile, for the largest theme-group of all is *The Sonnets of Exile*. The size and importance of this group in the poet's life has been obscured by the insertion of sonnets addressing 'Mr. W.H.' which have been scattered throughout the sequence breaking up this largest group in particular, and confusing the story-line by distracting the attention of the reader. The juxtapositioning of sonnets which seem to be addressing the same person or relating to the same problem or situation, when in fact they can be shown to be completely different, is the device that has been cleverly used to conceal the real story.

Only when one has the real poet, Christopher Marlowe, in one's sights is it possible to see how all this subtle mix-up is separable and clearly reveals its hidden tale of a tragic life, yet one that was also blessed with the unshakable loyalty of his dear friend and patron who sustained him throughout his trouble. The story of loyal, true friendship that "*alters not ... But bears it out even to the edge of doom*", testified in that most beautiful *Sonnet 116*, "*Let me not to the marriage of true minds /Admit impediments*" is the central theme of the Sonnets, confirming that the True Patron is indeed Thomas Walsingham, his ever-faithful friend and patron who engineered the faked death that saved his life and gave posterity the genius we know as Shakespeare.

The True Patron's presence has been obscured by the clever presentation of 'Mr. W.H.' as the 'ONLIE BEGETTER', who is, in fact, a kind of mirage to mislead the would-be conundrum-solver into believing he has found the patron in "Will Hatliv", and thereupon ceasing to look further and applying the entire sonnet-story to him. Such an interpretation is impossible and is subject to confusion worse confounded by the deliberate a-chronological mix-up of the sonnet-sequence. It is hardly surprising that unravelling all this confusion has defied so many, including even Dr. Hotson, who accepted 'Prince' Will Hatcliffe as the sole patron, with an unconvincing result. Hatcliffe's patronage of his poet was probably as ephemeral as was his reign as the Prince of Purpoole, for his falseness as a friend soon became apparent. Reluctantly at first, but then with finality, Marlowe turned away and rejected him. This is clearly recorded in the 13-sonnet-group I have called 'The Friendship Turns Sour', dated early 1588.[43]

The Sonnets of Marlowe the Espionage Agent

This was Armada year, and the evidence that Marlowe, on returning from an urgent intelligence-gathering assignment in France, joined the English navy on board the ship the *Nonpareille* to fight against the Armada under Drake's old sea-dog, Captain Thomas Fenner, who was second-in-command in Drake's squadron, is marvellously confirmed in his 'Armada' *Sonnet 107*.[44] This poem is packed with references to the happy outcome of this historic naval encounter when "peace proclaims olives of endless age", and he exultantly declares that –

"Death to me subscribes,
Since spite of him I'll live in this poor rhyme".

He had recently experienced the closeness of Death in the battles of the greatest of all naval campaigns of the time, so graphically described in his 'Armada' play, **Edward the Third**, when the ships "Like fiery dragons"

> ..... from their smoky wombs
> Sent many grim ambassadors of death.
> Then gan the day to turn to gloomy night,
> And darkness did as well enclose the quick
> As those that were but newly reft of life.
> No leisure serv'd for friends to bid farewell;
> And, if it had, the hideous noise was such
> As each to other seemèd deaf and dumb.
> Purple the sea, whose channel fill'd as fast
> With streaming gore, that from the maimèd fell,
> As did her gushing moisture break into
> The crannied cleftures of the through-shot planks.
> Here flew a head, dissevered from the trunk,
> There mangled arms and legs were toss'd aloft,

---

[43] Wraight: *op. cit.*: pp.443-50

[44] Hotson: Originally published in *Shakespeare's Sonnets Dated* (1949) but repeated at length in *Mr. W.H.* (1964), pp.73-84. Hotson calls *Sonnet 107* "the chief 'dating sonnet'". It refers to a very important event in Marlowe's young life.
See my forthcoming book, *Christopher Marlowe and the Armada* (publication 1996) for evidence of Marlowe's involvement in the Armada campaign.

As when a whirlwind takes the summer dust
And scatters it in middle of the air.
Then might ye see the reeling vessels split,
And tottering sink into the ruthless flood,
Until their lofty tops were seen no more.

Act III Sc.1. 11.152-170

A few lines later in this splendid passage he mentions the *Nonpareille* "that brave ship", exhibiting the love which every sailor has for his own ship, determined to bring her into his play. The autobiographical content not only of the Sonnets, but of so many of Marlowe's plays, has been amply demonstrated in my Chapter XXI, 'Canterbury Tales' in *The Story That the Sonnets Tell*, which requires answering with adequately commensurate evidence by Stratfordians reluctant to accept the historical reality that Marlowe is the pseudonymous Shakespeare of both the Sonnets and the plays. The above passage is one of many in the apocryphal play *Edward the Third* that contain strong recollections of *Tamburlaine the Great*, which was on the boards in the autumn of 1587, so that *Edward the Third* was most likely the very next play Marlowe wrote if he was preoccupied with espionage assignments on the Continent at this crucial time of England's danger.

My attribution of this play to Marlowe is borne out by both internal stylistic evidence and the historic evidence of its Armada association, which argues strongly for the dramatist's personal celebration of this as his commemoration of an event that made a tremendous impact on him.[45] It was his first attempt at a play that was not a tragedy and contains a romantic 'Love Episode' which some scholars have argued was 'inserted' by Shakespeare, a theory that has been dismissed; it was also his first English history play, using Holinshed's *Chronicles* as his source, which set the fashion for two decades of contemporary dramatization of English history that produced about 220 plays in this genre between 1588 and 1606, as Felix Schelling has estimated. "The appetite for historical reading matter was enormous and the greatest poets and writers set out to satisfy this".[46] We note the date when this spate of historical drama began, and we also note that Marlowe was again the trend-setter of fashion. His was the great innovative genius that launched the age of Shakespearean drama which he can now rightly claim as his own.

It is also of interest that a line from *Sonnet 94* in the group critical of 'Prince' Will's *"lascivious"* and faithless behaviour is quoted verbatim in *Edward the Third* by the Earl of Warwick in his speech admonishing his daughter not to entertain the king's lustful advances to her, which reflect on his royal state dishonourably:

"Lilies that fester smell far worse than weeds"

Act II Sc.1, 1.451

---

[45] Wraight: *Christopher Marlowe and Edward Alleyn*, Chap.III 'An "Armada" English History Play' previews my unpublished book referred to above.

[46] Henry the Fifth: Introduct. Essay: 'The Mirror of Kingship', *The Folger Library General Readers' Shakespeare* (1960) ed. Louis B. Wright and Virginia A. la Mar.

This again, supports the date of this play as 1588 when he had only recently written these early sonnets. The play was not printed until 1596, with further editions in 1599, 1609, 1617, 1625 and we learn from Greene's reference to it that it was a great theatrical 'hit' with Edward Alleyn in the role of the Black Prince. Although an immature work it represents the effective companion piece to *Henry V*, as *Edward II* is the companion piece to *Richard II*, presenting close parallels in dramatic details and incidents as well as in the treatment of characters.

This love of dramatically reworking a theme is a characteristic of Marlowe's work on which fruitful research could be expanded almost indefinitely, seeking for parallels as well as contrasts. F. S. Boas has commented that *Hero and Leander* would have provided such another companion piece to *Romeo and Juliet* had Marlowe decided to write it as a play; and I suggest that, in a different genre, this is really how these two works on the theme of star-crossed lovers were, in fact, conceived – as companion pieces growing out of the same inspiration.[47]   One could go on to suggest comparisons and contrasts in *Scanderbeg* and *Tamburlaine the Great*, both about great warriors who fought the Turks; *The Jew of Malta* and *The Merchant of Venice*; *The Massacre at Paris* and *Love's Labour's Lost*, both about the King of Navarre, a Protestant hero, treated in wide contrast; *Dido Queen of Carthage* and *Antony and Cleopatra*, for Dido is undeniably an early portrait of Cleopatra; *Faustus* and *Macbeth*, for their invocation of the supernatural in its baleful aspect, which he then reworks as fairy characters in *A Midsummer Night's Dream* and *The Tempest*; and *Twelfth Night* and *King Lear*, each on a theme of madness of different kinds, as Hotson has shown; the merry madness of the former and the serious, tragic madness of the latter, each featuring a prominent Fool, with the linking of the Fool's song, "When that I was and a little tiny boy" of which another verse is sung in *Lear*. There is amazing, subtle interplay running like a thread right through the plays of Marlowe/Shakespeare from beginning to end, and in this canon *Edward the Third*, Marlowe's 'Armada' play, stands as an important link in the chain of the poet-dramatist's development.

The 'difficult' sonnets, *123* and *124*, are only to be understood when seen as written out of Marlowe's experiences as an espionage agent. *Sonnet 123* reflects a visit to Rome where he saw the "*pyramids*", i.e. those huge Egyptian obelisks brought to Rome by Caligula and long fallen which were re-erected by Pope Sixtus V's command – a feat of engineering skill that excited the amazement of Europe and brought visitors flocking to see them. The Pope had his portrait painted with these re-erected "*pyramids*" shown in the window. *Sonnet 124* comments on the recent political murder of Henry III of France – the final scene of Marlowe's *The Massacre at Paris* – and he ruefully considers the incidence of such murderous plots as that of Babington against his Queen, which he had been involved in preventing, commenting that these religious fanatics "*die for goodness, who have lived for crime*". This is the politically aware Marlowe writing apparently in 1589.[48]

---

[47]   F. S. Boas: *Christopher Marlowe* (1940), p.235

[48]   Hotson: *Mr. W.H.* pp.84-98. Originally published in *Shakespeare's Sonnets Dated* (1949)

Thomas Walsingham, the True Patron, and His Circle

We do not know when Marlowe became acquainted with Thomas Walsingham. My hunch is that it was during the Armada campaign, when many courtiers and noblemen made a last minute dash to board the English navy ships and join in the fight against the Spaniards. This happened as the fleet was passing the coast of Kent and boats of every kind were commandeered to ferry the eager passengers, bursting with patriotic fervour, to the ships as they were cruising within sight of the Downs. Although Thomas Walsingham is not named in the list of illustrious gentlemen who scrambled aboard, which included Raleigh and Northumberland, since Walsingham's home county was Kent it seems unlikely that he was not there too.[49] Alternately, he may, like Marlowe, have been engaged in the intensive espionage activity prior to the Armada's arrival, and been already aboard a ship of the navy. Ships were also used in gathering intelligence at sea.

In 1589 we find Marlowe closely associated with the Latin poet, sonneteer, dramatist and musician Thomas Watson, briefly involved in a duel with Watson's enemy, whom Watson then slew and both he and Marlowe landed in jail. Watson pleaded slaying in self-defence and was eventually freed with the Queen's pardon. He was in the patronage of Sir Francis Walsingham and may have introduced the brilliant young Marlowe to the Walsingham family circle. In November 1589 Thomas Walsingham, aged twenty-six, inherited his estate upon the death of his elder brother Edmund. He would then have had the means and status to become a patron of poets. No doubt he introduced Marlowe to the esoteric club of free-thinkers led by Sir Walter Raleigh and the young Henry Percy, 9th Earl of Northumberland, a man of exactly Marlowe's age, who had also recently fought against the Spaniards on board Drake's ship, the *Revenge*. Marlowe claimed that he knew the Earl of Northumberland well. He was a genuine seeker after knowledge who never stood on rank with men of genius, however humble, and was a great friend of Thomas Harriot, the scientist and brilliant mathematician, who was also Marlowe's best friend, together with Walter Warner, the philosopher and mathematician, and the other intellectual poets of this group, Matthew Roydon and George Chapman, the latter also in the patronage of Thomas Walsingham.

Although direct evidence is lacking there is good reason to believe that Thomas Walsingham, a discreet gentleman who was well trusted by the Queen, was also a member of Raleigh's and Northumberland's secret debating society, which met "behind closed doors"; for their investigation of the new scientific knowledge then emerging and their discussions of speculative philosophy were proscribed as dangerous 'atheism', the label 'atheist' given to them to blacken the reputation of any who dared to become interested in such 'heresies'. It was his involvement in the activities of Raleigh's circle that eventually led to Marlowe's arrest on a charge of 'atheism' by the reactionary Court

---

[49] Augustine Ryther: *A Discourse concerninge the Spanishe fleete inuadinge Englande in the year 1588* &c. (1590) translated by I.L. (James Lea?) who appends a prose passage and verses naming the courtiers who joined the navy.
See *Sonnet 107* which celebrates the peace after the victory:
> "*Now with the drops of this most balmy time*
> * *My love looks fresh, and Death to me subscribes,*
> *Since spite of him, I'll live in this poor rhyme.*"
* Is this a reference to his new patron, Thomas Walsingham?

of Star Chamber, which exercised control over men's minds comparable to that of a modern police state. At the universities even the knowledge gleaned by exploration of the flora and fauna of the American continent was not permitted to be disseminated. Raleigh's potatoes and tobacco were viewed with suspicion. As for the astronomical studies of Raleigh's and Northumberland's *protégé*, Thomas Harriot, who was in secret correspondence with Kepler about his discovery that the orbits of the planets were elliptical, this would be condemned as *"vile heresy"*.

The ignorance and superstition of the time gave rise to lurid stories that Raleigh's School of Night was engaged in raising the devil. The Earl of Northumberland was nicknamed "the Wizard Earl" because of his passion for conducting experiments in chemistry for which he had laboratories built in his houses. It is salutary to remind ourselves that Marlowe and Northumberland were both born in the same year as Galileo – together with William Shakespeare of Stratford of course, whose life, according to all the evidence we have, proceeded peacefully in the acquisition of property and theatrical shareholdings, unaffected by the momentous ideological struggle that characterized the English Renaissance. The trial of his exact contemporary Galileo would not take place until 1633 on a charge of heresy for maintaining that the earth moves round the sun. For so long was the power of reaction to dominate Western societies, which experienced an especially fierce outburst of persecution against heretics, whether adherents of the opposing religious faction or free-thinkers who advocated religious tolerance, such as Marlowe, that reached a climax in the 1590s. Of this Marlowe was a victim.

The Rival Poets and their Patron

On the evidence of his patronage of two such intellectual poets as Marlowe and Chapman, Thomas Walsingham is also perceived to have been of some intellectual stature. George Chapman's greatest achievement was his translation into English heroic couplets of the epic works of Homer. He was held in high esteem by his contemporaries as a poet, and admired by Keats, who wrote his ode *"On First Looking into Chapman's Homer"* as his accolade to Chapman's great work. The impression of a patron of a studious, intellectual nature with cultured tastes is reinforced by the tone of Chapman's dedications to Thomas Walsingham, who was also always a friend to his poets.[50]

It is Thomas Walsingham's patronage of the two leading poets of the School of Night that confirms him unequivocally as the True Patron of the Sonnets. Orthodox scholars have scoured the literary history of the period in their efforts to discover a patron with two poets who stand in a relation of rivalry over his patronage, hoping to find the Rival Poet of the Sonnets – to no avail. This sonnet-group is absolutely crucial to the identification of both the patron and the two poets. George Chapman has, in fact, been correctly identified by orthodox scholars from the apt and subtle descriptions of him in *Sonnets 80, 85 and 86*. They give a superbly accurate and evocative poetic portrait of him:

---

[50] Chapman's dedication to Thomas Walsingham of *The Conspiracy of Charles, Duke of Byron* (1608) addresses him "Constant Friend" and refers to him as his "ancient and worthy friend". His dedication of the comedy *All Fools* (1605) addresses him "My long loved and honourable Friend".

Was it the proud full sail of his great verse,
Bound for the prize of all-too-precious you,
That did my ripe thoughts in my brain inhearse,
Making their tomb the womb wherein they grew?
Was it his spirit, by spirits taught to write
Above a mortal pitch, that struck me dead?[51]
No, neither he, nor his compeers by night
Giving him aid, my verse astonished.
He, nor that affable familiar ghost
Which nightly gulls him with intelligence,
As victors of my silence cannot boast;
I was not sick of any fear from thence.
    But when your countenance fill'd up his line,
    Then lack'd I matter that enfeebled mine.

Sonnet 86

So clearly is George Chapman delineated to anyone who has studied him, that it is a cause of amazement that sophistical arguments have been advanced replacing him with others less suitable – even with Marlowe as the Rival Poet to Shakespeare (as author) – but in what rivalry over what hypothetical poem to which patron? Nothing fits in any of the alternatives put forward by desperate orthodox scholars determined to squeeze William Shakespeare into the picture. It can't be done. All frustration vanishes in a flash as History reveals her trump card – the true triangular situation appears with **Marlowe, Walsingham** and **Chapman** in our sights. Not only do we have our True Patron with his two poets *(Sonnet 83)*, but we have the precise reason and cause of the searing jealousy that beset Marlowe and engendered the only rift he ever had with his beloved friend and patron. This was over the completion of his unfinished masterpiece, *Hero and Leander*, an exquisite work, by his old friend George Chapman in 1598 as an epithalamium on the marriage of Sir Thomas Walsingham, newly knighted by the Queen to honour the occasion, to the Lady Audrey Shelton, one of her Maids of Honour.

The exact background to this traumatic episode is a complex one. In analysing it in detail I came to the conclusion that it was Thomas Walsingham himself who had asked their mutual good old friend George Chapman to complete Marlowe's poem. It was a well-intentioned gesture to have the completed poem published to do honour to his 'dead' poet (who could hardly have written the completion from beyond the grave) and thereby also to bring his bride, the Lady Audrey Walsingham, into the patronage of his two poets, for Chapman's completion is dedicated to her.[52] It was published at the same time as Marlowe's beautiful, unfinished fragment, which is dedicated to Sir Thomas Walsingham in the moving tribute written by the gentleman publisher Edward Blount, who was a good friend of both Marlowe and Walsingham.

---

[51] For good measure he gives us here a tiny hint about himself, the 'dead' poet. This is very typical of Marlowe, as we learn the more we read the plays with him in mind.

[52] Chapman's dedication to Lady Walsingham of his completion of *Hero and Leander* (1598) refers to Sir Thomas as "my honoured best friend". See Wraight: *The Story That the Sonnets Tell*, pp.167-80.

The dedication of Marlowe's exquisite fragment to his patron clearly indicates what was in the mind of Blount and doubtless Walsingham also; that the publication of *Hero and Leander* would rehabilitate Marlowe's tarnished reputation, and for this a completion of the story of the legendary star-crossed lovers was needed. The visualization of this completed edition, then already in hand for it followed almost immediately, seems to be hinted at by Blount's words.

To the Right Worshipful, Sir Thomas Walsingham, Knight ....

Sir, we think not ourselves discharged of the duty we owe to our friend, when we have brought the breathless body to the earth: for albeit the eye there taketh his ever farewell of that beloved object, yet the impression of the man that hath been dear unto us, living an after life in our memory, there putteth us in mind of farther obsequies due unto the deceased. And namely of the performance of whatsoever we may judge shall make to his living credit, and to the effecting of his determinations prevented by the stroke of death. By these meditations (as by an intellectual will) I suppose myself executor to the unhappily deceased author of this Poem, upon whom, knowing that in his life time you bestowed many kind favours, entertaining the parts of reckoning and worth which you found in him with good countenance and liberal affection, I cannot but see so far into the will of him dead, that whatsoever issue of his brain should chance to come abroad, that the first breath it should take might be the gentle air of your liking: for since his self had been accustomed thereunto, it would prove more agreeable & thriving to his right children, than any other foster countenance whatsoever.

The publication of the completed poem was indeed an enormous success, going into nine editions between 1598 and 1637, so enhancing the honour in which Marlowe's name as a poet was held and far from eclipsing his reputation with Chapman's substantial, longer completion of four sestiads to Marlowe's two, which was probably what had been Marlowe's greatest fear. To Walsingham's dismay this aroused a storm of grief and anguished jealousy in the heart of the absent, exiled Marlowe at the completion by the hand of another of the last work he had written in his own name, as the bitter accusations of the *Sonnets of the Rival Poet* testify. This represents a traumatic episode in the sonnet-story, and the spilling out of such passion could only have been engendered by a sufficient cause. This is precisely provided by the situation of the completion of an especially valued poetic work by the other poet in Walsingham's patronage, and offered as an epithalamium on the occasion of the marriage of their patron.

What a scenario this presents of hurt relationships! Eventually Walsingham was able to explain his reasons for having called on their mutual, good old friend, George Chapman, to complete Marlowe's unfinished gem. Having understood Walsingham's action as benevolent, there follow four moving sonnets of reconciliation in which the exiled Marlowe eloquently atones for his jealous outburst.

> What potions have I drunk of siren tears
> Distilled from limbecks foul as hell within,
> Applying fears to hopes, and hopes to fears,
> Still losing when I saw myself to win!
> What wretched errors hath my heart committed

Whilst it hath thought itself so blessed never!
How have mine eyes out of their spheres been fitted
In the distraction of this madding fever!
O benefit of ill! Now I find true
That better is by evil still made better,
And ruin'd love when it is built anew
Grows fairer than at first, more strong, far greater.
　　So I return rebuk'd to my content,
　　And gain by ills thrice more than I have spent.

Sonnet 119

Having endured the pangs of jealousy, which are indeed a kind of madness, he was the better able to express this corrosive emotion in his dramatic works on the theme of jealousy, notably **Othello**. It is very likely that this play was written about this time. Assessing the likely dates of composition of the plays is inherently hypothetical since many of them were revised before being published in the First Folio or at times between printings in quartos. The incidents of Marlowe's life and personal experiences we can glean from his Sonnets give a far more telling guide to the progress of his artistic output and probable dates of compositions of his plays. It opens up the possibility of getting to know Shakespeare as we had never thought possible.

THE CHRONOLOGY OF THE SONNETS IN RELATION TO MARLOWE'S LIFE HISTORY

The Sonnets reflect the vicissitudes of the life of Christopher Marlowe in remarkable detail, so that it has been possible accurately to date their composition for almost all of the fourteen theme-groups of the sequence.

1. **Sonnets in Praise of his First Patron**, 'Prince' Will Hatcliffe *alias* 'Mr. W.H.', opening with a poem of pure perfection, *Sonnet 18* at Christmas 1587/8.
    Sonnets: 18-22; 53-55; 59; 62-65; 105, 106.

2. **Sonnets of First Love**, *Sonnets 23* and *24* on falling head over heels in love with Luce Morgan, 1587/8, an overwhelming experience for the twenty-three-year-old Marlowe. At first it left him tongue-tied. This is how Marlowe describes falling in love in his play **Edward the Third**, written at this time. When he wrote **Tamburlaine** he had not yet had this experience, and Tamburlaine's reaction is one of a sudden flood of euphoric praise for his beloved in hyperbolic eulogy of her beauty with wild promises of how he would treat her, so much so that his friend Techelles remarks in alarm: "What now! In love?" To which Tamburlaine replies:

    "Techelles, women must be flattered:
    But this is she with whom I am in love."
    Tamburlaine the Great, Part One, Act I, Sc.2, ll.106-8

His own reaction of tongue-tied adoration is pictured in *As You Like It*. Marlowe places these two sonnets separately from the group to the Dark Lady, as they introduce the experience of First Love, whereas in the later sonnets their relationship is already established. This suggests that 'Prince' Will did not make his entry as rival immediately, perhaps because he was still enjoying his relationship with the first mistress he stole from his poet *(Sonnets 40, 41, 42)*. He appears to have been a fickle lover. These sonnets are included in the next group.

3.   The **Friendship Turns Sour**, comprising thirteen sonnets that are increasingly critical of his youthful patron. Both groups of sonnets to 'Mr. W.H.' are widely scattered either singly or in small groups of two, three or four throughout the sequence. This group dates from early 1588, I suggest.
Sonnets: 35; 40-42; 57, 58; 69, 70; 93-96; 126

4.   The **Sonnets to the Dark Lady**, dating from 1587/8 to perhaps as late as 1593 (?) are an unbroken group of twenty-five sonnets, in which *Sonnet 146* alone is not concerned with her, although the mood of despondency may have arisen out of his unhappiness in this passionate affair.
Sonnets: 23, 24; 127-145; 147-152

5.   **Sonnets of a Secret Agent**: three sonnets reflecting his experiences as an espionage agent: *Sonnet 107*, his 'Armada' sonnet which arose as a result of his involvement in intelligence work; *Sonnets 123* and *124* reflecting his patriotic and philosophic contemplation of the political scene of his professional assignments, dating from 1588 and 1589. This precise dating follows Leslie Hotson's research on the meaning of these sonnets.
Sonnets: 107, 123, 124

6.   **Sonnets to the True Patron**, Thomas Walsingham, praising him with devotion; dating probably from 1589 and continuing to an unknown late date towards the end of the poet's life. A widely chronological group which forms only a small part of the total of seventy-one sonnets that directly address him in their life-long friendship.
Sonnets: 25; 38; 100-104; 108; 115, 116

7.   The **Commissioned Sonnets** to Henry Wriothesley, 3rd Earl of Southampton, dated 1590, are placed separately at the beginning of Thorpe's edition as an unbroken group denoting that they are not autobiographical. These seventeen sonnets, numbered *1* to *17*, were commissioned by Lord Burghley as a gift for the seventeenth birthday of his Ward of Court, the Earl of Southampton, who had been placed in his care since he was eight years old when his father died. Burghley held the lucrative office of Guardian of these high-born Wards of Court, which entailed also the authority of arranging suitable marriages for them until they reached their majority, and was anxiously cajoling Southampton to accept the hand of his granddaughter, Lady Elizabeth de Vere, having arranged this match when Southampton was only sixteen. He was able to plead his youth as excuse for delaying the consummation, but by the end of the year he was still adamantly refusing to proceed with the marriage. Burghley accordingly hit upon the idea of persuading him to change his mind by means of sonneteering him, and who more suitable to compose these sonnets than the poet Christopher Marlowe who was right there at the court working

as his intelligence agent? Eloquent as these seventeen sonnets are, one sonnet for each year of the Earl's life, they did not succeed in inducing him to accept the match. Whereupon Burghley next commissioned another of his servants at court, his secretary John Clapham, to write a Latin prose narrative of the tale of the self-loving *Narcissus* as a moral example to impress his ward, but again Southampton remained obstinate, which eventually cost him dear – a fine of 5,000 pounds was imposed when he reached his majority still unwed. It was a crippling levy on his estate, the price he paid for eventually marrying for love.
Sonnets: 1-17

8. The **Sonnets of Exile** are a huge group beginning on 30th May 1593 when the first of his verse-letters (*Sonnet 26*) to Thomas Walsingham, the man who saved his life, was probably written on board the hoy bearing him away to the Continent and a life of anonymity and exile.
Sonnets: 26-37; 39; 43-52; 56; 60, 61; 71, 72; 75, 76; 81; 97-99; 109; 113, 114; 125

It was to be a seven-year exile, with at least one brief return in 1595, that he spent largely in Italy, home of the Renaissance, in which his burgeoning maturity came to its glorious flowering in the radiant comedies and the romantic tragedies of this Italian period. He began with the still somewhat immature Veronese play *The Two Gentlemen of Verona*, the first romantic comedy, aptly described as "an experiment which led to much; it was a repertory of dramatic ideas; it brought Italy and romance into Shakespeare's comedies".[53]

The plays deriving their plots, either wholly or in part, from the Northern Italian writers Boccaccio, Fiorento, Bandello and Cinthio include:

> *Romeo and Juliet*
> *The Merchant of Venice*
> *Measure for Measure*
> *All's Well that Ends Well*
> *Othello*
> *Twelfth Night*
> *Much Ado About Nothing*

Others showing Italian influences or reflecting knowledge of sixteenth century Italian life and customs include *The Taming of the Shrew, As You Like It, The Winter's Tale, Cymbeline*. Many of these argue a first-hand experience of sixteenth century Italy beyond what could have been gleaned from books or talking to Italians in London, according to research by the acknowledged authority in this field, Professor Ernesto Grillo.[54]

In the period of his exile from 1593 to 1600/1, there was also a rich crop of English history plays: *Richard III, Richard II, King John, Henry IV Parts 1 and 2, Henry V*,

---

[53] Edward Dowden ed. *The Warwick Shakespeare: Comedies* (1893), London. Introduction to *The Two Gentlemen of Verona*, p.80

[54] See Ernesto Grillo: *Shakespeare and Italy* (1949)

and from Roman history, *Julius Caesar*. *Titus Andronicus* was probably partly already written, possibly in collaboration with Kyd for his patron's company, the Earl of Sussex's Men, but taken with him abroad and completed after the Deptford incident as the first play to be sent to his playbroker, William Shakespeare. *Love's Labour's Lost* in its original form was also, I suggest, written before 1593 for a private performance, probably at Scadbury before members of his esoteric club at Christmas 1592/3, and later revised, as the 1598 quarto states that this was "newly corrected and augmented".

The Comedy of Errors, written in his exile, derives mainly from Plautus, who is discussed in Part Two as an important source for several of Shakespeare's plays. *A Midsummer Night's Dream* is an amalgam of multiple sources, including Kentish folklore. *The Merry Wives of Windsor* is full of nostalgic recollections of Canterbury transposed to Windsor (see *The Story That the Sonnets Tell*, pp.336-7).

All the dates of composition are conjectural, for even when contemporary incidents are reflected in the plays we cannot always be sure that these were not added later by the actors to introduce topical interest updating plays that were regularly played in repertoire. However, after 1601 the following are suggested with their probable dates according to scholarly orthodox research:

1602	*Hamlet*	The *Henry VI Trilogy* I attribute to
1603	*Troilus and Cressida*	Marlowe written in 1590, '91 and '92,
1606	*Macbeth*	endorsing the research of Tucker
1607	*Coriolanus*	Brooke, Bakeless and Gaw and now
1608	*King Lear*	further supported by the work of
	Antony and Cleopatra	Merriam and Matthews.
	Pericles	
1611	*The Winter's Tale*	
	Cymbeline	
	The Tempest	
1613	*Henry VIII*	

The last play was in performance at the Globe on 29th June 1613 when the thatch of the roof caught fire from the misfiring of a cannon ball and the theatre was burnt to the ground – luckily all the playscripts and properties saved. This play was completed by John Fletcher, an ex-alumnus of Marlowe's old college, Corpus Christi, but not his contemporary as he was a younger man. Towards the end of his life they seem to have collaborated also in *The Two Noble Kinsmen*, which is based on Chaucer's 'The Knight's Tale'. Chaucer would have been dear to the heart of our Canterbury poet-dramatist. This play is ascribed to Shakespeare by Stanley Wells and Gary Taylor in their meticulously researched edition of *The Complete Works* (1988). It would indeed be a fitting end for the great poet-dramatist to imagine that he might have been lying on his death-bed as his theatre, the Globe, was burning like a funeral pyre; but of course we shall never know. The obvious conclusion must be that he did die in 1613, for why else should Fletcher have finished this final English history play completing his great English history cycle with the christening of the infant Queen Elizabeth, and the millennial tone of Archbishop Cranmer's final speech?

Meanwhile, the playbroker William Shakespeare of Stratford-upon-Avon was reaping the rewards of the deal he had struck in Richard Field's print-shop as the flow of dramatic works of the pseudonymous, but anonymous poet-dramatist reached his hands *via* the channels of communication set up by Walsingham's expert knowledge of the espionage service. *Sonnets 44* and *45* speak of "large lengths of miles" that separate him from his friend, and refer to:

> ... those swift messengers return'd from thee,
> Who even but now come back again assured
> Of thy fair health, recounting it to me.

His journey to an unknown destination begins with *Sonnet 26*, a moving sonnet of gratitude to his dear Patron to whom he owes "*Duty so great, which wit so poor as mine /May make seem bare in wanting words to show it*" and he will not return till better times:

> Then may I dare to boast how I do love thee,
> Till then, not show my head where thou may'st prove me.

Sonnet 27 begins: "*Weary with toil, I haste me to my bed, /The dear repose for limbs with travel tired,*", the theme continues in *Sonnet 28*; and then in *Sonnet 29* we hear the full cry lamenting his fate:

> When in disgrace with Fortune and men's eyes,
> I all alone beweep my outcast state,
> And trouble deaf Heaven with my bootless cries,
> And look upon myself and curse my fate,
> Wishing me like to one more rich in hope,
> Featur'd like him, like him with friends possess'd,
> Desiring this man's art, and that man's scope,
> With what I most enjoy contented least:
> Yet in these thoughts myself almost despising,
> Haply I think on thee, and then my state,
> Like to the lark at break of day arising
> From sullen earth, sings hymns at Heaven's gate,
>   For thy sweet love remember'd such wealth brings,
>   That then I scorn to change my state with kings.

Then follows a sonnet-pair bewailing his loss of friends and "vanish'd sights" *Sonnets 30* and *31*, and *Sonnet 32* descants on "*that churl Death*". *Sonnet 33* describes mountain scenery and "*pale streams*" that suggest he is now travelling through the Alps. He tells us of the sudden eclipse of his fame in a cloud of disgrace when his sun "*did shine /With all triumphant splendour on my brow /But out, alack, he was but one hour mine, /The region cloud hath mask'd him from me now*". This poet was no nonentity, but had a reputation as a 'king' of poets, but now fate has cast him down. Some nameless "*disgrace*" has overtaken him.

Let me confess that we two must be twain,
Although our undivided loves are one,
So shall those blots that do with me remain,
Without thy help, by me be borne alone.

....

I may not evermore acknowledge thee,
Lest my bewailed guilt should do thee shame,
Nor thou with public kindness honour me,
Unless thou take that honour from thy name.

....

Sonnet 36

And travel he must, usually on horseback.

How heavy do I journey on the way,
When what I seek (my weary travel's end)
Doth teach that ease and that repose to say:
Thus far the miles are measur'd from thy friend.
The beast that bears me, tired with my woe,
Plods dully on, to bear that weight in me,
As if by some instinct the wretch did know
His rider lov'd not speed being made from thee.
The bloody spur cannot provoke him on,
That sometimes anger thrusts into his hide:
Which heavily he answers with a groan,
More sharp to me than spurring to his side;
   For that same groan doth put this in my mind:
   My grief lies onward and my joy behind.

Sonnet 50

Can anything other than a journey into exile explain these poems? This is the tenor of this theme-group with many variants, all intensely autobiographical, all of them verse-letters to his dear friend and patron who never deserted him, and to whom he is bound with ties of inexpressible gratitude. Some sonnets in this group speak also of his anonymity. *Sonnet 71* which speaks again of death, tells his friend: *"Do not so much as my poor name rehearse, /But let your love even with my life decay"*. This is echoed in *Sonnet 72: "My name be buried where my body is, /And live no more to shame nor me, nor you"*.

9. **Two Self-Identifying Sonnets:** We come now to the most significant autobiographical poems that are placed at the very heart of the sequence, *Sonnets 73* and *74*. *Sonnet 73* is a contemplative poem, looking back on his life to the days of his youth, when the poet is already in the sear and yellow of his age. His choirboy reflections are here combined with memories of playing amid the ruined arches of the great Abbey of St. Augustine very near his Canterbury home. Finally, he recollects the portrait painted at a turning point in his young life when in 1585, aged twenty-one, he celebrated his new career as the Queen's secret agent. This is an *impresa* portrait conveying the sitter's message, making a personal statement endorsed by his motto

QUOD ME NUTRIT ME DESTRUIT – an obscure Latin maxim perhaps hinting that the sitter is also a poet.[55] We find this same motto in an English version in the conclusion of this sonnet.

> That time of year thou mayst in me behold
> When yellow leaves, or none, or few do hang
> Upon those boughs which shake against the cold,
> Bare ruin'd choirs, where late the sweet birds sang.
> In me thou seest the twilight of such day
> As after sunset fadeth in the West,
> Which by and by black night doth take away,
> Death's second self that seals up all in rest.
> In me thou seest the glowing of such fire
> That on the ashes of his youth doth lie,
> As the death-bed, whereon it must expire,
> **Consum'd with that which it was nourish'd by**.
>> This thou perceiv'st, which makes thy love more strong
>> To love that well, which thou must leave ere long.

Sonnet 73

Sonnet 74 recollects the crucial turning point in his life, the faked murder at Deptford, preceded by his "*arrest*" and "*bail*" and ending with his autobiographical statement – "*my body being dead, /The coward conquest of a wretch's knife*".

> But be contented: when that fell **arrest**
> Without all **bail** shall carry me away,
> My life hath in this line some interest,
> Which for memorial still with thee shall stay.
> When thou reviewest this, thou dost review
> The very part was consecrate to thee.
> The earth can have but earth, which is his due;
> My spirit is thine, the better part of me.
> So then thou hast but lost the dregs of life,
> The prey of worms, **my body being dead**,
> **The coward conquest of a wretch's knife**,
> Too base of thee to be remembered.
>> The worth of that, is that which it contains,
>> And that is this, and this with thee remains.

Sonnet 74

I have critically and exhaustively investigated the circumstances and the persons involved in the Deptford affair, with the conclusion that this was a faked murder, skilfully plotted and successfully carried off with the help (fortuitously) also of

---

[55] A. D. Wraight & Virginia F. Stern: *In Search of Christopher Marlowe* (1965 London, & N.Y. paperback ed. 1993, London) pp.63-68 and pp.214-219, gives the full history of this portrait's discovery in 1953 at Corpus Christi College, Cambridge.

slander and gossip to seal it irrevocably.[56] His murdered reputation was the price he had to pay. This premise receives strong support not only from Shakespeare's autobiographical sonnets, but also from the plays, notably from *Measure for Measure*, which presents a most interesting analogy with what transpired at Deptford.

The Duke, having left his dukedom in the charge of Angelo, the seeming righteous man, returns in the guise of a holy friar to observe how Angelo is faring, and is dismayed to hear of the merciless and unjust imprisonment and condemnation of Claudio, who is to be executed peremptorily. To save Claudio's life he persuades the kindly Provost of the prison to execute another condemned prisoner and send his severed head to Angelo as commanded. The Provost is afraid that the substitution would be detected protesting: "Angelo hath seen them both, and will discover the favour". To which the Duke replies:

> O, death's a great disguiser, and you may add to it.
> Shave his head and tie the beard, and say it was the
> desire of the penitent to be so bar'd before his death.

Confidently the Duke continues:

> Put not yourself into amazement how these things should be;
> all difficulties are but easy when they are known. Call
> your executioner, and off with Barnardine's head. I will
> give him a present shrift, and advise him for a better place.
> Yet you are amaz'd, but this shall absolutely resolve you.
> Come away: it is almost clear dawn.
>
> *Act IV Sc.2, 11.165-196*

However, fate steps in so that there is no need for Barnardine's untimely execution. Another prisoner dies of a fever, who is "A man of Claudio's years, his beard and head /Just of his colour". Whereupon the Duke exclaims with relief:

> O, 'tis an accident that heaven provides!
>
> *Act IV Sc.3, 1.73*

Heaven, or natural causes, doubtless provided the body for the inquest at Deptford. Under the Royal Coroner Danby's official seal the body was immediately hastily buried in an unmarked grave in Deptford's parish churchyard. There was no exhumation to identify it. Lips at court and in the circle of Marlowe's friends were sealed. Almost as though by order, a curious silence descended on the gossiping court. Only the babbling gossip beyond the court grew louder, and false rumour about Marlowe's 'blasphemous atheism' spread to become a notorious myth that has spanned the centuries.

10. The **Sonnets of Vilification** are a small, intensely autobiographical group of four poems written after 1593 and probably belonging to the *Sonnets of Exile*, confessing his past indiscretion in proselytizing his belief in religious tolerance, exposing

---

[56] Wraight: *The Story That the Sonnets Tell*, p.127 and Chap.X 'The Death of Marlowe'

ignorant superstition – willing men "not be be afeared of bugbears and hobgoblins". [57] The accusations of his alleged atheism; the slanderous gossip; the Puritan pamphleteers who murdered his reputation following the events at Deptford, of which report was doubtless spread by the jurymen at the inquest on his dead body, *"The coward conquest of a wretch's knife"*; all this is repudiated in his bitter cry against the injustice of the blows that fate had dealt him.

> 'Tis better to be vile, than vile esteemed,
> When not to be, receives reproach of being.

Sonnet 121

The full enormity of the aftermath of the plot that saved his life, but murdered his reputation by depicting him as the aggressor in the ridiculous quarrel over the payment of the bill – *the reckoning* – for their day's hospitality at Dame Eleanor Bull's house in Deptford, did not strike home until later. Thomas Walsingham's servant Ingram Frizer only escaped the gallows by pleading that he had slain Marlowe in self-defence. His tale of Marlowe's unprovoked aggression was ably supported by the two experienced espionage agents, both consummate con-men, whom Walsingham had summoned to the rendezvous at Deptford to act as witnesses to the 'murder' that Frizer was to perpetrate there. The cock-and-bull story that these three presented at the inquest before the Queen's own coroner, William Danby, and sixteen jurymen was doubtless skilfully rehearsed, but it would not have convinced a modern court of law. It is doubtful that it convinced the Royal Coroner Danby, either. In fact, the evidence suggests that he, too, was party to the plot. Elizabethan coroners were providers of bodies at need, and a body there certainly was, lying on view, the stab wound duly measured and recorded as being "over his right eye", a facial wound, a convenient disguise.

We read of the anguish that the destruction of his reputation caused the exiled poet, helpless to defend himself, in the four *Sonnets of Vilification*:

> Your love and pity doth th'impression fill
> Which vulgar scandal stamp'd upon my brow,
> For what care I who calls me well or ill,
> So you o'er-green my bad, my good allow?
> You are my All the world, and I must strive
> To know my shames and praises from your tongue;
> None else to me, nor I to none alive,
> That my steel'd sense or changes right or wrong.
> In so profound abysm I throw all care
> Of others' voices, that my adder's sense
> To critic and flatterer stopped are.
> Mark how with my neglect I do dispense:
> > You are so strongly in my purpose bred,
> > That all the world besides me thinks y'are dead.

Sonnet 112

---

[57] Richard Baines's *Note:* B.L. *Harleian MS, 6848 f.186.*

That strange last line is as Thorpe printed it. We are forced to look at it. And to question? This is not a printer's error, I suggest, but a deliberate, obscure wording giving a hint of the hidden truth. Editors of the Sonnets have sometimes tried to 'improve' on Thorpe, but all have fallen wide of the author's intention and made an even greater nonsense than the original, which assuredly was deliberately altered for the publication in 1609 with a touch of wit, a hint of method in its madness, that makes us think. Note also the line: "*None else to me, nor I to none alive*".
Sonnets: 110-112; 121

11. The fourteen **Sonnets of the Rival Poet**, dated 1598, are perhaps the most anguished of all, wrung through with the exiled Marlowe's personal hurt. They testify how intensely he lived for and through his art in his exile. In *Sonnet 29* (*When in disgrace with Fortune and men's eyes, /I all alone beweep my outcast state*) he has told us that his solace is his writing in which he confesses himself the typically self-critical artist: "*With what I most enjoy, contented least*". To have given the completion of his most exquisite narrative poem to another poet seemed to him like a stab in the back. This is what engendered those fourteen bitterly anguished sonnets.

History presents us with the precise scenario of these sonnets in the **Marlowe-Walsingham-Chapman** triangle revealing the beloved patron with his two poets in rivalry over the completion of *Hero and Leander* as an epithalamium for his marriage.[58]
Sonnets: 78-80; 82-92

12. The four **Sonnets of Reconciliation**, dated perhaps 1599/1600, just before he returned from his seven-year exile, express his wretchedness in deep remorse for his jealous outburst. Most tenderly and significantly in *Sonnet 120*, in which every word, every phrase, conveys to us that this is Marlowe writing his moving tribute to his faithful friend and patron, Thomas Walsingham, whose magnanimous nature is here acknowledged in true humility by his erring poet-friend:

> That you were once unkind befriends me now,
> And for that sorrow which I then did feel
> Needs must I under my transgression bow,
> Unless my nerves were brass or hammered steel.
> For if you were by my unkindness shaken
> As I by yours, you've pass'd a hell of time,
> And I, a tyrant, have no leisure taken
> To weigh how once I suffered in your crime.
> O that our night of woe might have remembered
> My deepest sense, how hard true sorrow hits,
> And soon to you, as you to me then tendered
> The humble salve which wounded bosom fits!
>   But that your trespass now becomes a fee,
>   Mine ransom yours, and yours must ransom me.

---

[58] Wraight: *op. cit.*, pp.167-78

The recollection of their "*night of woe*", preceded by the reference to Walsingham's "crime", can only be the remembrance of what happened at Deptford – his departure into exile as the faked murder was being enacted at Dame Bull's house. It is evident that Marlowe had not been told the details of the 'murder' plot when he left Deptford, for when he learned of its full implications he was horrified. The tale that the three men, Poley, Skeres and Frizer, had concocted to protect Frizer, the 'murderer', condemned Marlowe to a murdered reputation as a man who had basely attacked Frizer "*from behind his back*", depicting him as the unprovoked aggressor in the petty quarrel over the settlement of the bill. Utterly dismayed that he was now powerless to refute this ugly story, which was soon spread through the grapevine by the jurors and eagerly embellished by gossip, destroying his good name down the ages, he could only spill out his grief in his *Sonnet 34*. This is included in the *Sonnets of Exile*, but I present it here as it has relevance to the above *Sonnet 120* which looks back on the tragic events for which Marlowe bore the consequences for the rest of his life. *Sonnet 34* is only understandable, and only makes complete sense when it is read in this context.

> Why didst thou promise such a beauteous day
> And make me travel forth without my cloak,
> To let base clouds o'ertake me in my way,
> Hiding thy brav'ry in their rotten smoke?
> 'Tis not enough that through the cloud thou break
> To dry the rain on my storm-beaten face,
> For no man well of such a salve can speak
> That heals the wound, and cures not the disgrace.
> Nor can thy shame give physic to my grief;
> Though thou repent, yet I have still the loss.
> Th'offender's sorrow lends but weak relief
> To him that bears the strong offence's cross.
>   Ah, but those tears are pearl which thy love sheds,
>   And they are rich, and ransom all ill deeds.

Clearly Walsingham was also deeply upset that he had not foreseen the consequences of the clever murder plot which aimed to protect all those involved, but which had in one important sense misfired, leaving him powerless to make amends. As Marlowe, in philosophic resignation, finally without bitterness put it:

> Now all is done; have what shall have no end.

Sonnet 110
(From the *Sonnets of Vilification*)
Sonnets: 117-120

13. There are two **minor group-themes**. (a) Two sonnets that describe the giving and receiving of a gift of a book with blank pages for recording thoughts or poems, and another of a gift of "tables". The book is perhaps a farewell gift to Master Will Hatcliffe, as the admonishing tone of *Sonnet 77* implies; the "tables" are a gift received by the poet, which he then gives away. This is obscure. The tone is of respect to the giver, who may or may not have been Walsingham.

(b) Four sonnets I have called **Problem Sonnets** are chronologically obscure, as is the subject of *Sonnets 67* and *68* who is referred to in the third person. All four sonnets are a lament for the evil times and the follies of men that spoil human existence, so that the poet longs for death; all four are philosophic in mood though bitter and critical, and more revealing of the intellectual poet himself than of the person or circumstances referred to. *Sonnet 146* is introspective, extracted from the Dark Lady group and disconsolate with himself; *Sonnet 66* is written out of his bitter disillusionment in society and the world. They all bear the hallmark of Marlowe's wit and could not have been written by such a self-evident non-intellectual as the man from Stratford.
Sonnets: 77; 122; 66-68; 146

14. L'Envoy, the sonnet-pair which concludes the sequence, was probably written for its publication in 1609. They are a rueful comment on his affair with the harlot Luce Morgan, in which he finally contracted gonorrhoea and had to take medicinal baths to seek a cure.
Sonnets: 153, 154

In the Sonnets we have the history of Christopher Marlowe clearly pictured from his strikingly successful arrival in London at the age of twenty-three in 1587, with his dramatization of the conquering *Tamburlaine the Great*, the play that was acclaimed, imitated, quoted, lampooned in the theatrical works of his contemporaries and beyond for more than seventy years. It was a world première worthy of our greatest dramatist, Shakespeare, and the impact he made as the innovative genius, the trend-setter and leading light of the Elizabethan stage in the 'pre-Shakespearean' period continued with momentum. He was hailed by his contemporaries as the "famous gracer of tragedians", and "the Muse's darling".[59] For six years his reign was supreme, and truly his sun "*did shine /With all triumphant splendour*" on his brow *(Sonnet 33)* until it suffered sudden eclipse at Deptford. Then followed his "*disgrace*" so deeply and constantly lamented in the Sonnets, and his years of exile.

It was amazing to find that every sonnet slotted into place chronologically and naturally to reveal the story of the life of Christopher Marlowe, not William Shakespeare of Stratford-upon-Avon who played his part as the playbroker. There are no contradictions, no anomalies. Once the deliberate a-chronological mix-up of Thorpe's cryptic edition was sorted out, what emerged was a seamless, coherent, historically valid record of a persecuted genius, whose strange fate was perhaps the fertile soil that nurtured his very special greatness.

---

[59] Greene's *Groatsworth of Wit*, Letter (1592) and George Peele: *The Honour of the Garter* (1593).

The Return from Exile

The return from his exile is traceable in an unique historic episode. This was the visit of Don Virginio Orsino, Duke of Bracciano, nephew of the Grand Duke of Tuscany, to the court of Queen Elizabeth in early January 1601 (new style). At the sumptuous marriage by proxy of his cousin, Maria de'Medici, to Henry IV of France, in October 1600 in Florence, Orsino had offended Pope Clement VIII by challenging his new decree concerning the pecking order of the Italian nobility. This decree had demoted the Orsini from their cherished position of priority granted by the late Pope Sixtus V, who was Don Virginio's great-uncle-in-law. It was a piece of typical Italian tribal in-fighting. To avoid facing the Pope's ire, Orsino decided secretly to extend his journey to France whither he had accompanied the newly-wed Queen, by visiting England – a risky thing for a Catholic prince to do. He would require assurance that his reception at the Protestant court would be especially warm and welcoming so that he could flaunt his friendship with that 'great Jezebel' Queen Elizabeth under the nose of the Pope! He was playing a diplomatic game of chess.[60]

Arriving *incognito* in London on 3rd January, he was received at court three days later on 6th January with the most extraordinarily, cordial courtesy by the Queen. That night, being Twelfth Night, a play was given in his honour. As Dr. Hotson's superlative research published in *The First Night of Twelfth Night* (1954) has established beyond all possible doubt, this play was Shakespeare's delightful *Twelfth Night*, featuring Duke Orsino to the life in the speaking portrait of this cultured, music-loving Italian nobleman, paying court to the Lady Olivia (Queen Elizabeth) in the established chivalric tradition of the times.[61] To argue that the actor, William Shakespeare, could have knocked up this exquisite play, perfect in all its courtly detail, in less than three days to honour the visit of Duke Orsino, whose arrival had been kept a close secret for diplomatic reasons, is more than even Dr. Hotson's skill can make convincing. Accordingly, this marvellous research has been largely ignored, for in all other respects it is unanswerable.

It was, of course, written by the returning exile, the pseudonymous Shakespeare, Christopher Marlowe, who had evidently been in the service of Duke Orsino during his last years in Italy. Documentary evidence for his service with Orsino is now being researched, logically following what is implied by the evidence presented in Part Two.

The delightful Saturnalian comedy, *Twelfth Night*, was, I believe, Marlowe's New Year gift to his Italian prince and the great Queen whom he had served as an intelligence agent for so many years. There is documentary evidence that supports Marlowe's presence in London in the cryptic letter by Thomas Thorpe to Edward Blount in late summer 1600 when he might have been sent as Orsino's envoy to arrange for his intended visit.[62] The spectacularly lavish welcome that Queen Elizabeth prepared for Orsino strongly supports this scenario, that it was a case of diplomatic collusion between

---

[60] Leslie Hotson: *The First Night of Twelfth Night* (1954, London) pp.50-4. Hotson's entire book is the invaluable source to be consulted.
See also Wraight: *The Story that the Sonnets Tell*, pp.385-90.

[61] Hotson: *op. cit.* pp.124-9.
Wraight: *op. cit.* pp.405-7.

[62] Wraight: *op. cit.* Chapter XXIV, 'Thorpe Writes a Letter', and pp.418-23.

Elizabeth and Orsino exploiting the papal snub to the full. And this was something that had to be arranged in advance. Who better to achieve this than the skilful, experienced and well-trusted intelligence agent Christopher Marlowe? He may not even have had to maintain a disguise to the Queen, as I have argued cogently that she was herself aware of the Deptford ruse to save the life of her foremost dramatist from the machinations of the Court of Star Chamber under the orders of her "little black husband", Archbishop Whitgift, with whose witch-hunt against the free-thinkers she would not have been pleased in this instance.[63]

Raleigh had been in disgrace for his clandestine marriage to Elizabeth Throckmorton, but that was the Queen's private affair, not political. By 1600 Raleigh had long been re-admitted to her grace and remained her favourite to the end of her days, and the free-thinkers were ever benignly regarded by this broad-minded woman. Elizabeth loved playing politics, and the visit of this Catholic prince was a timely opportunity to impress her Catholic enemies that she had a powerful friend in their camp – the extremely rich Grand Duke of Tuscany's own nephew, who was as a son to him, no less.

With this visit, Marlowe returned from his long exile and remained in England under the protection of the secret society of the Freemasons, which was headed by his good friend Francis Bacon, the Masonic Solomon. As my Masonic evidence will reveal, this was a Baconian society in which both Anthony Bacon and Christopher Marlowe held high positions, and it was through the agency of the Freemasons that Marlowe was enabled to return in safety. The seven years of his exile are reflected in the dominant group of the *Sonnets of Exile*.

Those informed scholars and sensitive poets who studied Thorpe's cryptic edition of the Sonnets, such as Auden, Spender, Barber, Boas, Harrison, Hotson, Wordsworth, have perceived that this is an autobiographical poetic journal even though obscurely presented in a deliberately confused mixed-up state, the mix-up certainly being the poet's own skilful arrangement for the purpose of the publication. Hotson's research establishing the precise numbering of certain sonnets in relation to their psalms (*Sonnet 107* with Psalm 107, and *Sonnet 124* with Psalm 124) is an amazing and significant revelation of the poet's intent in the subtle and extraordinarily sophisticated presentation of his sonnet-sequence.[64] Finally unravelled, its autobiographical story is now confirmed beyond possible doubt.

---

[63] *Ibid*: pp.116-23.

[64] Hotson: *Shakespeare's Sonnets Dated*, pp.4-20
    Mr. W.H., pp.73-84
    See also Wraight: *op. cit.*, pp.237-9 and p.256

Tracing Marlowe in Exile

Having been led step by step, in following the trail laid by the Sonnets as this complex story unravelled, to what is undoubtedly the historical truth about Marlowe, the conviction grew that more evidence must be lying somewhere as yet undiscovered and unresearched, if only one knew where to look. History does not conceal, but reveals her treasures willingly to the enquiring mind that is open to guidance and not hampered by preconceived notions stubbornly held. The clues are there: we need to have the mind to follow them – an open, questioning mind, not prone to jump to conclusions that are not tested rigorously, and always being prepared for surprises that are perhaps contrary to what one had expected to find!

A most important clue that presented itself was the cryptic nature of the First Folio, which led me to investigate the connections with Freemasonry already suggested by others (but followed through with fallacious assumptions) that are detectable in the life of Francis Bacon. Of relevance to the present paper, however, is his brother, Anthony Bacon, whose largely neglected archives of correspondence, sixteen volumes of manuscript papers in all, have yielded the amazing documentary evidence that is the concluding testimony revealing that Christopher Marlowe was alive in the years 1595 and 1596 and had evidently been living abroad, mainly in Italy.

In 1592 Anthony Bacon's declining health forced him to return to England after having lived for twelve years abroad, mainly in France and Switzerland, where he had worked as an intelligence agent for his uncle, Lord Burghley, and for the Secretary of State, Sir Francis Walsingham, until his death in 1590. The papers of Anthony Bacon had been made extensive use of in the 1750s by Thomas Birch for his *Memoirs of the Reign of Queen Elizabeth*, and Birch claims that they afford the most comprehensive source of information extant on French contemporary history gleaned, for the most part, from the reports of the intelligencers who worked for and with Bacon. Marlowe's employers were also Burghley and Sir Francis Walsingham, and there is the strongest presumptive conclusion that their intelligence work would have brought them into contact; that Anthony Bacon and Marlowe became well acquainted as early as the 1580s, and that their friendship led to a close collaboration between these like-minded men and Anthony's brother Francis, all three sharing the same aspirations for mankind, which found expression in the development of the great secret society of the Freemasons. Marlowe's close ties with Anthony Bacon, both as a fellow intelligence agent, and as a brother Freemason, are the thread that has led to the discovery of the documentary evidence to be presented here.

Dame Frances Yates has established that the last decade of the sixteenth century in particular exhibited the signs of instability associated with the *fin de siècle malaise* of Western societies. In such an atmosphere a renewed assault on heresy was to be expected. When Marlowe fled into exile on the Continent seeking a safe haven, he must have been aware that it would be essential to maintain acute vigilance. At this time Giordano Bruno was languishing in a Roman prison, eventually to be burned at the stake. The most sympathetic area would be Northern Italy, where the rich and powerful Grand Duke of Tuscany ruled, who was no puppet of the Pope, and was suspected of being secretly something of an Anglophile. His sumptuous court was at the Pitti Palace in Florence. His nephew, Don Virginio Orsino, Duke of Bracciano, whom he had brought up as his son from a tender age when the young prince was orphaned by the murderous marital intrigues of his parents, was often in Florence at the court helping his uncle in government affairs. Eventually, Marlowe was to find himself in some kind of service to Don Virginio, and to immortalize him as his Duke Orsino in *Twelfth Night*.[65]

As an experienced intelligence agent, we can assume that Marlowe would have continued to sustain himself by working as a professional intelligencer, using an assumed name as was the regular practice of secret agents when working in dangerous situations. He would have had the ready help of Thomas Walsingham who, even if no longer active in the secret service since his inheritance of the family estates in Kent, would have influence and contacts within the espionage network. But what this research highlights is the relationship between Anthony Bacon and Christopher Marlowe and the focus now shifts distinctly onto Anthony Bacon's activities as a master-intelligencer.

Although he had inherited a goodly estate in the counties of Hertfordshire and Middlesex at his father's death in 1579, Anthony, then aged twenty-one, set out on his travels and determined to live abroad. He first took up residence in Paris, where he was encouraged by his uncle, Lord Burghley, to form a close friendship with the exiled Catholic traitor, Dr. William Parry, with a view to keeping an eye on him. He thus began his highly successful career as an intelligence agent for the government. He corresponded regularly with Sir Francis Walsingham keeping the foreign secretary informed on every nuance of the political state of France, where he spent a considerable time at the court of King Henry of Navarre. Over the twelve years of his residence abroad he travelled widely on the Continent and settled for periods in Switzerland and Italy as well as France, building up an intelligence and espionage network of his own with trusted, hand-picked agents working and reporting directly to him. Two of his most valuable agents were devout Catholics who were loyal to England, a reflection of the non-sectarian, ecumenical attitude towards religion espoused by the Freemasons.

One of these, a zealous Catholic, was Anthony Standen who had originally left England on religious grounds and became a pensioner of King Philip of Spain, but he was won over to serve Queen Elizabeth by Sir Francis Walsingham with a pension of 100 l. a year and introduced by him to Anthony Bacon in Paris. Standen undertook to return to Spain to provide intelligence for Bacon. Ironically he was betrayed to the French authorities and accused of being a Spanish spy and was imprisoned in France, but Anthony Bacon managed to obtain his release with the help of English diplomatic pressure in 1591. It was at this time that Anthony Bacon's health suffered an aggravated attack of the rheumatic condition he had been afflicted with from childhood and, almost crippled, he made the decision to come home to England.

Standen did return to Spain to work for Anthony Bacon, and on leaving the country again in 1593 he wrote to Bacon saying how anxious he was that "poor Mr. Rolston" had not been able also to get out and he feared he might be in danger of being seized by the Spaniards and subjected to tortures. Standen intended to cross over from Calais requesting that someone meet him at Dover and accompany him to London, where he will impart his news from Spain by word of mouth, and requests "a quiet house, as near

---

[65] Hotson: *The First Night of Twelfth Night* (1954) pp.46-64 and p.205.
See Wraight: *op. cit.* pp.394-5 and pp.405-6.

you as might be, of no common resort, and in effect where it shall best like her Majesty, this purporting much her royal service for my return over again".[66] This implies that Standen would be reporting direct to the Queen.

There can be little doubt that the top secret agents did on occasion have confidential audiences with the Queen. Their services were highly valued as the indispensable eyes and ears of the government on whose information foreign policy was formulated. This applied also to Marlowe, particularly in connection with his intelligence for the 1588 Armada attack, as is shown in my forthcoming book on this historic encounter. Standen was eventually knighted by Queen Elizabeth for his services – despite being a Catholic! This puts a different light onto the role of the professional intelligencers and espionage agents, who have been depicted as rogues and essentially a part of the Elizabethan underworld of criminal elements of society by the prejudiced and superficial writers who set out to sensationalize the Elizabethan espionage service in order to gain interest in their books among a wider readership. The fact that men like Poley and Skeres were paid for their services and sometimes had to suffer spells in prison as part of their work, and were not all equally admirable, morally speaking, in their behaviour has nothing to do with it. Our members of Parliament are also capable of corruption and thereby demean their high calling, as do men of the church. But there were a great many well-educated, politically aware men of honesty and integrity and commitment who served the English Protestant Queen, often at great personal risk. Such men who either directly served or were in correspondence with Anthony Bacon included Anthony Standen and Anthony Rolston, both zealous Catholics, Edward Selwyn, Robert de La Fontaine, Edward Burnham, Godfrey Alleyn, Henry Hawkins, John Clapham, Anthony Ersfield, George Gilpin, James Combes, Edward Yates and others listed as "servants" of Anthony Bacon, who also when abroad furnished 'intelligence' on the political movements and local news items they observed, as did his good friend Jean Castol, Minister of the French church in London on his frequent trips to France. There were also two Italian merchants who acted as agents in Italy, Jacomo Marenco and Giovanni Bassadona of Venice. The latter has an evocative name that immediately suggests he may have been the inspiration for Bassanio in *The Merchant of Venice*. Here we are exploring the relationship of the exiled Marlowe with Anthony Bacon and their association in the intelligence service which we know they both served, and it would be a practical certainty that Marlowe would have known Bassadona in Venice.

Not only governments, but influential and ambitious noblemen employed men as private 'intelligencers' to bring them news from the Continental courts and countries, for they were all avid for news from abroad. Part of every gentleman's education was to travel; making the 'grand tour' of the Continent was the educated Elizabethan's finishing school. Those who travelled abroad on their own account, pursuing their personal interests or pleasures, assiduously gathered information on the countries they visited and often acted as unofficial intelligencers providing political news and observations as a lucrative side-line to their travels. A fine example of these intelligence-gathering travellers was the Elizabethan courtier Sir Stephen Powle, whose large cache of extant letters has been researched by Virginia F. Stern and significantly throws light on this activity.[67] His vast

---

[66] Thomas Birch: *Memoirs of the Reign of Queen Elizabeth* (1754) Vol.I, p.102.

[67] Virginia F. Stern: *Sir Stephen Powle of Court and Country* (1992) Associated University Presses. See esp. Chaps 4 & 5, 'Agent for Queen Elizabeth at Casimir's Court' and 'Agent for Queen Elizabeth in Italy'.

correspondence has yielded a rare, first-hand record of a much-travelled sixteenth-century gentleman's view of the European scene, including also Scotland and his own homeland and court. Powle is a meticulous and astute observer, cultured, scholarly, intelligent, highly motivated to serve his country and a devout Protestant, but pragmatic withal. On his travels he recorded everything, often in great detail, and also acted as a courier bearing important packets of letters to their Continental destinations. Inevitably and naturally he graduated to become an agent for Queen Elizabeth and much of his correspondence to Lord Burghley and Sir Francis Walsingham falls into the category of intelligence gathering, for which he would have received remuneration; though he was not in the government's secret service. The dividing line was thin. Powle was, undoubtedly, rendering honourable service in providing essential information to his Queen and her government.

When Anthony Bacon returned to England in 1592, he severed his professional relationship with his uncle Burghley, complaining that he had never remunerated him adequately for the work he had done for the government despite the fact that the Queen had herself often commended the excellence of his letters of intelligence. Instead, Anthony Bacon entered the service of the Earl of Essex, who had now acquired a seat on the Privy Council and had turned his ambition to gaining a great reputation as a statesman, rather than seeking the path of military glory. In this course he was advised by Francis Bacon, who had also joined Essex's service. To enhance his new position, an important aspect of Essex's policy was to have a ready supply of expert intelligence on foreign affairs with which to impress the Privy Council. To this end, late in 1595 Anthony Bacon had recommended to the Earl an intelligence agent with experience in Italy, for this is where the Earl especially desired to obtain information.

In the *Bacon Papers* there is extant the lengthy and very detailed assignment that was prepared for this new agent, who was duly introduced to the Earl as "a French gentleman" by the name of Monsieur Le Doux, for whom passports were issued dated at London February 10th 1595/6 and renewed at Richmond, whither the court had removed, on March 10th.[68] Monsieur Le Doux's instructions are appropriately written in French, in the hand of Anthony Bacon's clerk, Jaques Petit. These provide a most interesting insight into the range of information that an intelligence agent might be required to obtain. An intelligence agent acted quite often in an advisory capacity to his government or master, and consequently his position was of considerable standing and importance. This is reflected in the language employed in some of these reports indicating what actions and diplomacy should follow from the information provided. An experienced intelligencer was in the valued category of one whose word was listened to. Such a one was this Monsieur Le Doux, whose instructions, while very precise, also have a tone of respect.

This document headed "*Memoires Instructives*" is not signed, but is clearly speaking in the Earl's name. It is of interest to see it in full, here given in translation, as it is a rare example of an assignment from which we learn what countries the agent, Monsieur le Doux, would be visiting and what he would be doing.

---

[68]   Lambeth Palace Library, *Bacon Papers MS 655 f.191, MS 656 f.191*

Memoires Instructives[69]

Firstly, during the journey, you shall please remember to keep the ear open & the pen ready to advise by post of the reliable cities all the occurrences which you encounter & deem worth reporting.

Then, once arrived at the place where you propose to sojourn, such as at the court of the Emperor or elsewhere, I wish you to advise not only on the state & the affairs of the Imperial Court, but that which you can also find out there about Italy & Turkey.

Those points most noteworthy & memorable which you should inform on are: The death of Princes & important personages & who succeeds them. What are their successors' reputed expectations, sufficiency & means. The friendships & enmities between a State or a Prince & the other: And in what manner they proceed with one another. If they make war, who are the leaders & what armed forces are levied at sea or on land. To make peace what conditions & covenants do the two parties treat & with what pretensions is the peace concluded, & whether it is sought by both sides or through the mediation of a third party.

Afterwards you should observe well which alliances & confederacies are formed or renewed between the Princes of Germany & Italy or by each of them with foreigners. Which embassies are maintained by one Prince to another either between themselves or outside & what is their outcome.

The disturbances & seditions occurring in each Prince's State, their motives & chief points.

Who are the Princes' favourites & principal counsellors, & which significant personages are under their Prince's suspicions, the reason for jealousy & through what means such personages hold their positions & strengthen their influence.

What noteworthy sums in deniers are due from each Prince or State to the Italian banks.

And in case you should find a good commodity to go to Italy, particularly to that source of all news, Rome, to make some sojourn there, I entreat you to keep your ears open to discover the sources of intrigue, particularly touching anything concerning England or Scotland & the two Princes of these two Kingdoms. And as my misfortune has been such that God has never permitted me to see Italy, the Garden of Christendom, I must particularly enjoin you, for my own satisfaction, to take some trouble writing particular descriptions of each Principality of Italy, specifying for each of them the following points:

The size and superficies of each one. The revenue & how & from where it is derived. The fortified cities with their garrisons, what number of soldiers are kept in each State. The sea ports. The big rivers & famous cities of each Principality. The commodities which each land sells & where they are transported to: What merchandise comes from outside & by what laws & customs each State is governed & which counsellors & officers the Prince uses most.

Lastly, you should always remember that through the medium of the acquaintances which you will make in your place of residence you may gain the friendship of others who reside where the principal occurrences take place, such as [..?] & Spain of whom you should make no difficulty in assuring them, if they

---

[69]   *Ibid*: *MS 656 f.186^{r-v}*
    Text translated by Mme. Lucie Bouchon

56

furnish you with some good & valuable material of important & secret occurrences & not such as one finds in St Mark's Square, that they will be justly recompensed according to the value of their product. What may remain for you to advise or admonish I leave to your own judgement & discretion & to the events to come. *Nam res magis dant consilia hominibus homines rebus.*[70]

A great deal of research was envisaged providing a most valuable fund of information. My view of this is that it shows Francis Bacon's mind in the preparation of this assignment, guiding the wayward Earl into the paths of a successful political career. It was probably dictated to Petit, and doubtless a copy was made for Le Doux.

That name, Le Doux, immediately struck me as a *nom-de-guerre* adopted by an English agent who was posing as a Frenchman, for Anthony Bacon's experienced intelligencer Anthony Standen used the *nom-de-guerre* La Faye when operating in France. Standen, posing as Monsieur La Faye, reports an amusing incident to Anthony Bacon of his success in presenting himself as a born Frenchman who could not understand a word of English of which he convinced a party of Englishmen who had arrived in France; who then proceeded to converse freely with each other in English in his presence,[71] unaware that Monsieur La Faye was absorbing all the information he required! Standen was also introduced by Anthony Bacon to the service of Essex.

Was Monsieur Le Doux then perhaps also an English intelligence agent posing as "a French gentleman" and carefully maintaining this cover to the Earl of Essex who supplied him with instructions in French? He was highly recommended to the Earl by both the Bacon brothers. Was it possible that this might really be the cover for Christopher Marlowe, who had been living in exile in Italy? The connection with both the Bacons, his known experience as an intelligence agent, and the suggestion of his knowledge of Italy all seemed to point towards this as a possibility. If Standen could pull off his successful pose as a Frenchman who understood no word of English, we may be sure that Marlowe would have been able to do so. He was probably an excellent actor! Agents were adept at disguises, and how well Essex might have known Marlowe personally is doubtful. Whatever the case, Monsieur Le Doux was accepted as a *bona fide* Frenchman who was a skilled intelligencer, to whom a passport was accordingly issued.

My suspicions have now been put to the test. The evidence discovered in the archives of the voluminous correspondence extant in the Anthony Bacon Papers at Lambeth Palace Library has come up with the positive answer. As has happened so often in my long pursuit of the historical truth, the sort of evidence that turned up was a totally unexpected surprise. My search might just as well have drawn a blank, revealing nothing. What these amazing documents disclose speaks for itself.

In Part Two this evidence is analysed, testing the premise that Monsieur Le Doux can be none other than Christopher Marlowe, the pseudonymous William Shakespeare, alive and working in intelligence on the Continent for his friend Anthony Bacon in 1596.

---

[70] The Latin maxim translated is: For affairs influence men more than men do affairs
[71] L.P.L. *Bacon Papers MS 648, f.132ᵛ* In a long letter ff.132-133ᵛ signed La Faye.

PART TWO

MONSIEUR LE DOUX

Piecing together the jigsaw of the evidence discovered is an absorbing challenge that these amazing manuscript documents present. Here in the Bacon Papers, waiting to be researched, lay papers that had kept their secret for almost exactly four hundred years. They are the historical records relating to an intelligence agent who was introduced to the Earl of Essex as a "French gentleman" with the intriguing name *Monsieur Le Doux*. The correspondence is accordingly all in French, and in addition to his letters and a number of letters from others relating to him, there was the most exciting discovery of two vitally important documents:

(1) Monsieur Le Doux's personal library listing fifty-six books belonging to him.
(2) A list of the contents of his chest of assignment papers, numbering fifty-two bundles identifying their subject matter and naming the correspondents from whom he had received reports and confidential letters.

It is altogether an absolutely remarkable cache of documents! These will now be examined in some detail after briefly referring to some of the letters and setting the scene for Monsieur Le Doux's presence in England.

As 1595 drew to its close, a development in the Earl's requirement for intelligence from the Continent led to the engagement of another secret agent, who was to be sent to Germany to inform the Earl of the political affairs between the German Princes and their Italian counterparts. He would initially be at the Court of the Holy Roman Emperor, Rudolf II, probably moving later on to Italy, but he was not to depart immediately, it transpires, for arrangements were made for him to stay in England for a while, residing at the palatial home of the Haringtons, an aristocratic family who were good friends of Anthony Bacon, who were doing him a "favour" by taking Monsieur Le Doux into their household at Burley-on-the-Hill near Exton in Rutland.

One of the first mentions of Le Doux is in a letter from Anthony Bacon's Gascon secretary, Jaques Petit, dated 10th December 1595,[1] when Le Doux was at Burley, in Rutland, employed by Sir John (later 1st Baron) Harington as tutor to his three-year-old son. This was not the same Sir John Harington as the translator of Ariosto's *Orlando Furioso*, notorious godson to the Queen, and inventor of the flush toilet! That was his cousin, who lived, appropriately, at Bath, famous for its ancient Roman baths. "Taking the baths" (for medicinal purposes rather than ablution in those days) may have been where he dreamed up the water-closet?

Petit joined Le Doux at Burley as his "valet" and was to remain with him for several months. His frequent letters to his master, "Monsieur de Bacon" as he calls him, present a fascinating picture of events at Burley and tell us much about both Le Doux and

---

[1] *Bacon Papers*, Lambeth Palace Library, MS 654 f.70. (In the following documents, the spelling of the name varies between 'Le Doux' or 'le Doux', 'le Douz' and 'le Doulx'. I have used the first of these throughout.)

Jaques Petit. These interesting and entertaining letters are investigated in detail in Part Three.

Le Doux had been residing at Burley from an as yet unknown date by October 1595 until about 25th January, when he left temporarily, accompanied by Sir John. Two weeks later, a passport is issued to Monsieur Le Doux, over the signature of the Earl of Essex, as follows:

> Whereas the bearer of proof Monsr le Doux a french gentleman being repaired into England for the dispatch of some necessarie business, intending now presentlie to returne into Germanie by the low Countries: These are to will & require you & evrye of you to whome it may app[er]taine that you permitt & suffer him quiettlie to passe & to embarke himselfe with his servant in any of Her Ma[jes]ties porte without any your lette, stay, molestation or hinderance whereof you must not faile. And this shall be your sufficient warrant in that behalfe. At London the 10 of February 1595
>
> *Essex*
>
> To all Maiors, Sheriffs, Bayliffs, Constables, Headboroughes, allsoe to all Customers, Comptrollers, Searchers & other Her Ma[jes]ties officers to whome it may appertaine and to everye of them.[2]

The year 1595 is shown thus to indicate that this is according to the Elizabethan calendar in which the New Year began for all ecclesiastical, legal and official purposes on Lady Day, 25th March, not on 1st January, so that the early months until that date were taken as part of the previous year. However, there was fairly general inconsistency in actual practice. Henslowe's *Diary* typically shows him crossing out the year to alter it, and sometimes he switches from one year to another in mid-list undecided as to whether he is in the New Year or the Old. Writers of letters also sometimes fail to make clear which calendar they are using. Happily Anthony Bacon's clerks consistently use 1st January as the start of a new year in endorsing these papers. In addition, England still adhered to the Julian Calendar whereas the Continental countries had adopted the Gregorian Calendar of Pope Gregory XIII in 1582 by which they leapt forward eleven days. Travellers like Le Doux and Jaques Petit had to adjust the date each time when hopping back and forth to the Continent. This anomaly remained for over 150 years, until the Calendar Act of 1751 set the New Year officially as 1st January, and removed the days between 2nd September and 14th September, 1752. People rioted in the streets, demanding the return of their 'lost' days, accusing the government of shortening their lives!

In February Le Doux departed for the Continent, but only briefly. He evidently returned to England, for a second similarly worded passport was issued at Richmond on 10th

---

[2] L.P.L., *Bacon Papers:* MS 655 f.191.

March.[3] Meanwhile, the long list of instructions – *Memoires Instructives* – provided for him by the Earl of Essex, reveals that he is being sent to Germany where he is to "keep an ear open and the pen ready to advise by post" of everything interesting that he discovers, and subsequently is to proceed to Italy. He is instructed to "advise not only the state and the affairs of the Imperial Court, but that which you can also find out there about Italy and Turkey". There follows a long list of the many things that he is to report back upon, all in the general area of 'Foreign Affairs', but in addition, if he finds it possible to get to Italy he is to provide "particular descriptions of each principality".

We first hear from Le Doux himself on 5th April, when he sends a very short note (Appendix 2a), giving no indication of where he is, but obviously still in contact with Jaques Petit.[4] He expresses some concern that, in a desire to "avenge" himself, Petit has sought the help of "Mr. Castol", although Le Doux is consoled by the fact that Castol is "prudent" and devoted to Anthony Bacon. Castol was minister of the French Church[5] in London and a very good friend of Anthony Bacon. The next reference to Le Doux on 12th April, is a letter from Petit to the French King's Ambassador, Nicholas Harlay, Seigneur de Sancy, concerning a passport for Le Doux.[6]

Another letter (Appendix 2b) is sent by Le Doux on 20th April, about a Spaniard called "Cyprian", whose son had worked for the late "Mr. Welsinghan" (presumably this is his spelling of Walsingham. The Elizabethans were remarkably casual in their variation of the way they spelt even their *own* names). Cyprian wants help in getting a book of his printed – a Latin version of the story of Bacon's friend, Antonio Perez, who will figure again later on in this story. It is of interest that Le Doux should mention a 'Mr. Walsingham' who is now deceased, since it indicates that he had been known both to Le Doux and to Bacon. Who this is will be discussed later (see p.113). Thomas Walsingham, to whom the *Sonnets of Exile* are written, was Marlowe's dear patron, and he is therefore likely to have found any mention of that family of immediate interest.

The final letter from him (Appendix 2c) comes from Middelburg, near Flushing in the Netherlands, dated 22nd June,[7] and translates as follows:

> Sir, my lord & master writing to you I have done this short note to serve as a cover to his letters, while waiting for us to arrive in Brabant, of which we will write amply to you. Meanwhile Monsr the Count Maurice is getting ready to forestall the designs that Archduke Albert has on Hulst, Axel & Ostend. His soldiers are leaving this evening. I think that their lord the Count will also depart from here tonight. The Cardinal was at Neuport only four days ago. Monsr Eberbach, both by his own humanity and for love of you, has shown me very great friendship. He is completely yours and will write to you at the right moment and when he

---

[3] *Ibid*, MS 656 f.191.

[4] *Ibid*. MS 656 f.371.

[5] *Index to the Papers of Anthony Bacon in Lambeth Palace Library* (1974) p.20.

[6] L.P.L., *Bacon Papers*: MS 656 f.252.

[7] *Ibid.*, MS 657 f.227, trans. L. Bouchon.

will present some subjects worthy of you. Meanwhile he and I pray that God will give you, Sir, fulfilment of your most noble desires.

From Mittelburg the 22nd of June 1596

Your very affectionate
humble servant
Le Doulx

Who 'Count Maurice' was has not been traced, but 'Albert' is certainly Cardinal Albert, Archduke of Austria and Duke of Brabant. Henri d'Eberbach was the servant of John Dionisius, Baron Zeirotine, ambassador from the Emperor.[8] Among the same papers is a passport issued for the Baron, also on 10th March 1595/6, and signed by members of the Privy Council, to assist him in his wish to visit the 'Realme of Scotlande'.[9] The first of the letters from Le Doux had in fact been written on behalf of *Mr le baron*, so it looks as though his initial assignment was as a servant to the Emperor's Ambassador. Did Le Doux perhaps await his return from Scotland before accompanying him to the Netherlands? Whatever the case, no further mention of Le Doux is to be found in the Library's index. Presumably he carried out his commission, and the extent of these voluminous papers allows us to hope that more evidence may yet be discovered to tell us what happened to Monsieur Le Doux.

But what is it that most clearly links these documents with the works of William Shakespeare and the playwright and intelligence agent Christopher Marlowe? To establish this, we need to examine two other astonishing sets of papers that have lain undiscovered until now among the Anthony Bacon Papers.

MONSIEUR LE DOUX AND WILLIAM SHAKESPEARE

Of outstanding relevance to the case for Le Doux as **'William Shakespeare'** is a list of books which he had apparently purchased during his time overseas (Appendix 3). It is annotated *"Catalogue des livres de m^r le Doux le 15me de feurier 1596"*.[10]

The various items in the original list are arranged mainly according to the language in which they have been published. To bring out their relevance to the works of Shakespeare, however, these have been rearranged according to the subject matter of the books as best ascertained from their titles. In each case, the item as given in the catalogue is shown in italics, together with an informed guess as to what it might actually be, and (in brackets) the language in which this copy has been published.

---

[8] *Index: op. cit.,* pp.29,30.
[9] L.P.L., *Bacon Papers:* MS 656 f.98.
[10] *Ibid.,* MS 655 ff.185-6.

Languages

Onomasticon 7. linguarum Junij	Junius's Lexicon of 7 languages
Nomenclator Junij	Junius's Nomenclature (Latin)
Nomenclator quatrilinguis	Nomenclature of four languages
Dittionario volgare e francese	Italian/French dictionary
Vocabulario de las dos lenguas Tos. y Castellona	Tuscan and Castilian vocabularies
Reglas Grammaticales	Rules of grammar (Spanish)
Giambularj della lingua fiorentina	Giambullari's language of Florence
the french Alphabet	A French handbook

The above collection of eight lexicons and language reference books testifies to the importance of a mastery of foreign tongues for a competent intelligence agent working abroad. Since Le Doux is now working for the Earl of Essex, it is odd that our "French gentleman" does not include an English dictionary in his list. The first thing that strikes one about this whole catalogue is that, except for one bible, none of the items is either **in** English or **by** an English person. Discarding the possibility that he spoke no English, this whole list would appear to be a record of books he purchased overseas, probably in those countries in which they had been printed in their native languages, and this indicates that by 1595 he had had postings in France, Italy and Spain.

A comparison of the number of books in each language is of interest: in Latin he owned twelve, in French twelve, in Spanish ten, and in Italian sixteen; in English only one, and in Latin and Italian combined four. This does not include dictionaries or books in more than two languages, or not specified. Since he is supposedly French, the highest proportion of Italian books purchased suggests that he had been mainly domiciled in Italy. This accords precisely with what the Italian influence in the plays of Shakespeare's maturity after 1593 indicates.[11] There are twelve Latin works in this library, but none in Greek, these being represented in translations into Latin. There is no evidence that Marlowe was a good Greek scholar, all his own translations being from the Latin.

The **Junius** referred to is not the famous Franciscus Junius, a well-known language scholar, but Adrianus Junius, author of the *Onomasticon* and *Nomenclator*. The seven languages are Latin, Greek, German, Dutch, French, Italian and Spanish. Le Doux is clearly a serious student of languages *other* than English which is curiously absent.

Pier Francisco **Giambullari** (1495-1555) was a Florentine writer best known for his *Istoria d'Europe* (887-94).[12] He also wrote on the Florentine language or dialect, and his *Giambularj della lingua fiorentina* was printed at Florence in 1549 in 8°, and again in 1551 by the same Florentine printer under the more explicit title, *De la lingua che si parla in Fierenze*, but presumably Le Doux owned the earlier edition. This shows that Le Doux was probably resident in Florence for a time, where the Grand Duke of Tuscany had his Pitti Palace at which his orphaned nephew, Don Virginio Orsino, was brought up, and where, when he grew up and became the Duke of Bracciano, he often returned to take an active part in government business. As an agent Le Doux or

---

[11] See Wraight: *The Story That the Sonnets Tell*, Chapter XXIII, 'The Italian Years'.

[12] F. M. Schweitzer & H. E. Wedeck, ed. *Dictionary of the Renaissance* (1967) p.269.

Marlowe would have hoped to find employment at the Florentine court. Interestingly, 'giambulari' were also satirical verses (hence the name, iambic[13]) and Francisco's brother, Bernardo Giambullari (1450-1529) was a poet and minor playwright of comedies.

Lastly, one cannot help wondering why someone named Le Doux would want *the french Alphabet*, a small 8° handbook written by N. G. Delamothe as an aid to learning good French presenting "the Treasure of the french Tung containing the rarest Sentences, proverbs &c.".[14] It was published in 1595 in London, so Le Doux must have bought it very recently (to improve his image as a "French gentleman"?).

The Bible and religious works

La Bibbia	The Bible (Italian)
Bible dorée en Anglois	Gilt Bible (in English)
Psalmos de David	The Psalms of David (Spanish)
Il nuouo testamento latino e volgare	The New Testament (Latin & Italian)
Evangelios y actos de los Apostoles con coment	The Gospels & Acts of the Apostles, with commentary (Spanish)
Dos tratados del papa y de la missa	Two tracts on the Pope & the Mass (Spanish)
fiorettj della lingua volgare e latina	'Little Flowers of St Francis' (Italian & Latin)

A secret agent operating in this period of fierce religious conflict would have to be well grounded in the rites, practices and theological tenets of either faith, able to pass himself off as a staunch Protestant or devout Catholic, perhaps to don the garb of a priest as a disguise, or pose as a student of divinity. The list of seven religious works represents what would be an essential adjunct to his library. Of special significance, however, is Monsieur Le Doux's possession of an English bible with the familiar gilt-edged pages, his *only* English book.

As a divinity student intended for the priesthood, Marlowe became deeply interested in questions of theology, which has been distorted by superficially researched commentary on his supposed Atheism which better acquaintance with his writings dismisses as utterly false. Matters of theology were keenly debated by Anthony Bacon, whose dearest friends included Jean Castol, the French Huguenot minister in London, and the great Swiss theologian, Theodore Beza, in whose household he had lived for a time during his residence abroad.

It is worth quoting Robert C. Fox,[15] who said, "There is hardly a scene in any of the Shakespeare plays that does not contain some Biblical quotation, paraphrase, allusion or parallel", and Robert Noble has found at least one hundred and fifty references to the Psalms alone.[16] Shakespeare's will disclosed that he did not even possess a bible.

---

13 J. H. Whitfield, *A Short History of Italian Literature* (1960) Penguin, p.124.

14 *Hazlitt's Handbook to the ... Literature of Great Britain* (1867) p.152.

15 Robert C. Fox in *A Shakespeare Encyclopaedia* (1966), Methuen, p.70.

16 Robert Noble, *Shakespeare's Biblical Knowledge* (1975).

Plays

The Roman comic dramatist **Plautus** (c.254-184 BC) was one of the major influences on the works of Shakespeare. According to *A Shakespeare Encyclopaedia*, "The plays of Shakespeare show Plautine elements down to the very end of his literary activity. Generally, however, the resemblances are more marked in the early plays". No fewer than fourteen of Shakespeare's works are cited by name.[17] The plot of *The Comedy of Errors* was taken straight from Plautus' *Menaechmi*, with some of his *Amphitryo* for good measure.[18] Some of the sub-plots and characters in *The Merchant of Venice*,[19] *Twelfth Night*[20] and *The Merry Wives of Windsor*[21] have also been discussed as possibly coming from Plautus. He created several stock comic characters, such as 'The Trickster' and the 'Braggart Soldier', whom we find splendidly recreated in such plays as *The Winter's Tale* (Autolycus) and *Henry IV* (Pistol and Falstaff).[22]

Whereas Plautus mainly employed ridicule, it was from the comic dramatist **Terence** (Publius Terentius Afer, c.95-c.59 BC) that Shakespeare learned the irony at which he, Shakespeare, excelled. From him he is also said to have learned elements of plot, style, characterization and, most of all, structure.[23] In 1610, the poet John Davies actually addressed Shakespeare as "our English Terence, Mr. Will Shake-speare".[24] Note that he uses the hyphenated form of the name indicating that he was aware that this is a pseudonym, so recognized by several contemporary poets and writers who also use it (e.g. Heywood, Webster, Digges and I. M. in the First Folio). The significance of this, modern scholars have totally failed to grasp.

Both *Twelfth Night* and *A Midsummer Night's Dream* are said to have taken a part of their plots from Terence's *Andria*.[25] There has also been a suggestion that his **Hecyra** may be referred to in *All's Well that Ends Well*.[26] It is worth noting too that the name 'Dromio' in *The Comedy of Errors* probably comes from 'Dromo', the type name for a slave in many plays by Terence.[27] *The Taming of the Shrew* was partially based upon Ariosto's *I Suppositi* about which Ariosto himself said, "and the author confesses to you that in this matter he has followed both Plautus and Terence".[28]

---

[17] Murray Hartman in *A Shakespeare Encyclopaedia* (1966), Methuen, p.635.

[18] R. A. Foakes, ed. *The Comedy of Errors* (1962) The Arden Shakespeare, Methuen, pp.xxiv & xxvii.

[19] Murray Hartman, *op. cit.*

[20] J. M. Lothian & T. W. Craik, eds. *Twelfth Night* (1975) The Arden Shakespeare, Methuen, p.xlvii.

[21] H. J. Oliver, ed. *The Merry Wives of Windsor* (1971) The Arden Shakespeare, Methuen, p.lix.

[22] A. R. Humphreys, ed. *Henry IV part I* (1960) The Arden Shakespeare, Methuen, p.xlii.

[23] Murray Hartman, *op. cit.* p.863.

[24] John Davies, *The Scourge of Folly* (1610).

[25] Murray Hartman, *op. cit.* p.864.

[26] G. K. Hunter, ed. *All's Well that Ends Well* (1959) The Arden Shakespeare, Methuen.

[27] R. A. Foakes, *op. cit.* p.xxxiii note.

[28] Brian Morris, ed. *The Taming of the Shrew* (1981) The Arden Shakespeare, Methuen, p.79.

History

Commentarij Caesaris	Caesar's Commentaries (Latin)
Commentaires de Caesar de Vigenere in 4°	Caesar's Commentaries (French)
Sallustio volgare	Sallust (Italian)
Sallustius latine	Sallust (Latin)
Cornelius Tacitus	Tacitus (Latin)
Historia Imperial	History of the Empire (Spanish)
Le vite de glj Imperatorj	The Lives of the Emperors (Italian)
Sleidano	A work by Sleidanus (Italian)
Sleidan des 4 empires	Sleidanus on the 4 empires (French)
Mussulmannica historia Leuenclauij in f°	History of Islam by Levenclavius (Latin)
Paralipomena hist Turcicae Leuencla. in 4°	History of Turkey by Levenclavius (Latin)
De Origine Turcarum & Scanderbegj histo. in f°	Turkish history by Baptiste Ignatius (Latin)
Cronica del Principe Castrioto	Chronicles of Prince Castrioto, i.e. Scanderbeg (Italian)
Historia Ethiopica	History of Ethiopia (Spanish)

Caesar's *Commentaries* were familiar to any Latin speaker, but it is still worth recalling the words in *2 Henry VI*, about Marlowe's own county, Kent :

> Kent, in the Commentaries Caesar writ,
> Is term'd the civil'st place of all this isle.
> Act IV scene 7 lines 59-60

This play is attributed to Marlowe by several eminent scholars. As well as the general relevance of the events of history told by the Roman historians, **Julius Caesar, Sallust** and **Tacitus**, a dramatist would also glean much about political personalities, corruption and party rivalries from Sallust[29] and about high level politics from Tacitus.[30]

Ioannes **Sleidanus** (c.1506-1556) was a German humanist, and classical scholar, historian and diplomat, best known as the author of *On the State of Religion and Government under the Emperor Charles V*.[31] This, his life's work, is considered the most valuable history of the times of the Reformation written from the Protestant point of view which Sleidanus espoused. He was also a student of ancient languages. The four empires in the book listed in Le Doux's library above are the Babylonian, Persian, Greek and Roman empires. From this background information for Shakespeare's Roman and Greek plays, *Julius Caesar, Antony and Cleopatra, Coriolanus, Timon of Athens* and *Troilus and Cressida* could be gleaned. A characteristic of Marlowe that is equally evident in the works of the author Shakespeare is a wide reading of historical sources.

The *History of Ethiopia* is the *Æthiopica* by a Portuguese Jesuit missionary to Abyssinia, Pedro Paez **Xaramillo** (1564-1622).[32] Marlowe's interest in Africa is testified in *Tamburlaine*.

---

[29] *Encyclopaedia Britannica* (1991) 15th edition.

[30] *Ibid.*

[31] F. M. Schweitzer & H. E. Wedeck, *op. cit.* p.553.

[32] F. M. Schweitzer & H. E. Wedeck, *op. cit.*

The items concerning **Scanderbeg** are significant because of **Marlowe's** own association with this name, his (now lost) play, *The True History of George Scanderbeg*.[33] Gabriel Harvey in his cryptic poem *Gorgon or the wonderfull yeare*, is certainly referring to the death of Marlowe, this being the year 1593 (not the year 1588 for which wonderful events had been forecast), which has caused Harvey amazement!

> *"I mus'd awhile: and having mus'd awhile,*
> *Jesu, (quoth I) is that* Gargantua minde
> *Conquer'd and left no* **Scanderbeg** *behinde?*
> *Vow'd he not to Powles* A Second bile?
> What bile, or kibe? *(quoth that same early Spright?)*
> Have you forgot the **Scanderbegging** wight?"

He refers to Marlowe as both "Tamberlaine" ("Weepe Powles, thy Tamberlaine voutsafes to die"), and as Scanderbeg, identifying the man with his famous plays on Turkish history,[34] for Harvey's *New Letter*, to which the poem is an addendum, is much concerned with the then current wars against the Turks. The group of books about Turkey and 'Mussulmannica' would be of special relevance to Marlowe, including a history of the Mongol and Ottoman Empires. We are therefore right in the world not only of Scanderbeg, but also of the plays that made Marlowe famous, the two parts of *Tamburlaine the Great*.

Discussing the sources for *Tamburlaine*, Bakeless refers to *The Annals of the Turks*, written in Turkish, which was brought from the East and translated "into Latin by a certain Leuenclavius", presumably the second of the **Levenclavius** books on our list. He also mentions **Baptista Ignatius's** *De Origine Turcarum Libellus*, a copy of which had been in the library of Corpus Christi in Marlowe's time, as a minor source.[35] The background to Marlowe's play *The Jew of Malta* is of course also that of a war against the Turks.

Verse

Gierusalemme liberata	Tasso's 'Jerusalem Delivered' (Italian)
La deliurance de Hierusalem in 4°	Tasso's 'Jerusalem Delivered' (French)
Gierusalemme conquistata	Tasso's 'The Conquest of Jerusalem' (Italian)
Hierusalem en rime francoise	'The Conquest of Jerusalem'? (French)
Les sepmaines du Bartas	du Bartas's 'La Semaine' (French)

Torquato **Tasso** (1544-1595), the greatest Italian poet of the late Renaissance, was clearly a favourite, as he had been (presumably) with Marlowe and his friend Tom Watson. Don Virginio Orsino, Duke of Bracciano, in whose service I believe Marlowe eventually became an agent, and who, according to Dr. Leslie Hotson, was the original Orsino of *Twelfth Night*, was Tasso's patron. Shakespeare is also said to have drawn upon Tasso's *Gerusalemme liberata* in writing his **Cymbeline**.[36]

---

[33] John Bakeless, *The Tragicall History of Christopher Marlowe* (1942) Harvard Univ. Press. Reprinted Greenwood Press, 1970. Vol.II, p.285.

[34] See Wraight: *op. cit.* Chapter XI, 'Gorgon, or the wonderfull yeare", pp.129-37.

[35] John Bakeless, *op. cit.* Vol.I, p.215 and p.61.

[36] *A Shakespeare Encyclopaedia, op. cit.* p.852.

Guillaume de Salluste, Seigneur **du Bartas** (1544-1590) is best known as author (in 1578) of *La Semaine*, a poem about the creation of the world. Its Protestant message was apparently more acceptable in England than in France, however, and both Sir Philip Sidney and Edmund Spenser were said to have been influenced by it.[37] Writing of *Venus and Adonis*, Sir George Greenwood said, "Then for his description of 'the ideal horse' he goes to Virgil as imitated and expanded by **Du Bartas** (in *La Semaine*) ... Sylvester's translation of this ... was not published till 1598".[38] Greenwood also draws attention to how Autolycus's song in *The Winter's Tale* ("The lark that tirra-lirra chants") echoes *La Semaine*'s "La gentille allouette avec son tire-lire".[39]

Prose

La fabrica del mondo	The works of great writers (Italian)
Operae succisiuae Camerarij	Successive works by Camerarius (Latin)
Les fables d'Esope en taille doulce	Line engravings of Aesop's Fables (French?)
Il Corteggiano in 3 lingue	Castiglione's 'The Courtier' (in 3 languages)
Las epistolas de Gueuara	Guevara's letters (Spanish)
Hecatonmithi	Stories by Cinthio (Italian)
Essays de Montaigne	Montaigne's Essays (French)
Lettere del Tasso in 4°	Tasso's letters (Italian)
Constantia Lipsij	'De constantia' by Lipsius (Latin)
Auenturas de Antonio Perez	The adventures of Antonio Perez (Spanish)
Dialogj Castalionis	Castalian Dialogues (Latin)

La fabrica del mondo is a collection of the writings of the best Italian authors made by Francesco **Alunno**, first published in 1548 in Venice. Many later editions followed, all printed in Venice. It claims to contain "all the words of Dante, Petrarch, Boccaccio and other good authors" (*"nella quale si contengeno tutte le voci de Dante, del Petrarca, de Boccaccio & d'altri buoni autori"*).[40] It was one of Le Doux's expensive folio books priced at 11s.

Operae succisiuae Camerarij are the works of Philippus **Camerarius**, not of his more famous contemporary Joachim Camerarius, being a collection of his meditations and observations, "historical, natural, moral, political and poetical".[41]

A few references to **Aesop** in Shakespeare are the Fox and the Grapes *(All's Well That Ends Well*, Act II sc.1 line 69), the Wolf in Sheep's Clothing *(1 Henry VI*, Act I sc.4 line 54) and the Ant and the Grasshopper in *Edward III* (Act II sc.2 line 17).

Il libro de Corteggiano (The Courtier) by Baldassare **Castiglione** (1478-1529), is certainly relevant. Shakespeare is thought to have based the relationship between his characters Beatrice and Benedick in *Much Ado About Nothing* on Lady Emilia Pia and Pallavicino

---

[37] *Encyclopaedia Britannica* (1991) 15th edition.

[38] Sir George Greenwood, *op. cit.* p.59.

[39] *Ibid.*, p.433.

[40] B.L. *Short-title Catalogue of Books printed in Italy ... 1465-1600* (1 58) p.21.

[41] Philippus Camerarius, *Operae horarum sub cisivarum, sive meditationes historicae ... &c.* (1506) Frankfurt.

in this work[42] and, as the Arden edition says about the play as a whole, "the seminal inspiration was that of Baldassare Castiglione's *Il Corteggiano*, the outstanding example of Renaissance social doctrine".[43] In addition, a discussion to be found in it upon the nature of nobility is reflected in *The Tempest*.[44]

Antonio de **Guevara** (1480-1545), a Spanish court preacher and man of letters, was, according to Britannica, "A rhetorician, more concerned with developing golden prose than with content". His *Epistolas familiares* covered the period from 1539 to 1542. His realm was court politics and manners and he wrote advice to rulers in much the same way as that early influence on the young Marlowe, Niccolo Machiavelli.

With *Hecatommithi*, by **Cinthio** (Giovanni Battista Giraldi, 1504-1573) we strike gold again. Amongst the stories contained in this work are *Disdemona and the Moor*[45] (*Othello*, of course) and *I and Epitea*, given as a source for *Measure for Measure*.[46] No English translation of these stories is known to have been made before 1753.[47]

The essays of Michel Eyquem de **Montaigne** (1533-1592) would not be translated into English by Marlowe's friend, John Florio, until 1603. To quote the Arden edition, "The only undisputed source for any part of *The Tempest* is Montaigne's essay *On Cannibals*".[48] The argument contained in this essay is also central to *The Winter's Tale*,[49] and the essay *Apology for Raymond Sebonde* is said to have provided several major themes for *King Lear*. According to the Arden edition, no fewer than 23 passages in *King Lear* are echoes of Montaigne.[50] Harold Jenkins also points out traces in *Hamlet*.[51]

De constantia, by the Flemish humanist, classical scholar and moral and political theorist, Justus **Lipsius** (1547-1606) has some marginal relevance. Lipsius was an enthusiastic supporter of **Seneca** and this is described as a 'Senecan tract'. Seneca's influence on *Titus Andronicus* and on *Macbeth*[52] is usually mentioned. There is also an interesting snippet in the Arden *Measure for Measure*, implying that Lipsius had written a version of the story, but unfortunately no reference is given for this.[53]

The *Adventures of Antonio Perez* are of particular interest. A former Secretary of State to Philip II of Spain, Antonio Perez (c.1540-1611) was involved in a number of political and amorous intrigues, and had to flee the country at the risk of his life. He was at the court of Henry of Navarre for a while, but finished up a member of the Earl of Essex's

---

[42] A. R. Humphreys, ed. *Much Ado About Nothing* (1981) The Arden Shakespeare, Methuen, p.15.
[43] *Ibid.*, p.16.
[44] Frank Kermode, ed. *The Tempest* (1954) The Arden Shakespeare, Methuen, p.xliv.
[45] M. R. Ridley, ed. *Othello, Moor of Venice* (1958) The Arden Shakespeare, Methuen, p.xv.
[46] J. W. Lever, ed. *Measure for Measure* (1965) The Arden Shakespeare, Methuen, p.xxxv.
[47] M. R. Ridley, *op. cit.*
[48] Frank Kermode, *op. cit.* p.xxxiv.
[49] J. H. P. Pafford, ed, *The Winter's Tale* (1963) The Arden Shakespeare, Methuen, p.xxxvi.
[50] Kenneth Muir, ed. *King Lear* (1952) The Arden Shakespeare, Methuen, p.249.
[51] Harold Jenkins, ed. *Hamlet* (1982) The Arden Shakespeare, Methuen, p.108.
[52] Kenneth Muir, ed. *Macbeth* (1951) The Arden Shakespeare, Methuen, p.xiii.
[53] J. W. Lever, *op. cit.* p.xxxvii.

household, having been a correspondent of Anthony Bacon for several years, and apparently of Le Doux as well, as the contents of the trunk (described later) indicates. One wonders if this is the book of which the Spaniard Cyprian, mentioned above, was offering a Latin version. If Perez was with Henry of Navarre when Anthony Bacon and Marlowe were perhaps there at the same time, the link with Shakespeare would be given historic credibility for the character Don Armado in *Love's Labours Lost* is said to have been based on Antonio Perez.[54]

The *Dialogj Castalionis* are presumably by the Italian writer Josephus **Castalio**, under whose name more than thirty titles are listed in the British Library, though none is exactly identifiable as Le Doux's book. His subjects ranged from the ancient Greek and Roman writers, Virgil, Plautus, Seneca, Horace, Plato, Aristotle and other philosophers and men of letters to commentaries on the popes and great families such as the Ursini and Aldobrandini, and topography. His books appeared from 1586 onwards, all printed in Rome.

Miscellaneous

Les harangues militaires	Military speeches (French)
Hercolano del varchi	Varchi's 'Hercules' (Italian)
paedagogus freigij	A Latin primer
Medicina Weckerj in f°	Wecker's 'Medicine' (Latin)
Trattenimentj del Bargaglj	Bargagli's 'Diversions' (Italian)
Lhore dj recreatione	The hours of recreation (Italian)
Le coffre de bonne ésperance	'The Chest of Good Hope' (French)
Mons' petit un angelot	'Mr Petit's a cherub'?!

Military speeches are clearly of interest to both Marlowe and Shakespeare. Consider only *Tamburlaine*, *Edward III*, Marlowe's first English history play written in 1588,[55] which links both *Tamburlaine* and *Henry V*, *Julius Caesar* and *Coriolanus*, all great military dramas. *Les harangues militaires* may be *The Orator* by Alexandre **Silvain**, which was coming out at about this time and has been mentioned as a source of the scene in which Coriolanus faces the tribunes,[56] and also of *The Merchant of Venice*;[57] but there are several other books on military speeches that qualify for consideration. Whoever the author may be, its ownership by Le Doux as the most expensive book in his library (he paid 13s for it) testifies to his keen interest in military matters, identical to Marlowe's as discussed later under 'Marlowe and the Art of War' (see pp.87-90).

Benedetto **Varchi** (1503-1565) was another admirer of **Seneca**[58] so one wonders if his *Hercolano* could have been a translation of the latter's *Hercules Oetaeus* and/or *Hercules Furens*, both of which are mentioned in connection with Shakespeare's 'most Senecan'

[54] Robert Gittings, *Shakespeare's Rival* (1960).
[55] Wraight: *Christopher Marlowe and Edward Alleyn* (1993) Chapter III, previewing research in my forthcoming *Christopher Marlowe & the Armada*.
[56] Philip Brockbank, *op. cit.*, p.31.
[57] John Russell Brown, ed. *The Merchant of Venice* (1981) The Arden Shakespeare, Methuen, p.xxxi.
[58] J. H. Whitfield, *op. cit.*, p.164.

plays, *Macbeth*[59] and *Richard III*,[60] the latter a play adjudged by many Shakespearean scholars as particularly indebted to Marlowe in style and influence if not actually partly written by him.[61]

The *paedagogus freigij*[62] was a Latin primer by Ioannes Thomas **Freigius**. This might have been useful to Le Doux as a reference book on the conjugation of Latin verbs and Latin grammatical construction at times; or he may on occasion have turned his hand to tutoring, for we learn from Jaques Petit's letters that Le Doux was engaged as tutor to Sir John Harington's precocious little son (though not in Latin as he was hardly more than an infant). The delightful portraits of worldly-wise children in Shakespeare's plays reflect acute observation of Elizabethan childhood in which precocity was encouraged and lauded.

Wecker's *Medicina* by Hanss Jacob **Wecker** was Le Doux's second most expensive book, priced at 12s, considered one of the most valuable and widely respected medical books of the period. It is of interest that books have been written about Shakespeare's medical knowledge.[63]

Scipione **Bargagli** was the author of the *Trattenimentj*, a book on games, stories and love songs printed by B. Guinti in Venice in 1587 in quarto, followed by a second quarto edition in 1592. Either edition might therefore have been in Le Doux's library, and this again links him with Venice.[64] Games figure in several Shakespeare plays; the implication is that the dramatist was a keen gamester: Bo-peep *(King Lear)*; Bowls *(Richard II)*; Cards *(Antony & Cleopatra, King John)*; Cherry-pit *(Twelfth Night)*; Chess *(The Tempest)*; Dice *(Antony & Cleopatra, Henry V)*; Leapfrog *(Henry V)*; Loggets *(Hamlet)*; Nine Men's Morris *(A Midsummer Night's Dream)*; Primero *(Henry VIII)*; Push-Pin *(Love's Labours Lost)*; Quoits *(2 Henry IV)*; Shove-Groat *(2 Henry IV)*; Tables *(Love's Labours Lost)*; Tennis *(Hamlet, 2 Henry IV, Henry V, Pericles)*; Tick-Tack *(Measure for Measure)*; Tray-Trip *(Twelfth Night)*; and Troll-my-Dames *(The Winter's Tale)*.

Lhore dj recreatione has been identified (surprisingly) as a manual for learning French and Italian! Surprising, that is, if Monsieur Le Doux is really a genuine "French gentleman"; but if he is, in fact, the agent and poet-dramatist Christopher Marlowe, such a book would have been a virtual necessity to enable him to assume the identity of a French national and to help him to settle into his adopted country of exile Italy, effectually losing his English identity in total anonymity.

Le coffre de bonne ésperance is another of Le Doux's most expensive books, doubtless a folio edition, priced at 12s. So far it has not been traced, but it sounds like a collection of literary excerpts from various authors.

---

[59] Kenneth Muir, *op. cit.* (1951), p.xlii.

[60] Antony Hammond, ed. *Richard III* (1981) The Arden Shakespeare, Methuen.

[61] Bakeless: *op. cit.* Vol. II, pp.246-248.

[62] *Paedagogus*, printed 8° at Basle, 1582. B.M: *Catalogue of Books Printed in the German-speaking Countries ... from 1455-1600* (1962) p.320.

[63] Sir George Greenwood, *op. cit.* p.379 note.

[64] B.M: *Catalogue of Books printed in Italy 1470-1600*, p.172.

The book entitled *Mons' petit un angelot* is of some curiosity interest, being the name of Anthony Bacon's secretary, Jaques Petit, who was not only a prolific letter-writer with a dry wit, but also wrote poetry. This may be a book of Petit's poems.

Why the list?

Against each and every item on the above catalogue appears a sum of money, <u>in shillings and pence</u>. If Le Doux was just an intelligence agent with a taste in literature identical to Shakespeare's and Marlowe's, it is difficult to see why such a price-list would be needed. If, on the other hand, he was really the poet/playwright Christopher Marlowe, these would be the books he had purchased abroad to furnish himself with a library, replacing what he had lost when he fled from Deptford and must have been sorely missing. In that case, this would surely be an account of approximately how much they have cost him, with a view to his being reimbursed by his patron, Thomas Walsingham. The tradition of patronage was to provide some financial support, including payment of such expenses. The Earl of Pembroke granted Ben Jonson an annuity of £20 a year for the purchase of books. Being always short of money himself, Anthony Bacon may have encouraged Marlowe to seek reimbursement. The total sum involved is £14-9s-0d.

One assumes that if the owner, Le Doux, is really Marlowe, these would represent his purchases since 1593, and he would have taken at least one or two of his most treasured books with him. We know he was a bibliophile, and one of these would doubtless have been his copy of the indispensable Holinshed's *Chronicles*.

The Catalogue and Shakespeare

In examining the Le Doux catalogue for possible connections with Shakespeare and Marlowe – and over **half** of its books did have some clear relevance – some of the associations may be just a bit remote. Therefore let us take a longer view to see which of the connections can be fully justified.

If we exclude Shakespeare's histories, all of which rely almost entirely upon English sources, the remaining canon of his plays numbers about twenty-seven. **Ten** of these (i.e. more than a third of them) have had one of the above-named books specifically mentioned by expert commentators as being among their presumed sources. Depending upon which plays of Plautus and Terence were in Le Doux' collection, a further five plays could be added to the list, bringing the total to fifteen. Beyond this, we have a definite contributor to *Venus and Adonis* and the obvious relevance of the religious books, the historical items – particularly the Roman ones – and for Marlowe the Turkish histories. It is therefore almost impossible to escape the conclusion that what we have here is a list of books collected by 'Shakespeare' himself conjoined with the agent and playwright, Marlowe, while staying in France, Italy and Spain. It is certainly just such a personal library as this that one might have expected to find in the <u>author</u> William Shakespeare's possession. Such a library would certainly have been in the possession of Christopher Marlowe in exile, who was observed as being frequently a browser at the bookstalls in St. Paul's churchyard, one of his favourite haunts before 1593.

LE COFFRE DE M. LE DOUX

The second exciting and very important discovery is a list of the contents of a trunk – *"le coffre de Mr le Doux"*[65] (Appendix 4). Parts of it are somewhat illegible, as in nearly all these old manuscripts, but a transcript is provided. The trunk seems to have been a 'filing cabinet' of documents collected by the owner over several years acting as a government agent. They precisely match what one might have expected Christopher Marlowe's files to have contained, although some date from before his time as a secret agent and would in this case have presumably been passed on to him for information in connection with work he was doing. At the death of Sir Francis Walsingham in 1590 many of his papers would naturally have passed to his most trusted agents, of whom Marlowe was undoubtedly one.

There is correspondence with Sir Francis Walsingham and his secretaries, together with letters from Lord Burghley. There are also letters from other agents, particularly Anthony Bacon's friends, Anthony Standen, Antonio Perez and Anthony Rolston. As Appendix 4 shows, only brief headings are given, with no indication of the number of letters and in only five instances is a date given. The trunk also apparently contained many documents about the countries in which the owner had lived or which he had visited: France and Scotland in particular, with 'secret memories' of the latter. The Low Countries are also represented and, as well as information about Spain, there is what appears to have been a declaration made by him to 'Mr. Wade' – presumably William Waad, one of Sir Francis Walsingham's officers, later Clerk to the Privy Council – before being sent there.

England itself is not neglected, with details of its forces, ceremonies, and "orders". Her majesty's offices (sic) "as well publick as particuler" are listed and "some ministers discourse to her majestie for matters of state". There are details of the "detestable" plot by "Dr. Lopez" to poison the Queen, and a few items in praise of her. There are in fact two items concerning this Dr. Roderigo Lopez, a Jewish Portuguese physician who had counted among his patients not only Walsingham and Leicester, but also the Queen. In January 1594, however, Essex had apparently uncovered a plan for Lopez to murder her. Of particular interest is that the Shakespearean scholar Sir Sidney Lee thought that Shakespeare's character Shylock had been based on Lopez.[66] Bakeless discussed at some length the effect of this trial on the popularity of *The Jew of Malta*,[67] and Marlowe himself had mentioned him in *Doctor Faustus*.

> *Horsecourser:* Alas, alas, doctor fustian, quotha, (mass,
> Doctor Lopus was never such a doctor) has given me a
> purgation, has purged me of forty dollars – I shall never see
> them more. Act IV scene 4 line 28

There are also discourses, essays and treatises, and another item of particular interest, given that one of the accusations levelled against Marlowe was that he had said, "that the Indians and many Authors of antiquity haue assuredly writen of aboue 16 thousand

---

[65] *Ibid.* MS 656 f.184r-v.

[66] Sidney Lee, *The Original of Shylock, the Gentleman's Magazine* (Feb. 1880) CCXLVI.

[67] John Bakeless, *op. cit.* Vol.I p.361.

yeares agone wheras Adam is proved to have lived within 6 thousand yeares".[68]   It is *"une astrologie depuis le commencement du monde"*, which may have been the work of Marlowe's friend, the famous astronomer Thomas Harriot. He too had been particularly interested in the faulty chronology of the Bible.

Finally, what might have been the particular relevance of the papers of Francis Walsingham, *estant Ambassadeur en france pour la Royme d'Angleterre*? Bakeless gives a possible answer when considering sources for Marlowe's *The Massacre at Paris*. "For the massacre itself, Marlowe may have in part relied upon the accounts of Francis Walsingham, who had been English ambassador in Paris at the time of the massacre".[69]

SOME CONCLUSIONS

An interesting aspect of the catalogue of books belonging to Monsieur Le Doux, which was written in his own hand, as we shall see, is the fact that he lists the books noting the edition as *4°* or *f°*, which is in the manner of a scholar. Le Doux is therefore evidently a university educated gentleman.

Taking a critical look at the book list, we can exclude all works of specific relevance to Le Doux's career as a secret agent. These would include the eight language reference books, adding *Lhore de recreatione* from the Miscellaneous list; and of his religious works, *Two Tracts on the Pope and the Mass* and the *Little Flowers of St. Francis*. Also Wecker's *Medicina*, Bargagli's 'Diversions', *The Chest of Good Hope*, the Latin primer and *Mons petit un angelot*.

Removing these 16 books leaves us with 40 volumes to review as regards their relevance as source books for Shakespeare's and/or Marlowe's works. Of these:

• 10 have been specifically mentioned by expert commentators as being direct sources for the works of Shakespeare;

• a further 4 are of obvious specific relevance to Marlowe's Turkish plays;

• 5 are biblical works that would be valuable both to a secret agent and of interest to the works of Marlowe (*Tamburlaine* and *Dr. Faustus*) and to Shakespeare's with their preponderance of biblical echoes;

• another 21 are relevant in varying degrees to the canon of Shakespeare's works, or are seen to reflect Marlowe's and/or Shakespeare's known interests, e.g. in history.

This gives us a total of 40 books out of the library of 56 which are directly or partly associated with the creative writing of Shakespeare and/or Marlowe and their known reading interests. In researching these books, a total of 25 plays out of the 36 in the First Folio, plus *Venus and Adonis*, have been cited as deriving their source or influence

---

[68]   BL. Harleian MS 6848, f.185, Baines' *Note*.

[69]   Bakeless, *op. cit.* Vol.II p.77.

from Monsieur Le Doux's library. An astonishing proportion! This is more than coincidence.

The book list has also presented evidence that Le Doux is not a genuine born "French gentleman", but an Englishman using this identity as his cover – an Englishman, moreover, with reading tastes exactly like the persecuted poet-playwright Marlowe and the author Shakespeare. Like Marlowe he was also an agent with exactly the same secret service connections. When we look at Le Doux's trunk we find that it contained:

- Contacts with **'spymasters'**: Instructions from Sir Francis Walsingham, a declaration to Walsingham's agent Waad ("Wade") on being posted to Spain, correspondence with Walsingham's secretary Faunt ("Fantis"), and correspondence with Lord Burghley himself ("my L. Tresorer").

- Correspondence with other **agents & rapporteurs** (Rolston, Standen, Perez, Bruz) and **diplomats** (Moresin, Cockburne) especially in Scotland.

- Papers about **current affairs** and **politics**: Of the princes and present state of Christendom; in England (offices, ceremonies, memories, orders, forces); Scotland (causes of disorders & mutinies, secret memories, correspondence with *"grand seigneures"*); France *("les affaires des pauvres Mastres", "traitte des ... Canons et autres ministres de l'estate de France")*; Spain *("L'estat d'Espaigne")*; the Low Countries *("touchant la droit ... du Brabant, Lothier et Limburg")*.

There is therefore little doubt that these are papers relating to intelligence work on behalf of Walsingham and Burghley showing that Le Doux had for several years been occupied in intelligence gathering for Sir Francis Walsingham and Lord Burghley as had Marlowe.

The coincidences pile up to become finally overwhelming. We have already seen that the book list reveals Le Doux as having an extraordinary interest in history, poetry and theatre, just as the author(s) of the works of both Shakespeare and Marlowe would have had. As well as having a remarkable correspondence with the works of 'Shakespeare', the list also contains several items of specific relevance to the works of Christopher Marlowe. It is the mutual association with both the works of the First Folio *and* Marlowe's canon that is especially striking.

We know that Marlowe was employed for several years as an agent of Sir Francis Walsingham and Lord Burghley, but that he had been reported dead some three years before. However, as the thorough examination of the circumstances at Deptford cogently argues, that 'death' could certainly have been faked and there were on that very day extremely urgent reasons for doing so. This therefore brings us to the conclusion that Christopher Marlowe had *not* in fact died in May 1593 and that *Monsieur Le Doux* was in fact the intelligence agent Christopher Marlowe in exile. Once we look at all of the above in the context of the moving story of *The Sonnets of Exile*, the conclusion that he was Marlowe *alias* Shakespeare becomes increasingly unavoidable.

We rest the case, while the evidence of these manuscripts, including the letters, is further reviewed in detail.

PART THREE

THE EVIDENCE REVIEWED

The deductive investigation of the new documentary evidence presented in Part Two is reviewed here in the wider context of the historical background. The handwriting of these manuscript documents will also be examined.

This has been an exciting historical detective investigation to track down an intelligence agent on the Continent within the parameters of the years 1593 and 1600, but more specifically hovering around the years 1595 to 1596/7. Thomas Birch's anecdotal reference to two intelligence agents in the service of Anthony Bacon on behalf of the Earl of Essex first directed me to the archives of Lambeth Palace Library to research the manuscript collection known as the Bacon Papers, which reached this ecclesiastical library by a fortuitous route through Archbishop Tenison. We owe a great deal to Archbishop Tenison.

Birch mentions two agents by name, La Faye and Le Doux, both apparently French gentlemen, but La Faye has already been revealed as the *nom-de-guerre* of the English agent Anthony Standen. He is listed in the Library Index to the Papers under Standen *alias* La Faye and *alias* Andrée Sandal, so he obviously used two cover-names. Numerous letters by him in his large scrawly hand appear in the MS over all three names, sometimes signed just 'S' with a fine, flamboyant flourish. However, of Le Doux no such alternative identity is given. This, in itself, seemed curious to me since he is obviously an agent, whose *"coffre"* of intelligence documents is actually listed in these Papers. His name sounds remarkably like a *nom-de-guerre*, almost as the partner of La Faye, and in his *"coffre"* we find reference to *"Ltres de Mr. Standen"*, so they evidently knew each other. What is perhaps significant in the list of items in the *"coffre"*, numbering fifty-two separate items or bundles of papers in all, which are mostly written in French, is that thirteen of the items are in English. The entire list is also written in an English secretary hand. This will be discussed later.

Even if Monsieur Le Doux were really a "French gentleman", on which the Book List has cast doubt, one would have expected that he would be using a cover-name, being an agent, irrespective of his nationality. His letters are always signed Le Doux, and his library of books and his *"coffre"* are also presented under this name. This poses the questions: Is this his real name? Is he really a Frenchman? Or is extraordinary care being taken to keep his real identity undetected? How did he come to know Anthony Bacon who, from the tone and content of his letters, is not someone he had met for the first time in 1595? If Le Doux had worked in intelligence for some time during the years Anthony Bacon was domiciled in France, he could, of course, have come to know him then. The search for Le Doux is therefore not yet ended. However, sufficient evidence about him has already been found to identify him as a singularly important historical figure, hence every reference to him assumes a high degree of interest.

Monsieur Le Doux's whereabouts in England are revealed in Jaques Petit's letter to Anthony Bacon, dated 10th December 1595, telling his master of his journey to the home of the *"Chevallier"* Harington in Rutland, where Le Doux is awaiting him and is overjoyed to welcome him there. Petit's very amusing epistle describing this eventful journey sets the scene. The assumption readily made from the correspondence is that Le Doux is residing under the roof of Sir John Harington (the *"Chevallier"*) at his stately home in Rutland – something that had evidently been 'arranged' by Anthony Bacon, whose servant Jaques Petit is being sent there to join Le Doux for Christmas.

There are only three letters from Le Doux, all written to Anthony Bacon in the first half of 1596, after he had departed for the Continent; and five letters from Petit to Anthony Bacon that refer to Le Doux by name have been discovered, written between 10th December 1595 and 3rd February 1595/6. There are also two letters from the French womanservant, Ide du Vault, employed in the Harington household (of whom more in due course), who refers to Monsieur Le Doux as the carrier of her letters. A letter from Jean Castol, minister of the French Church in London, gives us important information about Le Doux whom he names his "friend". A single letter from Anthony Bacon to Le Doux exists, dated 29th January 1595/6, instructing him to return from Rutland, with a similar note to Jaques Petit.

Le Doux then evidently went abroad, for shortly afterwards the first of three letters from him to Anthony Bacon written from somewhere on the Continent (either the Low Countries or France, we think) appears in the correspondence. (These are reproduced at Appendix 2a, 2b, 2c.) Le Doux's last letter is dated 22nd June, after which the trail runs cold. The *Memoires Instructives*, the Book List and the *"coffre"*, together with the two passports in his name, complete the records uncovered to date that refer to Monsieur Le Doux. The correspondence is all in French.

The letters are of particular fascination because they throw light on Le Doux's character and his relationships with the people in this episode in his life: Jaques Petit, Anthony Bacon, Jean Castol, the woman Ide du Vault and, by inference, we detect a friendly relationship with his host Sir John Harington. We are given an intimate glimpse of the courtly circle of this sumptuous stately mansion at which aristocratic friends and family congregate for Christmas.

Anthony Bacon's only extant letter to Le Doux, dated 29th January 1595/6, written in French,[1] requests that Jaques be sent back to him immediately as he needs him (he had been with Le Doux for eight weeks) and he especially asks him to express his sincere thanks to his host, Sir John Harington, for the favour he had done him. This presupposes that Le Doux had ready contact with the *"Chevallier"* while residing under his roof. Anthony's brief note to Petit signed *"votre bon maitre"* informs him that Le Doux has been instructed to send him back *"en toute dilligence"* and also reminds Jaques to give special thanks to *"Chevallier Harrington"* for the favour he has done him – presumably on Le Doux's behalf. This concludes their visit.

---

[1]   Lambeth Palace Library: *Bacon Papers, MS 654, f.248.*

Intelligence Agent Extraordinary

Sir John Harington was evidently a very good friend of Anthony Bacon for he had done him a favour for which he and Le Doux are very grateful. What was the precise nature of this favour? The obvious answer would be the provision of a 'safe house' offering protection to Anthony's agent, who was evidently in need of it. This, again, points to Marlowe's special circumstances if he were now back in England. An ordinary intelligence agent would not have required such special 'protection' in England, beyond an official letter to allay malicious or ignorant rumour that might lead to the suspicion that he was a traitor if it were known he had spent time abroad in a Catholic enemy country such as Spain. This is the kind of protection that Anthony Rolston was seeking when he wrote to Anthony Bacon from *"Fontarabie"* in Spain on 26th February 1596:

> "I am now to trie my fortune in going home shortlye to my contry in hope
> that I shall find by yr good helpe friends and protection, for I do protest
> that I am to my prince and contry in all points as a dutifull subiect and for
> my callinge as readye to serve as any man liuing".[2]

We recall that Christopher Marlowe was accused of having turned traitor when it was leaked that he had been to Rheims whilst yet a student at Cambridge, on an espionage assignment that was probably his first major task for his spy-master, Sir Francis Walsingham, in connection with the then fomenting Babington Plot in 1585. The Privy Council's letter of 29th June 1587[3] is testimony of the need to quell such paranoid anti-Catholic rumours which branded as plotting traitors anyone who had been abroad in a Catholic country in suspicious circumstances. The question always hovered, Was the returning traveller innocent, or had he turned traitor, or double-agent? Temptation to do so with lucrative bribes was an ever-present trap, and the returning student furnished suddenly with unexplained money, which one can well imagine the generous nature of young Christopher Marlowe would lead him to treat his friends to a drink at the buttery bar, perhaps, would soon have engendered whispered comments about the source of his affluence. He learnt early in his new career of the double dangers, both at home and abroad, to which he would be exposed.

The emphasis given in both the Privy Council's letter assuring the Cambridge authorities that Marlowe had acted *"discreetly"* and *"deserved to be rewarded for his faithful dealing"*, and in Rolston's letter above, testifies to the importance of official protection for these government agents. Without this vital protection many a loyal government servant would have found himself in prison accused of treason, and once tainted the hope of justice was slight. Working in intelligence required a cool head and astute awareness of the swirl of political motivation in which the men in this profession were caught up.

In his special circumstances, Christopher Marlowe would, however, have been doubly endangered. As a secret agent, the normal hazards of a dangerous profession would have beset him; and as a fugitive from the Court of Star Chamber the danger of detection by an informer who might have been set on his track would have been an ever-

---

[2]   LPL: *Bacon Papers MS 656, f.109ʳ-ᵛ*.

[3]   MS *Acts of the Privy Council, vol. VI, 29 June 1587*.

present cause of fear. The anxiety under which he lived is a recurring emotion that haunts the *Sonnets of Exile*.

Again, if Le Doux is Marlowe, why did he not go to his patron and loyal friend Thomas Walsingham at Scadbury, since the Sonnets show that he was constantly in contact with his patron during his exile? Two reasons suggest themselves.

Firstly, it was imperative not to endanger Walsingham. If he had engineered the Deptford murder plot flouting the decree of the Court of Star Chamber, Marlowe's presence would be risky. If Marlowe were tracked down, Walsingham's position would have been unenviable. All their free-thinker friends would also have been endangered. Marlowe dared not take a foolish risk in exposing himself too confidently after only three years. Walsingham had saved his life once. He could never again involve him in mortal danger.

Secondly, by this time Walsingham appears to have retired from his involvement in intelligence and espionage work, whereas Anthony Bacon was continuously active as his vast correspondence testifies.

Jaques Petit is very important in this scenario. He is the constant go-between of Anthony and Le Doux, the trusted liaison officer with his master's agents at home and abroad, and whilst Le Doux is in England, or near to the Channel coast on the Continent, Petit attends him as his "valet", who acts, in a sense, as his guardian on behalf of Anthony Bacon.

For Marlowe to have assumed the identity of a "French gentleman" would be particularly suitable. He had certainly heard French spoken from early childhood for there was a large French-speaking, immigrant community in his native city, Canterbury, and we know opportunities existed for children to learn French from immigrant language teachers. It is likely that his knowledge of French had recommended him for recruitment to carry out the urgent espionage assignment at Rheims in connection with the Babington Plot when he was still at Cambridge. The universities were the recruitment ground from which the government's intelligence agents were drawn. Educated men were needed for Sir Francis Walsingham's inner circle of trusted agents who were maintained out of his own purse. Of these Christopher Marlowe was certainly one.

His recruitment into government service when he was a young BA at Cambridge opened up a new career for the budding dramatist, which later led him into the court circles of the intelligentsia who were the free-thinkers. We should regard the sixteenth century free-thinkers as the historic brothers of the dissidents and liberal-minded fighters for freedom of thought in modern oppressive police states, or the underground movements in Nazi-occupied countries during the Second World War, who maintained close secrecy for mutual protection.

If the law-lords of the Court of Star Chamber, and in particular one thinks of Archbishop Whitgift, entertained any suspicions about the too convenient death of Christopher Marlowe on 30th May 1593, there is little doubt that there would have been an on-going witch-hunt against the great free-thinker, Christopher Marlowe, who was seen as an important quarry – the intellectual compeer of Raleigh, Harriot, Northumberland, Bruno, and a leading member of that band of early scientific thinkers who were feared by reactionary orthodoxy.

The 1590s was a decade of witch-hunting against the free-thinkers, not only in England but throughout Western Christendom. In pursuing his suspicions, the man whom Whitgift would most likely have set onto Marlowe's tracks would be the informer Richard Baines, whose task it had been to collect damning 'evidence' to bring Marlowe to trial in the Court of Star Chamber in 1593. Marlowe's disappearance into the arms of death had baulked the prosecuting authority of success in the witch-hunt against the free-thinkers. The Cerne Abbas inquiry against Raleigh's circle in 1594 petered out ineffectually after their chief witness had so fortuitously escaped into his unmarked grave.

There was good reason for Marlowe to have travelled as far as Italy in his exile. He needed to put *"large lengths of miles"* (*Sonnet 44*) between himself and any possible pursuers. In Richard Baines, the compiler of the infamous Baines *Note*, he had acquired a determined and crafty enemy. He is on record as bearing a grudge against Marlowe in the incident at Flushing in January 1592/3, when he spied on him and accused Marlowe of illicit coining.[4] Whether Baines had followed Marlowe to Flushing with hostile intent is not certain, but Marlowe appears to have been sent thither by Burghley to investigate the sources of extensive forging of money that was being carried on there to pay the Catholic army recruited by the English traitor, Sir William Stanley.

Meeting Baines at Flushing, Marlowe had ended up by sharing his rented room, perhaps offered in token of false friendship as a trap by the artful Baines? A third man occupied the room as their "chamber-fellow" who was a goldsmith. Was he also introduced by Baines? He was named Gifford Gilbert, a strange inversion of the name of the double agent from Rheims through whom the Babington Plot was uncovered. The goldsmith was *"induced"* either by Baines or by Marlowe (counter-accusations as to who had done the 'inducing' were later flung at each other) to demonstrate the art of counterfeiting money, and a Dutch shilling in the base metal pewter was *"uttered"* in Marlowe's presence by the goldsmith. Baines meanwhile dashed off to the governor of Flushing, Sir Robert Sidney, to report that this illicit coining was going on, and Marlowe and Gilbert were arrested 'red-handed'.[5]

Sir Robert felt inadequate to deal with so serious a charge and despatched Marlowe, described as *"a scholar"* who claimed he knew Lord Strange and the Earl of Northumberland well and declared his innocence, and the goldsmith, described as an *"excellent workman"*, back to London under guard, accompanied by the accusing Baines, there to face Lord Burghley and take their punishment. At this point the record dries up. There was no punishment meted out to Marlowe or the goldsmith so far as we know.[6] One must assume that Baines had once more 'put his foot in it' by interfering with Burghley's well laid plan to discover the source of the illicit coining that was a cause of concern.

---

[4] R. B. Wenham: 'Christopher Marlowe at Flushing in 1592' in *English Historical Review, vol. XCI* (1976) pp.344-5, SP *84/44 f.60* (calendered in LSAP *Foreign 3, No.81*).

[5] Charles Nicholl has an excellent account of this episode. See *The Reckoning: The Murder of Christopher Marlowe* (1992) pp.234-8.

[6] *Ibid.*

I cite this incident because it throws light on Baines' vengeful nature and devious actions, which seem to indicate that he was targeting Marlowe as his victim. There may be some connection with Baines' unsuccessful plot to poison the well of the Catholic Seminary at Rheims when Baines was there in 1583. His plot was exposed and Baines was arrested, but after a mere ten months' imprisonment he was once more a free man! It seems incredible that he escaped punishment. No one has ever been able to explain this.

My belief is that Baines made some kind of crafty deal with Cardinal Allen to undermine Sir Francis Walsingham's great espionage service, which time and again discovered Catholic plots to assassinate Queen Elizabeth so that these schemes came to nought. How could Baines have promised to breach this? By destroying the reputations of the English government's top agents, thus attacking the espionage service from *within*. That, at any rate, is what he appears to have been trying to do, and Marlowe was his chief target.

F. S. Boas believes that Marlowe lampooned Baines' well-poisoning incident in **The Jew of Malta** and made Baines the laughing stock of the secret service![7] Perhaps this is why Baines was seeking revenge. Both hypotheses are relevant to this case. Baines was certainly the villain in Marlowe's tragedy; but whether it was he who might still have been pursuing him in 1595 and 1596 is, of course, guesswork.

Whatever the actual facts of the Flushing incident, they came to nothing. But Baines did not let the matter rest there. When informing on Marlowe in 1593, he made sure to include the charge of illicit coining yet again in his *Note*. This was one of the items that was struck out by the correcting hand that 'edited' the copy of the *Note* to be presented to the Queen.[8] That correcting hand would logically have been the authoritative hand of Lord Burghley. The same hand also struck out the item accusing Marlowe of having commended sodomy with boys! Only someone with Burghley's authority would have dared to tamper with a criminal indictment destined to be presented to the Queen. Burghley was both a Privy Councillor and a lord of the Star Chamber Court. He also knew Marlowe as his secret agent of many years' standing. He *also* knew Baines and would have shrewdly assessed the qualities of these two men.

Three years after Deptford, Baines may still have been tracking his quarry, and if Marlowe had left the relative safety of Italy and surfaced nearer home in England, he might have walked into a trap. He would always be in danger of detection by an informer as the escapee from the Star Chamber Court in 1593. In 1592 Giordano Bruno had been apprehended in Venice when he returned inadvisedly to his native Italy, and was still languishing in a prison in Rome. Marlowe would undoubtedly have known about Bruno's fate, though not that he would eventually be burnt at the stake four years hence.

This is a hypothetical scenario, but such is the dramatic hypothesis that can logically be woven from the letters and the need for residence in a 'safe house' which suggests that he was now back somewhere in England. Where this place in England, well distant from London, was, is described in detail in a series of letters to be presented.

---

7 F. S. Boas: 'Informer against Marlowe' in *T.L.S. 16 September 1949.*

8 B.L. *Harleian MS 6853, fols. 307-308.*

The English Secretary Hand

Monsieur Le Doux's list of intelligence papers in his *"coffre"* is written in the English secretary hand, not in Italic, although it is mostly in French, but there are thirteen items in English:

Item 14	A collection of all her ma[*jes*]ties offices
Item 15	Ceremonies, memories & orders of ye Estates of England
Item 16	A register of her ma[*jes*]ties offices aswell publick as pticuler
Item 17	Observacons vppon a lible published in ye yeare 1592
Item 18	of ye Princes & present state of Christendome 1582
Item 20	Doctor Loppes confession to poison her ma[*jes*]tie & les instructions pour my Lord Wimes
Item 21	The tree of ye comon wealth
Item 23	Secrett memories of Scotland
Item 26	The Declaration giuen to Mr Wade being sent into Spaine
Item 27	The generall causes of ye disorders mutinies in ye Scotish comon wealth
Item 29	A true report of ye detestable treason intended by Doctor Lopes
Item 30	The praise of his soueraigne
Item 33	Some Ministers discourse to her ma[*jes*]tie for matters of state

It is evident from this that M. Le Doux was fluent in English, and his use of the English secretary hand throws some doubt on how French this "French gentleman" really was. The *"coffre"* list is not identifiable as a copy in the hand of any of Anthony Bacon's servants, but has every indication of being this agent's original and personal list written by himself, which had been deposited, probably for safekeeping, with Anthony Bacon while Le Doux was on his travels. It would have represented a heavy bundle of papers as there are fifty-two items in all.

The date of the list is 12th March 1596, and a comparison of the handwriting with the extant 'Leaf' of Marlowe's play *The Massacre at Paris*, which is also in the English secretary hand, will certainly be of interest. This 'Leaf', now in the Folger Shakespeare Library, was authenticated by Joseph Quincy Adams, custodian of the Folger manuscripts, and supported by F. S. Boas in 1940, and further corroborated by Seymour de Ricci, an authority on sixteenth century manuscripts. It is believed to have been one of the 'foul sheets' discarded, or possibly a first draft from which a fair copy was made.[9] This play has survived only in a pirated and very corrupt printed edition that is clearly a heavily cut version of the text. The speeches in the Folger 'Leaf' are more than twice as long as those in the printed edition, and the general consensus of opinion is that this 'Leaf' is in Marlowe's autograph. I have made a meticulously detailed study of this in connection with a forthcoming book, comparing the hand in the 'Leaf' with another document that I believe to be in Marlowe's hand, which is the subject of my study, *Christopher Marlowe & the Armada* (to be published 1997).

---

[9] J.Q. Adams: 'Massacre at Paris Leaf' in *The Library*, *XIV, March 1934*.
See photographic reproduction on p.84.

What had at first sight seemed a contradiction in the handwriting of the *coffre* list is, in fact, its strength in arguing the identity of the writer as none other than Christopher Marlowe. The list is separated from the 'Leaf' by about four years, possibly more, but not less. As Dr. S. A. Tannenbaum has stated: "It is a matter of ... universal experience that the handwriting of a person who writes much ... undergoes considerable change as he grows older ... But notwithstanding these changes, there always remain enough of his essential characteristics to enable the careful investigator to establish his identity".[10]

It will be of interest to refer to the *"coffre de M. Le Doux"* in Appendix 4(a) and 4(c) in the discussion below.

The development that has occurred in Marlowe's hand is his increasing use of a letter 'h' that has a loop, or squiggle, in the tail. Only one of these is present in the 'Leaf' in the fourth line from the bottom in the word *"thinkst"* showing a loop-tailed 'h':

"and when thou thinkst I have forgotten this". [11]

In examining the long list of titles of documents filed in *"le coffre de Mr Le Doux"*, which is, I believe, in the same hand as that of the 'Leaf', I counted 12 examples of what I have called 'h'(b) and 11 examples of the standard old-style 'h'(a). He always uses the latter in the word 'the', and sometimes uses one of each style in the same word where the letter 'h' occurs twice. The evidence of the list of contents of his *"coffre"* shows that he now uses two forms of 'h' interchangeably in a ratio of approximately 50:50, which varies with his mood and with the kind of word he is writing. *"Christendome"* and *"Scotish"* sport his new-style 'h'(b), while *"the"*, *"The"* and *"her"* and *"published"* are given old-style 'h'(a). He does not use the alternative standard secretary style 'h' that appears in the 'Leaf' for words beginning with 'h' because there are none in the list.

This kind of development in a writer's handwriting is indicative of growing maturity and self-confidence. He no longer feels he must conform to the standard handwriting taught rigorously in his Elizabethan education. In all other respects there seems to be essential agreement with the hand of the 'Leaf'; the identical, typical flow and pen pressure, slope of the writing, spacing, size of up-stroke and down-stroke, the overall style, character, and general 'feel' of the hand, as well as the formation of the individual letters. All the characteristics proclaim that these two examples of the English secretary hand were written by the same man. This must be left to further palaeographic examination to confirm.

We also have the extant signature of Christopher Marlowe in 1585 at the age of twenty-one, in which he spells his name *Christofer Marley* in an elegant English secretary hand, when witnessing the will of Mistress Katherine Benchkin in Canterbury, together with his father, who writes his name *Jhan marley*, and his maternal uncle, Thomas Arthur, and his brother-in-law, John Moore – a cluster of family names.[12]

---

[10] S. A. Tannenbaum: *The Booke of Sir Thomas More* (1927) p.59.

[11] See Marlowe's manuscript on p.84.

[12] Discovered by Frank W. Tyler in 1939. Benchkin Will, P.R.O. *Canterbury*, 16/86 now in the Kent Record Office, Maidstone.
John Bakeless: *The Tragicall History of Christopher Marlowe* (1942) Vol.1, pp.74-5.

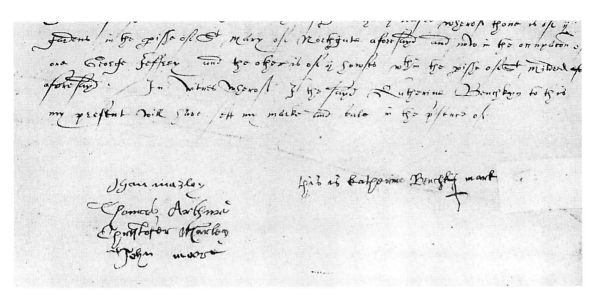

(Courtesy of Kent Record Office, Maidstone)

Signature of Christopher Marlowe discovered on the will of Mistress Katherine Benchkin. The signatories read:

Jhan marley
Thomas Arthure
Christofer Marley
John moore

John Marley is Christopher's father; Thomas Arthur is his uncle on his mother's side; and John Moore his brother-in-law, husband of his sister Joan and also a Canterbury shoe-maker. The will was witnessed in November 1585.

Enlargement of Christopher Marlowe's elegant signature. Like his father, he uses the spelling of his surname as 'Marley', and signs himself *Christofer Marley*.

Marlowe's Manuscript

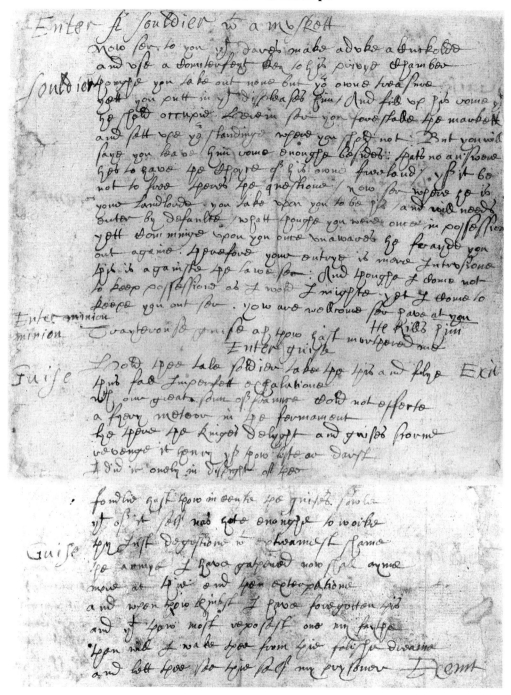

The so-called 'Collier Leaf' of Marlowe's *The Massacre at Paris* now in the Folger Shakespeare Library, *MS J.b.8.*

Marlowe's Manuscript 'Leaf' transcription

Enter A Souldier wth a muskett

Souldier   Now ser to you y^t dares make a duke a Cuckolde
and vse a Countrefeyt Key to his priuye Chamber
thoughe you take out none by yor owne treasure
yett you putt in y^t displeases him. And fill vp his rome y^t
he shold occupie. Herein ser you forestalle the markett
and sett vpe yor standinge where you shold not: But you will
saye you leaue him rome enoughe besides: thats no answere
hes to haue the Choyce of his owne freeland. yf it be
not to free theres the questione, now ser where he is
your Landlorde you take vpon you to be his and will needs
enter by defaulte whatt thoughe you were once in possession
yett Comminge vpon you once vnawares he frayde you
out againe. Therefore your entrye is mere Intrusione
this is againste the Lawe ser: And thoughe I Come not
to keep possessione as I wold I mighte yet I Come to
keepe you out ser. you are welcome ser haue at you.

Enter minion   *He kills him*

minion   Trayterouse guise ah thou hast murthered me

Enter guise

Guise   Hold thee tale soldier take the this and flye   *Exit*
thus fall Imperfett exhalatione
wch our greate sonn of fraunce Cold not effecte
a fyery meteor in the fermament
Lye there the kinges delyght and guises scorne
reuenge it henry yf thow liste or darst
I did it onely in dispyght of thee
fondlie hast thow in Censte the guises sowle
y^t of it self was hote enoughe to worke
thy Iust degestione wth extreamest shame
the armye I haue gathered now shall ayme
more at thie end then exterpatione
and when thow thinkts I haue foregotten this
and y^t thow most reposest one my faythe
then will I wake thee from thie folishe dreame
and lett thee see thie self my prysoner.

                                          Exeunt

Note: Wraight & Stern: *In Search of Christopher Marlowe* (1965 reissued paperback 1993), pp.226 and 231 show a photographic reproduction of **The Massacre at Paris** 'Leaf' both the whole page and an enlarged section.

The Italic Hand

Turning to the consideration of the documents in an italic hand, the most important of these is the list of *"les livres de Monsieur Le Doux"* comprising three full folios.[13]

There is very little italic writing in the 'Leaf' – only the words *"Enter"*, *"Souldier"*, *"minion"* and *"Guise"* with which comparison can be made. Nevertheless, from the pen pressure and all the other stylistic characteristics, the answer is positive, not negative. There is a very strong case for accepting the italic hand as identical with the 'Leaf'.

When we turn to the Le Doux letters, which are all in italic, being French, and italic seems to be more often used for this language, though not so in the *"coffre"*, there is nothing more certain than that the Book List is in the same hand as Le Doux's letters. The reader has only to look at the letters in the Appendix 2(a), 2(b) and 2(c) and compare them with the Book List 3(a), 3(b) and 3(c) to confirm that these are all in the same italic hand. Note the capital M in *Monsieur* and *Medicina*.

If the italic hand of Monsieur Le Doux in the Book List is identified as the same hand as his letters; and the English secretary hand of the *"coffre de M. Le Doux"* is identified as the same hand as in the 'Leaf' believed to be in Marlowe's autograph; and each is also identifiable with both the 'Leaf' and the *"coffre de M. Le Doux"*; then there is an unanswerable case for accepting that here, at last, we have the true handwriting of Shakespeare. Not those six dubious wobbly signatures, but the elegant, fluent hand of Christopher Marlowe, both italic and secretary.

The close scrutiny by palaeographers is invited to confirm the identification of the handwriting of these manuscripts.

There is evidence in the correspondence that Le Doux was in need of funds. Marlowe's characteristic independence would probably have made him diffident about asking Walsingham, to whom he owed such a great debt of gratitude, for money, and it may have been Anthony Bacon who obtained the Book List from Le Doux to present to Walsingham as an account. This alone seems to explain the existence of the Book List in the Bacon Papers.

When it came to matters of money, the Earl of Essex was always notoriously overspent, and Francis Bacon was hopeless at managing his financial affairs. Anthony Bacon had time and again to help his younger brother out of his indebtedness, thus leaving himself short of necessary funds. For Walsingham to reimburse Monsieur Le Doux would be an obvious course to take. Money expended on his books would not be like begging. The traditional role of the Renaissance patron was to support his poet with an allowance to purchase books. The marvellous plays he wrote from this list were his repayment to his patron for his bounty.

---

[13] L.P.L. *Bacon Papers MS 655 ff.185ʳ⁻ᵛ, 186ʳ*. See Appendix 3(a)(b)(c).

The striking relevance of the Book List to the plays of Shakespeare has been established in Part Two. Here its relevance to the works and interests of Marlowe will be investigated. This, too, is not negligible.

There are four items in the list that have an obvious relevance to Marlowe in a strongly individual aspect reflecting interests he held passionately in his early manhood.

De Origine Turcarum & Scanderbegj histo. in f°	Turkish history of Baptista Ignatius
Cronica del Principe Castrioto	Chronicles of Prince Castrioto (i.e. Scanderbeg)
Mussulmannica historia Leuenclauij in f°	The Annals of the Turks, trans. Levenclavius
Paralipomena hist Turcicæ Leuencla. in 4°	Supplement to the above

Marlowe was keenly interested in the history of Turkey as evidenced in the three plays he wrote dramatizing this: his lost play, which I believe was his first full length play, *The True History of George Scanderbeg*, sold to the Earl of Oxford's Men, who registered it for publication long afterwards when it had perhaps exhausted its stage life, in 1601;[14] and his first masterpiece, *Tamburlaine the Great, Part One & Two*, which launched him as a major poet-dramatist. These works dramatize the history of two great warriors who each conquered the Turks, who remained a much feared military threat to Western Christendom even in Marlowe's day.

To these four books in his library must be added those which evidence his abiding interest in the art of war, its conduct and the weapons and methods used, which is reflected in all his plays to greater or lesser degree. Even in *Dido Queen of Carthage* the most memorable great speech is given to Aeneas, in which he vividly describes his experiences in the final tragedy of the Trojan War, the Fall of Troy.

Marlowe and the Art of War

Tamburlaine the Great is a monumental military drama. Its dominant character is an historical figure whose life was a ceaseless campaign of warfare and conquest, fought against the main enemy of Western Christendom, the Turks, which made him a hero in Elizabethan eyes. The scene that reflects Marlowe's personal interest in military tactics is that in which Tamburlaine instructs his sons in the art of warfare, both offensive and defensive (Part Two, Act III, sc.2). Following the funeral ceremonies for the death of Zenocrate, Tamburlaine directs his sons' minds away from long grieving to the business of life, which for him meant waging war and conquering, ever to extend his empire:

---

[14]   Wraight: *The Story That the Sonnets Tell*, pp.208-9.
The True History of George Scanderbeg &c. S.R. *3 July 1601* licensed to Edward Alde.

> Boys, leave to mourn ....
> .... and list to me,
> That mean to teach you rudiments of war.

They must learn courage, and to endure physical hardship. The rigours of the campaign are painted forth: to sleep on the ground, march in armour, *"Sustain scorching heat and freezing cold"*; but above all to understand the techniques of successful warfare. How *"to scale a castle-wall, /Besiege a fort, to undermine a town, /And make whole cities caper in the air;"* how to build a fort:

> The ditches must be deep; the counterscarps
> Narrow and steep; the walls made high and broad;
> The bulwarks and the rampires large and strong,
> With cavalieros and thick countermines,
> And secret issuings to defend the ditch.

Bakeless has shown that Marlowe based this closely on Paul Ive's *Practice of Fortification* (1589) sometimes quoting from it verbatim, which suggests he had access to a manuscript as the book was dedicated to Sir Francis Walsingham among others.[15] Ive was a military engineer and may also have become a secret agent. William Urry has discovered Ive as the engineer supervising work being done on Canterbury's canal system.[16]

There was avid interest in military matters in the Northumberland/Raleigh/Harriot circle to which Marlowe belonged. Nina Taunton's recent paper, 'Harriot, Marlowe and the Art of War' has drawn largely on the Ninth Earl of Northumberland's manuscript on warfare,[17] and she has shown that Tamburlaine's instructions to his sons mirror the Earl of Northumberland's own instructions to his son, Algernon.[18] Harriot, who was in the Earl's patronage, was particularly interested in the problems of ballistics, and the mathematical application to aspects of the art of warfare, applying geometry to the design of fortifications, and working out the most advantageous numbers and deployment of troops. He compiled *"groundplatts vpon which may be orderly piled bullets"* in which he used "his knowledge of mathematical progression to facilitate the stacking of cannon-balls on sea-vessels".[19]

Harriot made diagrams of ballistics, and his friend Walter Warner, another mathematician in the patronage of Northumberland, worked on problems relating to the art of war. We have Kyd's testimony that those with whom Marlowe most frequently was

---

[15] Bakeless: *op. cit. Vol. I, pp.210-11.*

[16] William Urry: *Christopher Marlowe and Canterbury* (1988), ed. Andrew Butcher, p.68.
CCAL. *BAC Chamberlains' Accounts, s.a.*

[17] Nina Taunton: 'Harriot, Marlowe and the Art of War' (1993), *The Durham Thomas Harriot Seminar, Occasional Paper No.11, p.2.*

[18] *Ibid.*, p.33.
Instructions for the Lord Percy/ In His Trauells Giuen by/ E: of Northumb: HMC MS 24/1, fols. 4-5 (c.1615-1617).

[19] *Ibid.* p.2
B.L. *Add. MS 6786 ff.375ʳ-376ʳ.*

to be seen and *"conversed withal"* were **"Harriot, Warner, Roydon,** and some stationers in Paules churchyard".[20] Kyd was pointing his finger at these men as all *"of that vile opinion"*, i.e. Atheism. Among those subjects that featured in their conversation would have been discussion on the art of war. Both theoretical and practical aspects of warfare interested them, its *"deceits and stratagems"*, the construction of fortifications, and deployment and effectiveness of weaponry, and its philosophic and moral aspects. The question of conscience was addressed, *"whether it be lawfull for Christians to make Warres".*[21] Taunton points out that, "Tamburlaine's rhetoric is to impel the rulers of Asia to take up arms against the enemies of Christianity, and his transformation from shepherd to conquering hero is explained in the context of God's imperative to all Christians to defend their empire against the expansionism of the Infidel".[22]

These were the interests deeply shared by Marlowe with his friends, those friends he so sorely missed when in his exile *(Sonnet 30)* of whose stimulating company he was deprived, so that thinking on them he wept. He was right in the heart of this questioning, investigating, intellectual, scientifically-minded, debating social circle. When he came to refurbish himself with books, his purchases reflected these interests, just as his plays also dramatized history and warfare. Not only *Scanderbeg* and *Tamburlaine* about wars with the Turks, and *The Jew of Malta* (again it is war with the Turkish Selim Calymath, son to the Grand Seignior of the Turks) and *Edward the Third*, dramatizing the great naval battle of Sluys and England's most brilliant military campaign against France; but also references to warfare are in *Faustus, Edward II*, and there is a background of civil war in *The Massacre at Paris.*

In the agent Monsieur Le Doux's library we find:

Les harangues militaires	Military speeches (French)
Commentarij Caesaris	Caesar's Commentaries (Latin)
Commentaires de Caesar de *Vigenere in 4°*	Caesar's Commentaries (French)

Marlowe translated Lucan's *De Bello Civili VIII*, the First Book of his epic poem on the civil war between Caesar and Pompey while he was still at Cambridge. Thus early he demonstrated his interest in warfare, using Lucan's stirring epic to hone his skill in writing blank verse with characteristic innovation in his mastery of the metre. With Caesar he pauses to consider well before crossing the Rubicon:

> As soon as Caesar got unto the bank
> And bounds of Italy; "here, here," (saith he)
> "An end of peace; here end polluted laws;
> Hence leagues, and covenants; Fortune, thee I follow,
> War and the destinies shall try my cause."

---

[20] B.L. *Harleian MS 2849 ff.218-218ᵛ*
     See Wraight & Stern: *op. cit.* pp.314-5.
[21] Taunton: *op. cit.* p.37.
     Raimond de Fourquevaux: *Instructions for the Warres* (1589) Sig.B.
[22] *Ibid.* p.37.

This said, the restless general through the dark
(Swifter than bullets thrown from Spanish slings,
Or darts which Parthians backward shoot) march'd on.
. . . . . .
Day rose and view'd these tumults of the war;
Whether the gods, or blust'ring south were cause
I know not, but the cloudy air did frown;
The soldiers, having won the market place,
There spread the colours, with confused noise
Of trumpets' clang, shrill cornets, whistling fifes;
The people started; young men left their beds,
And snatch'd arms near their household gods hung up
Such as peace yields; worm-eaten leathern targets,
Through which the wood peer'd, headless darts, old swords
With ugly teeth of black rust foully scarr'd;
But seeing white Eagles, and Rome's flags well known,
And lofty Caesar in the thickest throng,
They shook for fear, and cold benumb'd their limbs.

Marlowe's *First Book of Lucan* 11.226-49

In addition, the library included nine more books on history, all of which would inevitably contain accounts of wars. War is man's oldest and most constant occupation! It was of endless interest to a man of Marlowe's intellectual quality and involvement in political activity. He would have had access to the great library of the Earl of Northumberland and all those in his circle were cultured, eager readers with libraries of their own. In exile he would have been lost without his own store of books and, as we have seen, he had laid out a large sum from his earnings to acquire what to him was essential food for the mind.

This library reflects not only the source books of Shakespeare's plays, but also the sources and interests of Christopher Marlowe, especially in its highly specialized acquisitions of books on Scanderbeg and Turkish history and on Caesar's wars and on military history and military rhetoric. In this we find Marlowe and Shakespeare side by side and of one mind.

Interpreting the Evidence

To sum up the hypothesis and the evidence of the documents, the following interpretation answers all the questions that these pose, bringing hypothesis and evidence together as the obverse and reverse of the same coin.

The hypothesis poses that the "French" intelligence agent Monsieur Le Doux is none other than Christopher Marlowe, who is in receipt of a significant assignment from his friend Anthony Bacon, on behalf of his lord, the Earl of Essex – probably at a time when Marlowe was in need of finding more work and short of money, hence the Book List.

Anthony, as the Earl's adviser on intelligence, with the backing of Francis, could readily have persuaded Essex that what he now needed was special intelligence concerning the relationship between the German and Italian states, all independent principalities with their own rulers, whether overtures of war and/or peace were being played out, so that he had advance knowledge of how the dice were falling, and could advise the Privy Council. The exceptionally detailed and comprehensive instructions for this assignment are designed to whisk Monsieur Le Doux away from the vicinity of any possible present danger to Germany, and to the Court of the Holy Roman Emperor, the eccentric Rudolf II, who was more interested in scientific or alchemical experiments than in politics, and thereafter back to Italy, keeping him employed for some time to come. My hunch is that this is when Marlowe first came into contact with Virginio Orsino, Duke of Bracciano, patron of Tasso, whose books were in Le Doux' library (see p.66).

With the new assignment came, perhaps, also a new identity as a *"French gentleman"* named Monsieur Le Doux, for whom official passports would be issued. A brief sojourn in England was also envisaged. Occasional reunions with his patron and dear friend, Thomas Walsingham, are reflected in the Sonnets with the expression of deeply felt joy, and sadness at parting again. They form a small sub-theme in the *Sonnets of Exile*, but whether these two met perhaps briefly on this occasion is not known. The assignment package would doubtless also have resolved his financial difficulties. It is perhaps significant that the date of the Book List is 15th February, a fortnight after Anthony Bacon's first letter to Le Doux. Then we hear from Le Doux himself with his first letter dated 5th April from somewhere on the Continent, when he seems to have entered the service of *"le baron"*, the ambassador from Emperor Rudolf, Baron Zeirotine, who is clearly well known to Anthony Bacon and sends a warm message (*"vous baise les mains"* – people were so wonderfully courteous in those days). Jaques Petit is once again with Le Doux.

The item in the Book List, *"Mons' petit un angelot"*[23] may be a volume of Petit's poems he had had printed privately and Le Doux bought a copy as a favour. The price at 10s is high (*un angelot* was equal to an English angel, i.e. 10s), which is perhaps reflected ruefully in Le Doux's title? *"Un angelot"* is also a 'cherub'. Did Jaques Petit have a chubby, cherubic appearance? If Le Doux is who we think he is, we could expect some witty word-play from him in his relationship with Jaques Petit, who was also a wit, as will be revealed in his letters, and a bit of a poet.

---

[23] See Appendix 3(b). Was Petit addicted to the French cheese named *"angelot"* cheese?

Jaques Petit

In the Bacon Papers, dispersed among the correspondence, are many poems written to Anthony Bacon, some composed in his honour, others sent to him by friends and correspondents for his interest and pleasure knowing his love of poetry. There are poems in Latin, Greek, French, Italian, Spanish and English, and one is an acrostic of his name ANTHONY BACON. He was evidently much loved and revered. Among these are several poems in French written by Jaques Petit, which are his own composition, most of them in praise of his *"bon maitre"* expressing his complete devotion in flattering terms, which to us sound obsequious but are very much in the spirit of the time.

Like many educated men of his day, though styled a servant, Jaques Petit seems often to have turned his hand to writing poetry in idle hours during his many travels. The book listed in *"les livres de M. Le Doux"* entitled *"Mons' petit un angelot"* was probably a collection of his verses which he had had printed. From the Bacon Papers here is one written as his farewell present to Sir Anthony Perez on 11th July 1595.

> Les soucys beau brillans des Oualles celestes,
> T'aillent Perez par tout fauorisant:
> Mon coeur cela va pour toy desirant
> De nostre Dieu par voeux & humbles gestes.
>
> Les Elemens ne te soint pas molestes;
> Que lair serain, te voise accompagnant;
> Que l'eau soit coy, 'allors qu'il va portant,
> Ton corps leger; au port des bons Athletes.
>
> Latorme soit, de toy tant glorieuse
> Qu'elle estim 'estié ne te soustenant bien
> Des allies la seule plus heureuse.
>
> Souhaitte encor' le tout puissant gardien
> Astr'nmiers tout agir & tenir coy,
> Pour ô bening, sauver mon doux Roy & toy.[24]

Sir Anthony Perez, as we learn from Le Doux's letter (MS. 656 f.372, Appendix 2b) was a cherished friend of Anthony Bacon. There are also some long poems by Petit; at the end of each he manages to weave in an eulogistic reference to his dear master Bacon, who is thus elevated to a position as his patron! Monsieur Jaques takes himself very seriously as a poet, polishing his lines with careful thought, and copying out his verses in an exquisite italic hand. He also wrote verses for Anthony Bacon to present to his friend Anthony Perez upon his departure on 11th July in 1595, two little mournful stanzas of four lines each, that speak on behalf of himself and Bacon. This places Petit more in a position of friend rather than servant, but his address to Bacon is always excessively humble and deeply respectful.

---

[24]   L.P.L. *Bacon Papers MS 653, f.108.* See Appendix 5(a) where a translation is given.

Anthony Bacon's Gascon servant was immensely versatile, acting as clerk, amanuensis and trusted agent (some of his letters give incidental intelligence, reporting military information and news of troop movements along with his general gossip) the constant go-between for his master and his other agents, sent here, there and everywhere, but particularly to France and the Netherlands. He is clearly indispensable to Anthony Bacon.

Petit's service with the rather eccentric, well-born Englishman, who preferred to keep the Channel between himself and that nagging, over-solicitous lady, his mother, Lady Ann Bacon, doubtless dated from the years when Anthony was resident in France for the greater part of his twelve years abroad from the age of eighteen. His father, Sir Nicholas Bacon, who was Queen Elizabeth's Lord Keeper of the Great Seal, died in February 1578/9 when Anthony was aged twenty, and he decided to remain in France rather than return home with his younger brother Francis. Anthony was a weakly child from birth, and when his failing health finally forced him to return to England, the indispensable Petit came too.

Petit obviously enjoyed putting quill to paper. His letters sometimes take the form of a diary record stating what happened each day of the week, and are especially useful in providing the background to this story. His descriptions of events are apt and vivid and afford a fascinating glimpse of the times, touched with his somewhat ironic sense of humour, spiced with Gallic wit.

It is through Petit that we know what was happening to Le Doux during his stay in England. The story begins with Petit's letter describing his three-days journey from St. Albans to the home of Sir John Harington (the *"Chevallier"*) in Rutland, where he was going to join Le Doux for Christmas. This is a very amusing letter with Petit's style of reportage in full spate, designed to entertain his master, Anthony Bacon. Here is an excerpt from his lengthy epistle.

> On Wednesday I wrote to you and spoke to the Earl's steward who told me that all those coming from you would receive only favour and courtesy. I left with the Earl, who mounted a horse a mile away from St Albans, and was baptized in the beautiful fount of the lake on the main road. Ten miles further on he stopped to douse himself with more holy water, and to leave his so well embroidered clothes. Then we spent the night in Bedford, where he was welcomed with ringing bells and where apples and wine were brought to him by the notables [officials?] of the city.

Petit's account of the dousing with *"holy water"* is doubtless intended ironically. It could hardly have been a baptismal bath that was taken in mid-winter. This is Petit's way of describing how the unfortunate nobleman was thrown by his horse with an almighty splash into a 'baptismal font' (*"fount"*) namely, a large puddle (*"the lake in the main road"*) and his clothes were splattered (*"embroidered"*) with mud! *"Le Comte"*, who was thus honoured little knowing how he would be reported by Petit to his master, would have been the Earl of Bedford. This was Edward Russell, the third Earl, who had married Lucy Harington, the sister of Sir John Harington, with whom they were going to spend Christmas. His Countess was doubtless following in their coach, when her husband decided to leave the jolting vehicle to take some exercise on horseback, which ended in discomfiture and he returned to the coach to change his mud-"embroidered" clothes.

At this stage Le Doux was not with Petit, who evidently began his journey with the Earl from Bacon's house, Gorhambury, at St Alban's. He meets up with Le Doux later at the house he calls *"Burley"*, which is in Rutland. We can trace this journey geographically from Hertfordshire to Bedfordshire and thence to Northamptonshire, travelling it seems from one stately home to another, and so is reunited with Le Doux at their destination for Christmas, which is evidently the palatial home of the Haringtons.

Petit continues his account of his journey:

> On Thursday we went to the house of Sir Edward Montague, but the retinue was sent back a mile away from there, where one was relying on oneself and God was for all. [Presumably Petit was in the retinue and not too pleased with his entertainment.]
> On Friday, the meeting place for the great and the small was a lunch at this knight's who, for once and as a farewell, treated us passably. As we left, two or three persons of the house accompanied my lord a fair way, well let's be fair to them, nearly 500 paces or a quarter of a mile. We arrived late here in Burley, where I was welcomed and well caressed by Mr Le Doux and the others. After the delivery of your letter to me together with the precious merchandise and your ornamental present to Mr Le Doux, I told him the words that you ordered me to say to Sir John Harington, which are (if I remember rightly) that you humbly kiss his hands and that, having heard from Mr Le Doux that he wanted one of your servants to come here, you had sent me there to offer my service and to learn, by his good leave, something from the said Mr Le Doux. He did not say anything to me. I begged him afterwards to see when Lord Harington would be available so that he could talk to him himself. He said that he would do that. Two days later, I asked him if he had spoken about it. He said he had, and on Tuesday he introduced me to him, who thanks you very much and assured me that I was welcome. As for the state of this house, it is a court in terms of expense and order. I shan't say more at the moment.[25]

It is clear from this that Le Doux has direct access to the lord of the house, while Petit is ranked more as a servant. Petit's description places this house as one of the stately homes of England, which were indeed like small courts. It was here at Burley-on-the-Hill, the main seat of the Haringtons, that Sir John entertained King James in 1603 when he was on his royal progress to London to be crowned King of England, and he created Sir John, 1st Baron Harington of Exton.

Jaques joined this household as "valet" to M. Le Doux, who was apparently acting as tutor to Sir John Harington's small son, which may have been arranged in exchange for hospitality given to Le Doux. The little boy, then aged almost four years, was also named John Harington. Elizabethan children were precocious, and he later acquired a reputation as a notable scholar at Cambridge with a mastery of Greek and Latin as well as other languages. He became the close friend of Prince Henry, the Protestant

---

[25] L.P.L. *Bacon Papers MS 654, ff.70ʳ⁻ᵛ*, trans. L. Bouchon.

champion of Europe, a great free-thinker who admired and befriended Raleigh in his imprisonment. The little boy's aunt, Lucy, was married to the Earl of Bedford (he who fell in the puddle!) and, as Countess of Bedford, became a renowned patroness of poets, including Ben Jonson, the friend of Francis Bacon, and with him closely associated in the production of the First Folio. The Haringtons were an advanced-thinking noble family, which suggests that their home would naturally have afforded a congenial place of safety for Monsieur Le Doux. They were obviously trusted friends of Anthony Bacon.

Jaques Petit's letters convey the day-to-day life-style of this aristocratic society. He seems to have made it his 'business' regularly to report on the people and the surroundings in which he finds himself when on his various embassies for Anthony Bacon, and he takes pains both to inform and entertain his master who, being a semi-invalid, moves very little in society.

Prior to their departure on the Christmas journey to Burley, Petit had evidently been at the great house of the Earl of Bedford, from whence he sent the following report to Anthony Bacon on 28th November 1595, not omitting to tell him how he has been treated and accommodated – always a subject of great interest to Petit.

> At about six in the evening I arrived in this city. I caught up with Mylord, who had departed from London 1 hour before me and having been quite nicely accommodated in his house, unknown among others, I saw him watch for his own entertainment a juggler performing conjuring and subtle tricks. He threaded a very new and thin needle (provided by the ladies) with three threads whilst rapidly turning and swirling round in the light of two candles and to the sound of two violins. Afterwards, whilst the meat was being served 4 or 5 trumpets were sounded for Mylord as is done at the Court for Her Majesty. All this which I relate is nonsense and empty words so I shall not dwell on it but shall go back to my business and, with my very humble and customary prayers to God for your health ....[26]

This letter does not mention Le Doux who, as we have learned, was already at Burley awaiting Petit and the Christmas guests. Petit then reports to Anthony Bacon describing the establishment he found at Burley, in a letter dated 14th December.

> With your permission I shall resume business to tell you how the people conduct themselves in these parts. They go hunting every single day, Madame la Comtesse as well as Monsieur le Comte, with their 4 horse carriages. The good knight Mylord Harrington pays alone the cost of these pleasures and buys expensively the grandeur of the name of Countess for his daughter, [Here Petit makes an error as the Countess is the sister of Lord Harington, not his daughter – a slip of the pen? Their father, Sir James Harington, died in 1592] and would like, so I hear, that everything which is done should be done over again. In the past he used devoutly to give his land without annual rent being able to admit or expel from his estate whomsoever he liked; now he is obliged to grant a lease to this one, a contract to that one for so many years and is obligated to everyone who gives him money in advance. Money has been brought to him (according

---

[26] L.P.L. *Bacon Papers MS.652 f.139*, trans. L. Bouchon.

to what the servants here tell me) for 3 or 4 weeks "more then a bushell and yet euery day et cometh in abondance". [Here he wrote in English.] Indeed he needs it as he has more than 100 persons going to bed and getting up in the house, 30 or 40 horses and as many or more couples of hounds: he entertains anyone coming or going, mainly on Sundays, to such an extent that I believe there is no ale-house in London laying as many tables for its guests as is done here. And moreover, afterwards a confusion of ruin is being invented and spread as this Christmas is the cause of much vain expense for tragedies and plays by Mr Disorder. But, as the custom is for all bad entertainment, one grins and bears it. Time goes slower than they think although the days are short.

Petit is no lover of the drama! After signing off with his usual expressions of excessive devotion he adds a postscript.

I am in great need of some Spanish wax to seal these letters and an Irish cap, brown-greenish with a ribbon of white Cyprus to follow my Castol.[27]

Jaques sees himself as a devout moralist, so he affects to dress in imitation of his master's admired friend Castol. Cyprus was a kind of crêpe, usually black not white, and worn as a sign of mourning.

The next day he writes again complaining of the post as his "last parcel", sent through Wilkinson, one of Sir John Harington's servants, would probably have reached Anthony Bacon before his previous letter "since the latter was sent through the customary carriers who usually have the speed of a snail" and he hopes that his master will not hold him responsible "for the disorder in their deliveries". He then comes to his "big news". At this time another Armada attack was expected. He reports:

.... one says here that the Spaniard claims he will come in harvest [time of harvest] as he did in the year 85 [sic but he means 88] that the Queen wants to send 20,000 men to France and that Sʳ John Harrington, for his part, is supposed to provide 50 of his servants.[28]

Two days later, on 17th December, he reports in typical Petit style that the sisters of Sir John Harington are now all become "Ladies" this news having been "given birth by the death of the Earl of Huntingdon who last Saturday went to see if his expectations looked more certain in the Kingdom of the Other World than in this one".[29] As a result, his inheritance and all his titles passed to the husband of the Lady Elizabeth, the younger of Sir John's sisters, the other being Lucy, Countess of Bedford. However, no sooner was this letter written than tragedy struck the Harington household a terrible blow with the sudden death of Lady Elizabeth's newly ennobled spouse, Sir Francis Hastings.

---

[27] L.P.L. *Bacon Papers MS.652 f.243*, trans. L. Bouchon.

[28] *Ibid: MS.652 f.239*, trans. L. Bouchon.

[29] *Ibid: MS.652 F.246*, trans. L. Bouchon.

My lord,

Before the enclosed letter left my hands again it befell that Sir John Harrington and all his kin are grief-stricken over the loss of Sir Francis Hastings who died having borne the name Mylord for 4 days only. He had for a wife one of the most beautiful sisters of Sir John Harrington who has taken to her bed so distraught and ill that one has almost lost hope for her life, all the more so because she is near to her child-bed. Her words are all extravagant. She says she no longer wants to live: that she does not care anymore about herself and her children, that whatever may happen it is all the same to her since she has lost all the solace of her life, the one who loved her and whom she loved beyond everything in the world. Sorrow is her comfort, tears and wailings are her food. Solitude is her only companion and entertains her far from all other company to let her thoughts dwell on the dismal departure of her dearly-beloved. She has three boys and two girls by the deceased, and the eldest has not yet reached the tenth year of her age. The good gentleman here was soon cast down from the joy he had to see his kin and their spouses ennobled, since that hour no one says a word. The master being dumb, so are all his servants and all is sorrow. The wife of the Earl of Huntingdon died six days after her husband. God of power eternal long preserve you. Your very humble & most faithful servant,

Petit[30]

Death was a frequent visitor in Elizabethan times. The distraught widow would eventually be consoled by Sir Edward Montagu, at whose residence, Boughton Castle in Northamptonshire, the party travelling to Burley for Christmas broke their journey, as described in Petit's letter of 10th December, and were entertained to "a lunch at this knight's, who, for once and as a farewell, treated us passably", as Petit comments. Sir Edward was high sheriff of Northamptonshire, and evidently a family friend of the Haringtons. He became Elizabeth's second husband. A wealthy widow was not long left on the shelf, especially if she was also beautiful.

After the high drama of tragic death at Burley, Petit's next letter, in complete contrast, reports the gaiety of the lavish Christmas festivities at the great house. He seems to have enjoyed himself and writes with a notable absence of irony. Among the entertainments was a performance of *Titus Andronicus*, of which Petit did not think highly, but he has already described plays as a "vain expense" to be laid at the door of "Mr Disorder" in his letter of 14th December. (This folio is damaged at the margins.)

My lord

After these idle days filled with pleasure and entertainment I have the temerity to greet your good grace very humbly in this letter which also will relate (if it please you) the excellent & magnificent order that was maintained in this house with all honest rejoicing this Christmas.

The organisation was such as to wine, dine and entertain [*veigner & entretenir*] 8 or 9 quit-rent neighbours who came every day to feast here. Twice a day there was a sermon in the church, in the morning and afternoon, and each day there

---

[30] L.P.L. *Bacon Papers MS.652 f.248*, trans. L. Bouchon.

was a new minister. The Earl and Madame the Countess attended for the most part.

The Earl was served with every possible honour and respect at dinner and supper. There was music [...?] 30 or 40 gentlemen serving when they carried the [...?] two or three knights and their ladies with a great many gentlemen and young ladies were at his table, then after the meal the dancing and pleasant games took place to make people laugh and to serve as recreation.

Sir John dined in the hall to welcome his neighbours and chief farmers and feasted them at extravagant expense with every sort of dish and every kind of wine.

His head butler was in attendance to see that nothing was lacking for anyone, ensuring that 4 or 5 long tables were loaded with meat for 80 or 100 persons who, having finished eating, withdrew to make room for as many others. Afterwards when everything was over, there were carried to the poor full hogsheads of meat and bread in such quantities that all were satisfied and still much remained.

New Year's Day showed the liberality of these [...?] and principally of the Countess for from the [highest?] to the smallest she gave ample proof of it, and I can even testify to it myself. The actors from London came here to receive their share. They were asked to play on the evening of their arrival and the next day they were sent on their way.

A masquerade composed by Sir Edward Wingfield was played here and also the tragedy of *Titus Andronicus*, but the performance was better than the subject matter. In addition to the above, what is even more appreciated is the fact that coming out of these festivities one is only entering them, as the good fare and entertainments are ever increasing and more pleasant and nothing is diminishing except the crowd and the excessive number of country folk.

I would be even happier if someone among your people could inform me – with your permission – whether six letters which I wrote to you were delivered to your Lordship. For it grieves me to trouble you knowing well that my method and style are not worth presenting to such judgement as yours. Yet my desire to serve you and prove to you my devotion and humble and sincere affection encourages me to bear my ignorance and heavy confusion, hoping in this way to earn your good grace through my faithfulness and diligence which will excuse the absence of that subtle finesse and sharpness of wit so apparent in others.

With this hope I humbly kiss your poor, ailing hands and pray God to bestow on them, as to your whole body, perfect and unalterable health with, at all times, honour and satisfaction to your mind.

Your ever humble, devoted and most faithful servant,

Petit

I send with this letter the two penknives [*ganivets* - an old word for 'canif'] which R. sent me in order to have more if they prove good as I have written to him.[31]

Petit's style in this letter is subdued, and he refers to his writing in a self-deprecatory way as though he is diffident and insecure about how his previous letters, in which he allowed

---

31 L.P.L. *Bacon Papers MS.654 f.253^{r-v}*, trans. L. Bouchon.

his ebullient touches of irony full vent, have been received. His is a nature that craves approval by his master, and one wonders whether his humble comparison of himself as "ignorant" compared with someone whose "finesse" and "sharpness of wit" are evidently admired by Anthony Bacon is a reference to Le Doux? Marlowe was much admired for these very qualities by his contemporaries, Thomas Thorpe acknowledging him as "that pure, elemental wit", and Michael Drayton called him "neat Marlowe", meaning one who is natural and free in expression, close to nature.

> Neat Marlowe, bathéd in the Thespian springs
> Had in him those brave translunary things
> That the first poets had; his raptures were
> All air and fire, which made his verses clear;
> For that fine madness still he did retain,
> Which rightly should possess a poet's brain.
> *Epistles of Poets and Poesy, 1635*

His *Hero and Leander* is an exquisite example of this. Marlowe was not only a poet of recognized genius, he was also a Cambridge Master of Arts, which counted for something in those days. Petit does not mention him unless there is a practical reason for doing so, and they evidently do not move in the same circle at Burley. This may, of course, also reflect the possibility that Le Doux kept a fairly low profile and did not, in fact, mix much in company, but he certainly had direct access to Sir John Harington when required. One hopes that he would have been present at the performance of *Titus Andronicus*!

However, we gain another picture from Petit's next letter, in which it is clear that trouble was brewing between him and Le Doux, the direct cause of which was a woman employee in the Harington household of whom the puritanical Jaques violently disapproves.

Jaques Petit, Monsieur Le Doux and the 'Nun'

Jaques Petit's letters, together with his poems give us a clue to his character, and if Anthony Bacon's Gascon servant was the sometime companion of Monsieur Le Doux, *alias* the exiled Marlowe/Shakespeare, as we suspect him to be, the relationship of these two gentlemen would be of considerable interest to us. In attempting a portrait of Jaques Petit, I imagine him as a Puckish figure, like his name, of a cherubic appearance, as perhaps indicated by Le Doux's sobriquet (?) *"un angelot"*, of short stature and perhaps fat? A man of the world, Petit at times reveals a critical, moralistic disapproval of the behaviour of his fellow human beings. He can even be quite stern!

We see this side of Petit in his letter expressing his disgust at the immoral goings-on he has discovered at the stately home of Sir John Harington, where he has been hospitably received into what was a very large establishment with many servants. His letter, endorsed as received by his master on 29th January 1596, shows him in an almost hysterical state over developments that have come to light since Christmas. He has discovered to his horror that among the female servants are some of loose morals − *"les paillardes domestiques"* (namely lewd, wanton, lecherous) one of whom is apparently having an affair with Monsieur Le Doux! She is even, so he fears, intending to seduce him, Petit, and he is desperate to escape from this place which he considers little more than an undercover brothel. Here is Petit's shocked letter in a translation, in which he refers satirically to this seductive woman as *"la nonain"*, the nun!

> Monseigneur,
> I beg you to send someone to take me away from here. I cannot stay any longer among fornicators and debauched domestic servants. I beg you to call me back without delay or I shall be the ruin of Mr Le Doux and the nun, whose deeds are so shameful as to be well in tune with those of the devil. The former confessed it, and the latter would take advantage of me if she could. If you, Monseigneur, do not send for me at once, and if they do not go away from here, they will run a great risk. I cannot bear the dishonour of those who extend me hospitality here. For the love that this old one bears you, I will keep silence still, provided they vacate this honourable house. I pray to God.
> Monseigneur,
> so manage it that among your servants this breed does not find itself.
> Your very humble and ever faithful
servant,
Petit.[32]

[He adds a P.S.] I don't know whether the truth lies in the name or the anagrammatist who presents it, but I found that the name of this whore, who is called *Ide du Wault* connotes that she wants *Du vi du valet*.

Translating Old French poses many problems, but *"vi"* is evidently *"le vit"*, which is the Old French word for the male organ. Petit's jest has definite sexual implications. We can guess what he is suggesting! He is intent on presenting Ide in the worst possible

---

[32] L.P.L. *Bacon Papers MS 654, f.69*, trans. L. Bouchon.
Petit spells her name du Vault with a **W** written as a double VV to get his anagram.

light. Presently we find Le Doux as the bearer of letters to Anthony, and we learn that Ide du Vault expects that she will be secretly dismissed and she is incensed with the "ill-natured valet". Clearly someone had been telling tales.

The question we have to ask is, was Ide du Vault really a nun? Or is this again just Petit's usual ironic way of describing people of whom he does not approve? If Ide du Vault *really* is a nun, Petit's extravagantly shocked reaction is the more justified and understandable. However, as we have seen, Petit is given to extravagant description of the people he is observing so keenly.

I confess that at first sight of Petit's shocked letter, I had read it as a piece of his typical satirical, wry humour naming this lady as *"la nonain"*, for it seemed unlikely that a nun would be employed in the Harington household as one of *"les paillardes domestiques"*. Then, suddenly, all was revealed. Peter Farey, trawling tirelessly through the microfilms of the Bacon Papers, came across a most important letter from Jean Castol, minister of the French Church in London to his long-standing friend Anthony Bacon, imparting personal confidential information. What a revelation this proved to be!

Below is the relevant excerpt from this letter, which throws a sharp light on the characters of both Jaques Petit and Le Doux and their relationship, and on Ide du Vault and the clandestine romance going on at Burley. He writes to Anthony:

> Our French Mercury has done Monsieur Le Doux and consequently myself a bad turn by obtaining for Monseigneur Harington a de-frocked nun, quarrelsome and incompatible, without the said *"Chevallier"* having requested it. It seems that, since a woman would be more suitable than a man to instruct a girl who is still but an infant, he meant to provide some opportunity to weary and scandalize one regarding the man who is a servant to you and a friend to me. But these are the mean and habitual traits, of which I have had my belly-full for a long time. We teach that we should not do to others that which we would not wish to have done to ourselves. And let us believe that it is enough. Let us not shrink from being subject to the same law. When all the running riot that one wants has been done, perhaps the conscience will awaken. I desire no other retribution.[33]

Here is revelation indeed! A de-frocked nun! The affair between Le Doux and "la nonain" had evidently been going on from the time when Le Doux arrived at Burley some months before Jaques joined him there, for Castol's letter is dated October 1595. We can now unravel the scenario.

It seems that it was Jaques Petit who had been instrumental in soliciting Ide du Vault, a French Huguenot who was known to be a de-frocked nun, for the position at Burley to take charge of Sir John Harington's infant daughter, while Anthony Bacon had sent Le Doux thither in a similar capacity to be tutor to his little son, who would be four years old in April 1596. The girl was an infant requiring a nanny rather than a tutor. Getting wind of the illicit love-affair that had developed, the decision had been taken to send Jaques Petit to Burley as Le Doux's "valet", but eventually, with Sir John's agreement, to replace him as tutor. (Perhaps this was the matter Le Doux was to broach

---

[33] L.P.L. *Bacon Papers MS.652 f.105*, trans. L. Bouchon.

to Sir John as inferred in Petit's first letter upon his arrival at Burley?) The fact that Anthony already knew of the affair was not disclosed to Petit, for in writing to Anthony Bacon he did not realize that this was not news to his master. Petit now made sure that the cat was out of the bag at Burley, despite his assurance of silence to his master.

Jean Castol's letter shows Jaques Petit in a very unfavourable light. He is apparently a known trouble-maker and of a misanthropic disposition. His attitude towards Le Doux is revealed as tainted with envy. This is also apparent in his own letters. Envy from lesser mortals had dogged Marlowe's life. We think of Gabriel Harvey, who displays this in his poem *Gorgon or the wonderfull yeare*. That iniquitous informer, Richard Baines's professional interest in him seems to have an element of personal malice springing from envy of the successful, well-favoured, young secret agent. Robert Greene, his envious colleague, comes to mind, at whose door the malicious gossip tainting the brilliant dramatist's reputation with 'godless' atheism can be laid, for he accused him of it outright in print in his deliberately damaging diatribe, his *Groatsworth of Wit*. Marlowe was peculiarly vulnerable to this baleful influence.

Le Doux is evidently known to his good friends, Anthony Bacon and Jean Castol, as susceptible to female charms. They may not approve, but neither do they censure him. At this point in the drama the best course was to extract him and find an assignment in intelligence-gathering for the Earl of Essex to whisk him away from temptation to the relative safety of Germany and thence back to Italy. We see here evidence of a benign concern for Le Doux. In the first place, what is he doing at Burley in far away Rutland? His profession as an intelligence agent hardly justifies such a placement in an aristocratic home of a good friend of Anthony, does it? That is, unless he were in need of special protection. In the light of Castol's letter Le Doux has some truly loyal friends who, while deploring his behaviour, are still always his zealous guardians. There is no suggestion of dismissing him or abandoning him, but he must be extricated from his entanglement with *"la nonain"* and sent on his way elsewhere.

Interestingly, if this is Marlowe in his undercover French disguise, it disposes once and for all of the myth that he was a homosexual, which I have questioned on several other grounds: his youthful translation of the decidedly heterosexual *Amores* of Ovid whilst at Cambridge, and the abiding influence this had on him, Ovid being the favourite Latin poet of Marlowe, as of Shakespeare; his choice of Scanderbeg, Prince of Epirro (now Albania) as the hero of his first full-length play written whilst in his teens, an almost legendary historic figure of high moral virtue who forbade his soldiers to rape women, and hated *"all vice especially that of the Citie of* **Gomorra**", and adored his wife.[34] It is, moreover, inconceivable that the tragic fate of the homosexual King Edward II could have been so horrifyingly and powerfully depicted by a homosexual dramatist, as it is in Marlowe's play.

If we consider the evidence of the Sonnets as autobiographical, there is an inference of this poet's libidinous behaviour in his *Sonnet 121*, in which he defends himself vigorously against those critics, who included censorious moralisers probably as much as the more virulent bigots who accused him falsely of the heretical sin of atheism, whereas his 'heresy' was the yearning for knowledge.

---

[34]   John Shute: *op. cit.* (See p.27, *n38* in the present text.)

'Tis better to be vile, than vile esteemed,
When not to be receives reproach of being,
And the just pleasure lost, which is so deemed,
Not by our feeling, but by others seeing.
For why should others false adulterate eyes
Give salutation to my sportive blood?
Or on my frailties why are frailer spies,
Which in their wills count bad what I think good?
No, I am that I am, and they that level
At my abuses, reckon up their own.
I may be straight though they themselves be bevel;
By their rank thoughts my deeds must not be shown.
  Unless this general evil they maintain,
  All men are bad and in their badness reign

Sonnet 121

The censure at Burley, stirred up by Petit one suspects, was felt keenly by Ide du Vault, and she complains bitterly in her letters (yes, this lady was literate) of a sense of ostracism by all and sundry as she awaits what is to become of her after Le Doux departs and she is bereft of his "consolation of the spirit". One can readily understand how Le Doux, especially if he is Marlowe, would have been attracted to her. As a Huguenot immigrant she would immediately have induced sympathy in her paramour (is she married, for she is also known as Madame Vallereine?), for as an eight-year-old boy he had vividly experienced the great influx of Huguenot refugees who arrived in Canterbury, telling tales of the terrible Massacre of St Bartholomew's Eve in Paris, an appalling blood-bath from which they had fled. Marlowe dramatized this horrific event in his play **The Massacre at Paris**, the last work he wrote under his own name. It was performed by the Lord Admiral's Men at the Rose with Edward Alleyn in the leading role of the Machiavellian Duke of Guise on 30th January 1592/3, a performance one imagines Marlowe would not have wished to miss.

Ide du Vault was, as her letters reveal, a lady in distress. France was still coming to terms with the aftermath of the years of turmoil and religious civil wars. She was clearly a Huguenot immigrant, and we may guess that she was either married and separated by the misfortune of the times, or perhaps a young widow who had taken refuge in a nunnery, but found the strict life of celibacy uncongenial. Her unfrocking implies some sort of scandal, and she refers in both her letters to a sense of guilt for having left her religion, for which she fears God is angry with her. Such a sinner would have appealed to the compassion in Marlowe *alias* Shakespeare.

We know from the Sonnets that the Poet's passionate love-affair with the Dark Lady was with a fallen woman, the beautiful black-eyed harlot, Luce Morgan. In that case, there is an intriguing suggestion of an historic repetition in this scenario, for Luce Morgan appeared at the mock court of the Prince of Purpoole in the guise of a nun! She posed as the "Abbess de *Clerkenwell*" who arrived to render her homage to the Prince in the form of "night service in *Cauda*" offering to provide "a choir of nuns, with burning lamps, to chant *Placebo* to the gentlemen of the Prince's privy-chamber". Marlowe was acting as the Prince's sonneteer and fell head-over-heels in love with the "nun" Luce Morgan.

Their passionate love-affair is recorded with extraordinary frankness in the Sonnets of the Dark Lady.

The identification of Marlowe as Le Doux throws up a strangely evocative, amorous association linking Luce Morgan and Ide du Vault – the one a mock nun, the other a de-frocked nun. Did her status evoke an echo in Le Doux's heart of his youthful passion that made him inevitably susceptible to Ide du Vault's charms? What Jaques Petit knew of Le Doux's past, one can only guess. The man was no fool. There is a somewhat sinister implication in Jean Castol's letter that Petit had set up Ide du Vault as a decoy for Le Doux hoping to provide some opportunity (*"donner quelque occasion"*) to disgrace Le Doux. If so, we have been given a glimpse into the black heart of envy.

We learn that Le Doux is due to depart for London to visit Anthony Bacon (perhaps to be confronted with the consequences of his behaviour? but certainly to discuss Petit's future) and he bears two letters entrusted to him by Ide for safe delivery. We learn more of the situation that was developing at Burley from these two letters written by Ide du Vault herself expressing her disgust with the "valet" (Jaques Petit), from which we also glean that she had a very sympathetic and confidential relationship with Monsieur Le Doux, and that she is held in some disgrace at Burley. What her disgrace is she does not spell out, but Petit has made this quite clear! Du Vault's letters are dated 24th January 1596 (new style) and in both she has much to say in her own defence. One is addressed to Mr. Jean Castol, minister of the French Church in London.

Jean Castol was a married man, hence Protestant, not a Catholic, and his many letters show him to have been a close friend of Anthony Bacon. In her letter Ide speaks with regret at having left her native land, coupling this with a reference to her "religion". She was evidently of a superior class of servant, a wide term, for both Jean Petit and Le Doux refer to themselves as Anthony Bacon's "humble servant" when signing off.

In her letter to Jean Castol she complains bitterly of Petit, who has been spreading malicious gossip:

> *"le valet de Mr Bacon ne fut jamais este icy quinse iour et ayant entendu ses parolles & deportimens que ie n'aye adverty Mr le doulx de ce quy reconnoit"*.[35]
> (Translated below)

She is distressed by Le Doux's departure and believes he had been dismissed, though this cannot have been the case for he returns to depart finally together with Petit, both having expressed their sincere gratitude (as specifically instructed by Anthony Bacon on his behalf) to Sir John Harington for his hospitality.

Here is a translation of Ide du Vault's letter to Jean Castol.

Sir,
    I humbly thank you for the honour you do me in remembering me by letters of Mr Le Doux, the present carrier. To my great regret my Lord's service is not retained. Mr Bacon's manservant had not been here fifteen days when, having

---

[35]   L.P.L. *Bacon Papers MS.654, f.186 verso.*

heard of his speeches and ill-doings, I warned Mr Le Doux of what he knows [about us?]. In effect, I am expecting as much [i.e. dismissal] one of these days having heard of the busy-body doings of Mademoiselle Molet. [She had apparently been busy finding a replacement for du Vault.] If this happens, at least there will be no reason to reproach those who had a hand in it for me. You have shown me a father's and a friend's solicitude for which I am obliged to you with all my heart. I have done nothing to my advantage in leaving my country and my religion to come to this place where I have no status and am put down [not appreciated]. When I expressed my misgivings Mr Le Doux dispelled them, but now I am deprived of this consolation of the spirit. I am extremely vexed that I cannot send money to Mr de Lignes. My wages are small, and my humiliations great. In this large establishment I withdraw myself from the others for several reasons. One is because I see myself held in such low esteem by madame [....?] and I beg you to excuse me for it to him [? here the writing is very obscure] you will oblige me the more to pray to God for you.

I kiss your hands and your wife's [*Madame votre femme*]. I pray God that he blesses the wedding of her sister to whom I send greetings.

Yours most humble for ever,

Du Vault[36]

de burley ce 24 Janvier

It would seem that she is in disfavour with my lady, and with the Countess (of Bedford) who is Sir John Harington's sister, of whom she has more to say in her other letter which was written on the same day to her friend, Madame Vilegre, in London to whom she unburdens herself. Her letter to Jean Castol is signed "Du Vault", but both letters are endorsed *"De Madame Vallereine à Mr Castol et Madame Vilegre, le mois de Janvier 1596"*.

With Le Doux absent poor Ide is in a state of despondency. She writes to her friend Madame Vilegre to air her grievances. These letters are given in a literal translation as interpreting them could possibly distort what the writer intends to convey. (Both letters are partly damaged at the right margin so that some guesswork is involved as indicated by the square brackets.)

Madam,

I entrust once more the gentleman leaving this house with this letter so that he can tell you some news of me as to a lady whom I wish to serve and obey in all things. Thus I shall tell you that during the Christmas festivities my lady told me that she had two people for one job [*pour une mesme chose* – which may mean to carry out the same duties?], and that if the present carrier [i.e. Le Doux] were going away my wages would be doubled since when [*du depuis*] one has given him [cut off at margin] a concealed dismissal [after?] the fashion of the court, and one does me a wrong and an insult in retaining [his?] manservant who knows nothing but bad [i.e. Gascon] French to teach the little one to read. I do not know if this is to make me give my notice, particularly as I saw some letters from Mademoiselle Molet, recently written, in which she tells the Countess [*madam la Comtesse*, who must be the Countess of Bedford then staying at Burley] that she has always prophesied to her that she would be the Sun of

---

[36] *Ibid, trans. L. Bouchon.*

England and her sister would be the Moon and that in order to help her she had chosen the most perfect young lady one could find in France to serve the little one, and a gentleman, and that they would come when they were wanted. I do not think that those who love change would refuse it. You will be told the three insults which I have received from the Countess herself which, if God does not help me, I shall remain charged with and in great shame for ever. I minimize the whole situation [try to make light of it] considering what bad times these are. However, if I thought that they wanted to give me my notice I would ask for it first, yet I shan't do anything of the sort until I have heard from you. One wonders if one is given one's notice or is supposed to ask for it. It is a great pity that I have left my country and my religion to come to a place where I am without any proper position and it is no wonder since God is angry and displeased with me, that my work is so thankless although I omit nothing of my duties, but I am ashamed to find myself in such bad repute with the others. Consequently I withdraw as much as I can [keep myself to myself]. Those of my disposition will never be welcome here as long as the Countess is present, who only loves vanities and those who run best at the hunt. Her tailor told me that I should not think that much notice is being taken of my bad situation [*son tailleur a dit que il ne me falloit pas penser que lon fit grand cas de moy estant si mal en point & que lon n'ayment pas cela ceans*]. They don't like that here. My mind is very disturbed. I pray God that he will take pity on me and that at least he does not take your good graces away from me. I beg you very humbly to send me a headdress of the same size as the first one you gave me, but it should be covered because my hair falls [*tombent* – cascades down? is long? or is falling out?] and it should have a peak, please[*]. I beg you to excuse my importunity since after God my recourse is to you. Thus I end by [cut off – kissing?] your hands praying God that he keeps dispensing his blessings on you.

Your most humble servant,[37]

(not signed)

[*] Her name for the headdress she requests is *"un moule"* which is a close fitting cap – literally a mould or cast made to fit.

It seems that Le Doux and du Vault are both employed to instruct, and/or take charge of Sir John Harington's little children, and that if Le Doux leaves, his position as tutor had been promised to du Vault, and she would receive double wages. Now she is furious to discover that his valet, Jaques Petit (who speaks abominable Gascon French) would take over Le Doux's job. A double blow for Ide; she loses her lover and his wages, which has set her fuming.

Ide du Vault's letters, as preserved in the Anthony Bacon Papers, are copies of the originals written by Petit; the one to Mme Vilegre is on the recto with her letter to Mr Jean Castol on the verso of the same folio. This is confirmed by Jaques Petit's letter, also written on 24th January, stating that he is sending copies of Du Vault's letters to Anthony Bacon for his information on the lady. But whether Petit made these copies

---

[37] L.P.L. *Bacon Papers MS.654, f.186 recto,* trans. L. Bouchon

with Le Doux's knowledge before his departure carrying post to London we can only guess. Jaques is playing a crafty game! Here is Petit's letter:

My Lord,
    The day preceding the departure of Mr Le Doux with Sir John Harington I received the letters from your page and from my compatriot. The first did not bring me any happiness because it informed me of the continuation of your severe illness.
[He then refers at length to his receipt of a New Year's gift of a hat and a "small angel" or coin from his master, over which there was some misunderstanding on his part.]
All the rest of the aforementioned letters do not enlighten me on your will. Please let me know if you have received 6 to 7 letters which I wrote to your lordship since my arrival. The last one was short and on its own.
[This would have been his urgent plea to be recalled at once from his present situation at Burley because he is so shocked by the immoral goings-on.]
I beg you, Sir, to allow someone to write it to me since it is like a death to your Gascon not to know the success of the business he undertakes. I shall not say anything about Mr Le Doux. I shall only relate to your lordship the will of "Miss-worth-nothing" [*Mzel Vaultrien* − which is another play on her name!] who says that she would like you to borrow her head and her tongue to scold Mr Le Doux for his sudden dep ... [cut off − probably *departure*] which she calls precipitated. I send you a copy [cut off at margin] of her letters which she thinks she has sent through her − Mr her am ... [cut off − could be *amant* − her lover] so that you know what good there is in her head and her tongue. I have nothing else to tell you further, as I speak little. I am sure you will hear much news. If I remain here any longer, some masterpiece shall be created, I mean regarding the education of Sir John's son. [This child developed into a brilliant scholar.] If I leave, some undertaking upon which I have reflected for a long time shall begin, that is to know what fortune to find in Gascony so that I can gallop after it if it is good, and run away from it if it is bad and withdraw to the Temple of Virtue to resist it. I shall not tell where this Temple is so that you do not think I am too much of a flatterer, but it is enough for me to know and recognize it. These are my plans. Choose whichever you would like me to finish or begin, since in everything and everywhere I shall be all yours.

He adds a postscript complaining of Mr Le Doux with whom he is obviously greatly displeased.

PS I owe 10 l^i to Mr Le Doux but, although he has already been paid by your liberality, because of his avarice, he counts them and asks them of me, and this to save 150 ecus [crowns] and more, which he has in gold.[38]

There is friction building up between Jaques Petit and Le Doux on several counts. Petit's letters reveal him as an eccentric character holding strong opinions, who is clearly a prey to envy, and cunning with it. He is probably also a misogynist. The contrast

---

[38] L.P.L. *Bacon Papers MS.654, f.13, dated 24 Jan. Rec'vd 30 Jan.*, trans. L. Bouchon.

between the strait-laced, puritanical Petit and the life-embracing, responsive, forbearing and susceptible nature of Le Doux is well illustrated in the episode at Burley. Petit later accompanies Le Doux abroad, and one wonders how these two opposites rubbed along together. One is tempted to see a reflection of their relationship in *As You Like It*, which is a play set in exile in some imaginary Forest of Arden, which some have suggested was the Ardennes. The plot is taken from Thomas Lodge's *Rosalynde*, but the characters of Touchstone and Jaques are the dramatist's own. I have given ample evidence elsewhere of the way Marlowe used episodes and characters from his life in the plays in the brief canon of his accredited works and in the canon of the Shakespeare plays, which is one of the strongest arguments for his authorship.[39] These are infinitely more appropriate and telling than the supposed reflections sophistically argued for the spurious authorship theories of de Vere, or of Francis Bacon. *As You Like It* is indeed notable for its *direct* references to Marlowe (the probable explanation for the curious fact that it was not licensed for printing by the Stationers' authority but was "stayed" in 1600). Here, in the scene showing the rather touchy relationship between Jaques and Orlando, it is not difficult to see another autobiographical reflection as he paints a portrait of his companion in exile, Jaques Petit, thinly disguised as the melancholy philosopher whose character is acutely observed. This is offered as a feasible hypothesis of the genesis of this scene.

Jaques:	*(to Orlando)* I thank you for your company, but, good faith, I had as lief have been myself alone.
Orlando:	And so had I. But yet for fashion's sake, I thank you too for your society.
Jaques:	God b'wi'you; let's meet as little as we can.
Orlando:	I do desire we may be better strangers.
Jaques:	I pray you mar no more trees with writing love songs in their barks.
Orlando:	I pray you mar no more of my verses with reading them ill-favouredly.
Jaques:	Rosalind is your love's name?
Orlando:	Yes, just.
Jaques:	I do not like her name.
Orlando:	There was no thought of pleasing you when she was christened.
Jaques:	What stature is she of?
Orlando:	Just as high as my heart.
Jaques:	You are full of pretty answers. Have you not been acquainted with goldsmiths' wives, and conn'd them out of rings?
Orlando:	Not so; but I answer you right painted cloth, from whence you have studied your questions.
Jaques:	You have a nimble wit; I think 'twas made of Atalanta's heels. Will you sit down with me? and we two will rail against our mistress the world, and all our misery.
Orlando:	I will chide no breather in the world but myself, against whom I know most faults.

---

[39] Wraight: *The Story That the Sonnets Tell: Chapter XXI, 'Canterbury Tales'*.

Jaques:	The worst fault you have is to be in love.
Orlando:	'Tis a fault I will not change for your best virtue. I am weary of you.
Jaques:	By my troth, I was seeking for a fool when I found you.
Orlando:	He is drown'd in the brook; look but in, and you shall see him.
Jaques:	There I shall see mine own figure.
Orlando:	Which I take to be either a fool or a cipher.
Jaques:	I'll tarry no longer with you; farewell, good Signior Love.
Orlando:	I am glad of your departure; adieu, good Monsieur Melancholy.

As You Like It, Act 3, scene 2, 11.238-277

In Petit's verses he certainly affects the melancholy mode, and his critically philosophizing disposition has many points of affinity with the character of Jaques, so that it is perhaps not too fanciful to see in him that rather prudish old acquaintance of Le Doux who inspired *Monsieur* Melancholy in a play whose setting is exile. Jaques is clearly indicated as a Frenchman.

Petit and Le Doux were each in different ways close to Anthony Bacon, but there would have been some friction between two such very different characters, and this is borne out by the letters. Jaques was a foil to that *"French gentleman"* Le Doux, who was really very English, and undercurrents of their relationship surface sharply in Jaques' emotional plea to Anthony to "Get me out of this place of fornication!" Bacon answered immediately on receipt of the letter on 29th January. It had taken six days to reach him. Meanwhile, Petit, having made his moan, wrote again to mitigate his outburst against Le Doux and his sexual liaison with Ide du Vault. He is evidently now a very worried man, wondering what Le Doux, who has gone to see Anthony Bacon in London, might say about him. Would his master be annoyed and discharge him to pass his services on permanently to Sir John Harington as tutor to his little son?

This letter has presented more than the usual translation problems as Jaques tends to become slightly incoherent when he launches into a high-flown, emotional eulogy of "Antoine de Bacon", as he addresses his idolized master. (This fault also applies to some of his poetry.)

My lord,
    As my duty governs all my affections and actions I shall obey you in everything you will decide about me in accordance with what Monsieur Le Doux will suggest concerning my residing here to teach Sir Jehan Harington's little son. Whatever you wish, My lord, I shall do with a cheerful and gay heart: should you want me back at your feet, I wish it too; and if you should want me to stay here, I desire to do so, for you have been and are my [....?] good weal; and for this reason I desire it for the hope I have to deserve thanks and obligation and by my pains and industry to earn for myself the favour of these noble Lords and Ladies the which may some day earn me advancement. Advise me, My lord, whatever commandments you are pleased to impose and whatsoever they are [....?] all will be to my contentment. You are my first [ma...? cut off ... master?] and if it please God will be the last also for I do not change my choice [but rarely?] which immutable and perpetual is for you. Notwithstanding My lord, I

beg you to consider benevolently a creature who is so much yours and honour it at this time by writing to Monsieur and Madame [....?] of the affection that I have for you and by this I shall know that during the long time I have served you I have gained some rank among your good servants and if my faithfulness is held in esteem I shall know whether the hope I entertain and have entertained can turn to certitude or into despair and thus I shall know also whether I am banned from your Ocean. That is to say, from your boundless graces, from your bounty and great love, and to say it better, even more from you yourself. For I have found that Antoine de Bacon, tells me, Banned from your Ocean [? ...] knowing what to think I have applied it as you see and declare assuredly [....?] that as my Apollo and true Oracle you will [cut off ...] me of doubt as to what you will do so that I know that having responded in a pleasing and desirable sound [voice? manner?] is making me hear in grace is love. [This entire passage is very obscure.]

I beg you My lord to accept these confused words [*"brouillard"* literally means "fog"] (which can do nothing but mistify you) in good part, because they come from a heart which I have wholly dedicated and devoted to your service and which always with as much zeal as of affection will pray the Divine and unique Oracle My lord to grant you perfect health and to bless your worthy designs.

Your Petit[40]

The scheming Jaques is in quite a state imagining that he will have to change masters, but having licked his beloved Antoine de Bacon's boots his fears prove groundless. His stay at Burley was not destined to become permanent. Anthony Bacon had been very ill again, but by the end of January was convalescing, and this may have been the diplomatic excuse offered for recalling Petit home urgently because his services were now much needed. He writes a brief note to confirm this:

Jaques,
This is only to warn you that I have asked Mr Le Doux to send you back to me as soon as possible and to thank Lord Harrington very affectionately for the favour he did me and assure him that I shall always be ready to do him some good favour in return when I am in a position to do so. You too, do not fail to do your duty when you leave and show all your gratitude and humility towards him.
Your good master.[41]

Accordingly, Petit and Le Doux departed after expressing their thanks for the hospitality received under the roof of Sir John Harington's palatial mansion at Burley-on-the-Hill, three miles from Exton in Rutland where the family had a second home, Exton Hall. This was a necessity for such great households to which the family would move while major cleaning and airing of their former residence was being undertaken. This periodical exodus from palace to palace was the *modus vivendi* of the royal court of the realm. As Petit had commented to Anthony Bacon on his arrival at Burley, "the state of this house ... is a court in terms of expense and order". These letters from his stylish

---

40   L.P.L. *Bacon Papers MS.654, f.95*, trans. L. Bouchon. This folio is also damaged at the edges.
41   *Ibid: MS.654, f.248*. Undated. Written in Anthony Bacon's own hand.

pen have given a most interesting and detailed description of a sixteenth century great house during the festive Christmas season, and the way of life there, both 'upstairs' and 'downstairs'.

It is thanks to Jaques Petit's busy quill that we now know more about the man whose sudden, brief emergence as Monsieur Le Doux suggests that by incredible luck we have found the secret agent, Christopher Marlowe, in his exile, filling out the picture that the *Sonnets of Exile* so movingly convey. These letters have highlighted an episode in his life that has given us an unique, intimate glimpse of the real man, warts and all, a genius, who is also a flesh and blood human being, not an obscure figure of myth, who was and is our pseudonymous Shakespeare. He has suddenly materialized as Monsieur Le Doux, and then as suddenly he vanishes again, leaving us wondering what happened to his liaison with Ide du Vault, to whom he had given such "consolation of the spirit" as she delicately puts it?

Le Doux's first passport was issued on 10th February, and he must then have gone abroad, but returned, for his passport was renewed on 10th March. Petit apparently accompanied him on the first leg of his travels in his intelligence service for the Earl of Essex; but letters from Jaques Petit dated September and October 1596, describing in detail events that appear to be connected with preparations to meet a second Armada threat – in which he is sometimes on board ship with many gentlemen of importance and nobility who are all mentioned by name – no longer include any reference to Monsieur Le Doux. By the autumn of 1596 it seems that Jaques and Le Doux had parted company and gone their separate ways.

Le Doux and Thomas Walsingham

The most important of the letters from Le Doux is that of 20th April in which he writes mostly about books, having just met the Spaniard John de Cypriano, *alias* Cardenas, who had been in touch with the Earl of Essex in 1595 and again in 1596.[42] This gentleman has arrived in the town where Le Doux is residing expressly to get in touch with printers who are evidently friends of Sir Antonio Perez, who may be interested in publishing Cypriano's Latin *"histoire"*, presumably a biography, of Perez, described as *"sa version latine de l'histoire"* of Sir Antonio Perez. Whether a translation into Latin or his original work is not clear.

Below is an English translation of this interesting letter.

> Sir,   Yesterday evening I met a Spaniard named Cyprian and reputed a man of virtue and learning, whose son had done service with the late Mr. Walsingham. This Cyprian told me that he had come from *"Neübüry"* to this town expressly for the purpose of finding out if any friend of Sir Anthony Perez would be interested to have his Latin version of the history of the aforesaid Sir printed, and told me that he would be content with a modest reward for his labours, either in money or in the form of a certain number of copies. I know your affection for the said Sir, and how much you value anything concerning him. And for the duty I owe you, I also wish him every satisfaction. This is why I wanted to advise you about this and beg you to let me know your opinion and wishes regarding the above. And do not trouble yourself too much. A little will be plenty. Our Frenchmen are not very happy with the man who is in your library. Your friends are of various opinions. They all sympathize with you. The others pass this by [take no notice?].[43]

There is no signature as here the page has been torn off, leaving a slightly jagged edge. It is endorsed "from Monsieur Le Doux" and we know it is from him both by the handwriting and the content, and it is filed immediately next to his signed letter of 5th April. (See Appendix 2a and 2b.) One is intrigued to conjecture, what might have been written on that torn off half page? Monsieur Le Doux evidently had something secret to impart, and since this is a personal letter we can assume that it would have been private information and not connected with his espionage work, for which ciphers were used to impart sensitive information.

The town of *"Neübüry"* was probably Neuburg an der Donau, as his use of the **u** *umlaut* suggests (although, in fact, it is wrongly used, but German was one language of which Marlowe/Shakespeare shows no knowledge). Neuburg, northwest of Munich, was at that time a thriving centre of learning.[44]

---

[42] *Ibid. MS 650, f.40.* Letter from Essex to Cardenas *alias* Cypriano.
      Also, *MS 654, f.135.*

[43] L.P.L. *Bacon Papers MS 656, f.372*, trans. L. Bouchon. See Appendix 2(b).

[44] I am indebted to Prof. T. W. Craik for suggesting that the town named is probably Neuburg, rather than Newbury in Berkshire.

The important clue this letter gives is the mention of the name "*Mr. Welsinghan*" (written "Welsingha*n*" which is obviously intended as "ha*m*"), who is clearly someone of great interest to Le Doux, who is also well known to Anthony Bacon. Apparently Le Doux learns that the son of this Cypriano had been in the service of the late "*Mr. Welsinghan*", a small point of mutual interest to both himself and Anthony which he is passing on in what is a personal letter, not one imparting intelligence matters in his professional capacity. Who, then, can the *late Mr.* Walsingham have been? He was not Sir Francis Walsingham, who died in 1590, as it would be a mark of respect in this class conscious society to refer to him as 'Sir'. Nor is it Marlowe's patron, Mr. Thomas Walsingham, who was very much alive; he would be knighted by Queen Elizabeth in the autumn of 1597 in preparation for his marriage to one of her favourite Maids of Honour, the Lady Audrey Shelton. This can, therefore, only be a reference to the elder brother of Thomas, the *late Mr* Edmund Walsingham, who died six months before Sir Francis, in November 1589 when Thomas inherited the family estates. Edmund Walsingham had also been employed in the intelligence and espionage service run by his cousin, Sir Francis. Marlowe would doubtless have known him, for his relationship with the Walsingham family was entirely circular in employment, friendship and patronage.

Edmund had inherited the Walsingham estates in 1584 on the death of his father, Sir Thomas Walsingham III, but he only lived to enjoy them for five years, when his cultured younger brother became the lord of Scadbury. This moated manor house would undoubtedly have had a fine library. The mention of Walsingham is in the context of a letter about books and publishing, and also refers rather critically to Anthony's librarian. "*Noz francois ne sont pas beaucoup contents de l'homme q'est en votre librairie.*" This is interesting to say the least, and also significant in providing a direct link between Monsieur Le Doux and the late "*Mr Welsinghan*", who was the brother of Marlowe's patron, whom he would doubtless have known at Scadbury or at Court.

The library of Monsieur Le Doux has been examined and shown to provide evidence of just such interests as Marlowe is known to have had, and the massive research done by scholars on the source books of Shakespeare's plays has revealed an impressive correlation between this personal library and the works of the First Folio. From the Book List, mention of no less than twenty-five Shakespeare plays has emerged:

> *The Comedy of Errors*
> *The Merchant of Venice*
> *Twelfth Night*
> *The Merry Wives of Windsor*
> *The Winter's Tale*
> *Henry IV*
> *A Midsummer Night's Dream*
> *All's Well That Ends Well*
> *The Taming of the Shrew*
> *Cymbeline*
> *Julius Caesar*
> *Henry V*
> *Edward III*
> *Henry VI, Part 2*
> *Much Ado About Nothing*

The Tempest
Othello
Measure for Measure
King Lear
Hamlet
Love's Labour's Lost
Coriolanus
Titus Andronicus
Macbeth
Richard III

When we add ***Venus and Adonis***, and Marlowe's lost play, ***The True History of George Scanderbeg***, with which he is personally identified by Gabriel Harvey in his cryptic elegiac poem on Marlowe's problematic death in 1593, *Gorgon or the Wonderfull Yeare* in which the wonderful year noted for miracles and strange happenings is not 1588 but 1593! the conclusion is irresistible.[45]

Bearing in mind *where* the Book List of this personal library was found, in the correspondence of the Anthony Bacon Papers, together with other documentary evidence relating to Le Doux, the logical progression is obvious and compelling.

The discovery of these documents, with the listing of numerous source books for Shakespeare's *and* Marlowe's plays in the personal library of an intelligence agent who also knew Thomas Walsingham's brother, and who was working for Marlowe's friend and colleague Anthony Bacon, preserved among Anthony's Papers, and endorsed by name, *"le coffre de M. Le Doux"* and the *"catalogue des livres de Monsieur Le Doux"*, presents a clear case of identification. Can it be doubted that the somewhat mysterious agent Monsieur Le Doux is indeed our lost genius, Christopher Marlowe, the Muse's darling, found again as the exiled pseudonymous William Shakespeare?

---

[45] See Wraight: *The Story That the Sonnets Tell*, pp.132-38.

MARLOWE AND SHAKESPEARE

William Shakespeare of Stratford-upon-Avon rose from obscure poverty to affluence rapidly from 1594 onwards. Within four years of joining the Lord Chamberlain's Men he had purchased the largest house in Stratford-upon-Avon. He was content to make good money from his role as playbroker in an age when copyright passed to the actors' company with every play sold to them, and authorship was of secondary importance, or none. Although a man of means, he owned no books or manuscripts, not even an English Bible.

In his great two-volume biography of Marlowe, *The Tragicall History of Christopher Marlowe*, John Bakeless had the courage to question the problem of his relationship to Shakespeare. He pondered this for years but finally had to admit defeat.

> "The exact relationship between the work of Marlowe and the work of Shakespeare will remain in doubt for ever."[46]

So inscrutable did their puzzlingly close stylistic relationship appear to him in 1942, that he felt that it would never be resolved. Bakeless squarely faces up to the remarkable *similarities* in the works of Marlowe and Shakespeare, which he sees as undeniable. Today such similarity is ignored or under dispute.

Academic fashion has conveniently forgotten that prior to 1930, or thereabout, the halls of academia resounded with heated debate on how much of Marlowe's work was actually incorporated in the earlier plays, *Titus Andronicus* and *Richard III* especially; whilst *Henry VI 2 and 3* were attributed by a galaxy of eminent scholars to Marlowe in their extant originals in the 1594 and 1595 quartos, *The Contention betwixt the Two Famous Houses of York and Lancaster*, and *The True Tragedy of Richard Duke of York*, which each comprises a major part of the text in the First Folio plays. This latter attribution was confirmed by C. F. Tucker Brooke and John Bakeless, and Allison Gaw added *Henry VI, Part 1* as Marlowe's play in collaboration with Peele and Greene and a fourth minor writer, thus making the whole of the *Henry VI Trilogy* the acknowledged 'Achilles heel' of the First Folio.[47]

The contention over Marlowe's contribution to the Shakespearean plays did not stop there, however. Bakeless writes:

> "Discarding the extremes of speculation, we may make the following list of Shakespeare's source plays in which the influence of Marlowe appears to be important:

---

[46] Bakeless: *op. cit.* Vol.II, p.205.

[47] C. F. Tucker Brooke: *The Authorship of the Second and Third Parts of 'King Henry VI'* (1921).
John Bakeless: *The Tragicall History of Christopher Marlowe* (1942) Vol.II
Allison Gaw: *The Origin and Development of 1 Henry VI: In Relation to Shakespeare, Marlowe, Peele and Greene* (1926).

Merchant of Venice	*Richard III*
Henry VI	*Taming of a Shrew*
Contention and True Tragedie	*Titus Andronicus*
Richard II	*Julius Caesar*"[48]

Richard III has already been mentioned, and added are other plays in which definite traces of Marlowe's hand have been detected:

> *Romeo and Juliet*
> *Henry V*
> *Midsummer Night's Dream*
> *Henry IV*
> *Macbeth*
> *Much Ado About Nothing*
> *King John*
> *Troilus and Cressida*
> *As You Like It*
> *Antony and Cleopatra*
> *Merry Wives of Windsor*
> *Hamlet*
> *King Lear*

The poems *Venus and Adonis*, *Lucrece* and some of the *Sonnets* are also included. A surprisingly catholic list, but given that these opinions were held by scholars of distinction the problem cannot just be summarily dismissed. This, however, was what was done by Professor Peter Alexander, who weighed in with his unprecedented attack on Marlowe in his *Shakespeare's Henry VI and Richard III* in 1929, launching his 'new orthodoxy', debasing Marlowe and elevating Shakespeare with an array of blatantly sophistical arguments. Scorning the total lack of evidence, he averred that Shakespeare had already written *Richard II* *before* Marlowe wrote *Edward II* for the Earl of Pembroke's Men, which he claims Marlowe wrote in imitation of Shakespeare's *Richard II*, thus turning the tables with a vengeance. Marlowe was no longer to be seen as the 'Morning Star' and great innovating genius of the Elizabethan drama, he was merely Shakespeare's egregious plagiarist. This view Alexander promoted vehemently in his *Shakespeare* (1964).[49]

Alexander's forceful intervention to quell the debate was his attempt to save the First Folio from disintegration, which was in itself an admirable objective, but to do so he had to do injury to literary evidence. His academic confrontation with Tucker Brooke over the attribution to Marlowe of *The Contention* and *The True Tragedy* (comprising one half and two-thirds respectively of the text in the First Folio) has been revisited in my study *Christopher Marlowe and Edward Alleyn* (1993), and Alexander's arguments are mercilessly exposed. I regret the necessity for this, but Alexander's wrong turning has been followed too closely to the detriment of generations of scholarly research. Today it is still too often only acceptable in teaching Shakespearean studies to ignore the numerous similarities and emphasize any differences between the styles of Marlowe's and Shakespeare's works, and the fact that they are printed under two different names does

---

[48] Bakeless: *op. cit.* Vol.II, p.217.
[49] See Wraight: *Christopher Marlowe and Edward Alleyn* (1993) pp.113-115.

the rest in ensuring a blinkered appraisal. This approach is in complete contradiction to the findings of scholars prior to Alexander's counterblast which brought the academic world to heel in orthodox unison: with the notable and courageous exception of John Bakeless who, despite the advent of World War Two, managed in 1942 to complete his monumental, definitive biography of Christopher Marlowe, and was still amazed to find that Marlowe's influence or stylistic similarity detectable in the works of Shakespeare was not to be denied. Speculating boldly he wrote attempting to find a rational explanation for this:

> The first and obvious suggestion is that Shakespeare wrote, as most young writers do, under the powerful influence of the foremost author of the moment.
> The second is that the two writers collaborated, Marlowe perhaps aiding in the construction – which in most of these plays is usually typical of his workmanship – and the less experienced dramatist doing most of the actual writing, except for very important scenes. Over the whole result Marlowe may have cast a critical eye, and into it, in rewriting, he may have worked the typical and unmistakable mighty lines which stud these plays.
> *The third is that Marlowe actually wrote the plays in question and that their attribution to Shakespeare is entirely erroneous.* [My emphasis]
> Still a fourth view, one which also accords well with Elizabethan stage practice, is that Shakespeare used as sources early Marlowe plays, which were already forgotten and have now been lost completely; and that in reworking them he had intelligence and literary feeling sufficient to let the more magnificently sonorous passages stand unchanged.[50]

In these suggestions Bakeless is groping for a hypothetical scenario which allows for the learning period of Shakespeare, which presents a total blank until the appearance of *Venus and Adonis* upon the disappearance of Marlowe, both aged twenty-nine. Marlowe had achieved his pre-eminent position as England's premier dramatist beginning his career by writing tragedy – in 1592 Greene hailed him as "Thou famous gracer of tragedians" – and historical drama. The apocryphal *Edward the Third*, an immature work compared with *Edward II*, stands in relation to the great Shakespearean English history cycle as *The Two Gentlemen of Verona* stands in relation to the romantic comedies, as "a beginning; it was an experiment which led to much, it was a repertory of dramatic ideas," which he developed further.[51] What is conveniently overlooked in evaluating the relationship of the plays of Marlowe's canon, many of which have come down to us only in a mutilated condition, and the thirty-six plays of the First Folio, is that the former represent the works of his youth. Of Shakespeare's youthful essays in dramatic composition we have nothing. Up to the age of thirty when *Titus Andronicus* appeared, there is a complete blank. The Marlowe canon stands in relation to the works of Shakespeare as those youthful works Shakespeare would have written, but which are missing.

According to the pundits who cannot see the similarities in the works of Marlowe and Shakespeare, but only concentrate their gaze on the differences, genius is not allowed to develop. The differences are the result of development, but the similarities remain

---

[50] Bakeless, *op. cit.*, p.215.

[51] Edward Dowden ed. *The Warwick Shakespeare: The Comedies* (1893) p.80.

throughout from early works to the end, hence even *King Lear* bears signs of Marlowe's inimitable touch.

The techniques used by Bakeless and all those nineteenth century and early twentieth century scholars who were struck by the similarities of style, expression, vocabulary, dramatic techniques and stage craft in the plays of Marlowe and Shakespeare were the skills of personal experience and judgement of Elizabethan dramatic writing, and their only yardstick the parallelism. This is the unconscious repetition of words, phrases and expressions that are scattered throughout any writer's works. An example of a very close parallelism is the following:

> Dumaine: Sweet Duke of Guise, our prop to lean upon,
> Now thou art dead, here is no stay for us.
> *The Massacre at Paris*, 11.1122-23

> Edward: Sweet Duke of York, our prop to lean upon,
> Now thou art gone, there is no hope for us.
> *Henry VI, 3*, Act II, sc.i, 11.68-69

A close *dramatic* parallelism is the deposition scene in *Edward II* and the deposition scene in *Richard II*: the identical dramatic technique is used in each, even to the inclusion of an interruption by the attending lord, who is angrily cut short by the distressed king half-way through his long speech in this, the most memorable scene in each play, in which each deposed king destroys an object in his despair − King Edward tears up a letter, King Richard shatters a mirror; each king handles his crown, delaying the act of divesting himself of his kingship, using his diadem as an emotive stage prop to heighten the dramatic effect.

The structure of the plays, the use of language and the way in which Marlowe varies his decasyllabic scansion to reflect changes in the mood of the dialogue, have been most sensitively analysed by Bakeless. For instance, to convey the brutality with which Tamburlaine's captives are treated in *Tamburlaine, Part One*, Marlowe adopts short, irregular lines in passages containing abrupt verses "to suggest the bluntness of the soldier:

> "Bring óut/ my fóot-stool
> 1. 1445

> Chide her/ Annípe
> 1. 1315

> Put him ín /agáin.
> 1. 1526" [52]

Marlowe freely adapted his blank verse to suit his characters and their situations. He also uses extra-metrical words and hypermetrical syllables to emphasise emotional tension.

---

[52]   Bakeless, *op. cit.* Vol.II, p.198.

No, nó/ then wíll/ I héad/ long rún/ intó the éarth.
Dr. Faustus 11.1440-41[53]

Again, he sometimes writes in tetrameters, discarding a foot. He does this even as early as in *Dido Queen of Carthage*:

Cárthage,/ my friénd/ ly hóst,/ adiéu.
1. 1151[54]

These tricks, and others used by Marlowe, Shakespeare also uses. As I have shown elsewhere, Marlowe's creation of his "high astounding terms" was, I believe, his deliberate attempt to find a medium to express the "high astounding" persona of the great Scythian conqueror who is the hero of his two-part dramatisation of the astonishing career of the historical Tamburlaine.[55] After *Tamburlaine* he dropped it. This is development even early on in his youthful career. To suggest that such a highly creative genius would stop developing as he matured is contrary to all the laws of genius.

Such subtleties of style as these are not reflected in the stylometric computerised analyses now being undertaken on the comparison of texts. This method can claim to be scientific as compared with the unscientific method of textual analysis aided by the yardstick of the parallelism, which is bound to be subjective. Its value, however, is that this old-fashioned yardstick can be understood and evaluated by the reader. On the other hand, a stylometric assessment is unfortunately not open to critical evaluation by the layman who has no means of checking the figures so coldly, presented as evidence of authorship; the statistical evidence has to be taken on trust. If an error of judgement is incorporated in the computer program, this cannot be detected except by an expert. A weakness in such stylometric techniques is that there is no way of building into the programme the historic element. We do not know, nor can we **hope** to know, precisely when each of Shakespeare's plays was first conceived by **mere examination** of the printed text as they have probably all, to some extent, undergone later revision. The 1598 publication of *Love's Labour's Lost* states definitely that it is "Newly corrected and augmented". How many other plays were revised during their existence as playscripts, in many cases until 1623?

Every writer or composer knows full well that their works undergo alteration, often drastic, before publication. In Shakespeare's works this is particularly relevant to the Sonnets which, as I have shown, were undoubtedly extremely carefully revised by their author for the late publication in 1609 in a deliberately cryptic edition, presenting a subtle a-chronological mix-up to obscure the autobiographical story they tell. This cryptic intent, once perceived, is in fact the most revealing aspect of Thorpe's clever edition.

Each method has its limitations, but today we are increasingly able to cite confirmation from old and new techniques, to show that we are at last on the right road to the discovery of the *real* Shakespeare.

---

[53] *Ibid.* p.197.
[54] *Ibid.* p.199.
[55] Wraight: *op. cit.* pp.9-10 and pp.63-4.

WHO WAS MONSIEUR LE DOUX?

Who, then, was Monsieur Le Doux? This is the intriguing question we can now attempt to answer with confidence, drawing on all the known facts that history has presented.

1. From the analysis of the Book List of *"Les livres de M. Le Doux"* it is to be concluded that he was in fact an Englishman who was an intelligence agent posing as a "French gentleman" as his cover. We have seen that he possessed lexicons and language reference books on all the other relevant Continental languages, *with the exception of English*. He also recently bought in London a newly-published handbook which was an aid to learning French at a sophisticated level, and possessed another which was an aid to learning French and Italian, as a "recreation" and not as a school book, so evidently for his personal use.

2. He is now working for the Earl of Essex having gained this assignment through his friend and colleague Anthony Bacon, the well-born nephew of Lord Burghley, both of whom were closely associated with Marlowe.

3. *"Le coffre de M. Le Doux"* reveals that he had worked for Lord Burghley and Sir Francis Walsingham and had done intelligence work concerning Scotland, as had Marlowe.

4. He receives what looks like *special* protection and assistance from Anthony Bacon while in England, being sent to Rutland to be accommodated at Burley as a "favour" by Sir John Harington, head of the sympathetic, advanced-thinking (free-thinking) family well known to Anthony Bacon. This suggests that they were also Freemasons whose ethical tradition is to give aid to brother Freemasons in trouble, as Marlowe then was. (See my forthcoming book, *The Legend of Hiram*.)

5. Le Doux owns a library of 56 books of which 16 relate to subjects relevant to either his intelligence career or other interests, and the remaining 40 are all to some degree associated with the creative writing of the works of Shakespeare or Marlowe's canon prior to 1593.

6. Le Doux appears suddenly from nowhere and as suddenly disappears again. He has no known Christian name suggesting that Le Doux is indeed a cover-name as was La Faye, used by his colleague Anthony Standen, with the difference that Standen is identified unequivocally, and Le Doux's identity remains a mystery, and this obscurity seems to be quite deliberate.

7. Le Doux claims to have a good knowledge of Italy and he is directed to return there to complete his extensive assignment for Essex. Italy is indicated as the place of Marlowe's exile by (i) the need to put "large lengths of miles" ... "of both sea and land" between him and possible pursuers suspicious of the Deptford murder; (ii) the undeniable Italian influence in the Shakespeare plays now emerging from the pen of a dramatist of thirty years, whose creative powers had matured.

8. The Deptford 'murder' has aroused suspicion and incredulity even among scholars whose perception of Marlowe is coloured and blurred by the pressures of academic

orthodoxy. The reasons for assessing it as a faked murder devised by his good friend and patron, Thomas Walsingham, a Master secret service agent who had all the expertise necessary for accomplishing this, are obvious to the unprejudiced mind, and are only rejected by those who have a vested personal interest in ignoring this compelling evidence with ostrich-like irrationality.

9. Marlowe's faked death and exile are confirmed by the testimony of SHAKE-SPEARES SONNETS as a historic autobiographical fact in his *Sonnet 74* and the deeply moving record of *The Sonnets of Exile*.

10. The Le Doux manuscripts have been favourably compared with the manuscript of Marlowe's **Massacre at Paris**, this verdict to be confirmed pending examination by experts in the identification of Elizabethan autographs. The fact that Le Doux's *"coffre"* list is written in the English Secretary hand, and not in the Italic hand normally used by French writers, also has significance.

11. Internal literary evidence is abundantly provided in the works of Shakespeare: (i) by the autobiographical SONNETS, printed in a cryptic and sophisticated a-chronological format; (ii) by the plays which are the mature works of the dramatist who had already established his dominance over the English stage as the great innovative genius of the dramatic form we know as 'Shakespearean' blank verse drama, outstripping all his contemporaries. Even orthodox Shakespearean scholars have to admit that Marlowe preceded Shakespeare in all essentials and made straight the path he was to follow.

12. As a poet Marlowe had matured early, while he had yet a lot to learn about stage-craft and dramatic interpretation and presentation in his bold break with the principle of the Three Unities. His exquisite narrative poem *Hero and Leander* outshines *Venus and Adonis* as a more mature work (though supposedly written by Shakespeare at precisely the same age as Marlowe in 1593). *Venus and Adonis* was Marlowe's own earlier narrative poem, written c. 1590 for the young Earl of Southampton when he had composed seventeen sonnets to the Earl as a commission from his employer, Lord Burghley, to persuade the seventeen-year-old Earl to marry. It was not printed until 1593 as "the first heir of my invention" over the chosen name of his pseudonym, 'William Shakespeare', after having contracted a deal with the said William Shakespeare through the printer Richard Field, who hailed from Stratford-upon-Avon. The latter is a logical deduction from the historical context and fits all the facts.

These are historically verifiable facts, not a concocted theory, which together all support each other to form a web of valid evidence that satisfactorily answers the question. Monsieur Le Doux and Christopher Marlowe are one and the same person. Christopher Marlowe adopted the cover-name Monsieur Le Doux while paying a visit to England in 1595 and 1596. Amazingly, he left a trail of personal manuscripts behind by which it has been possible to identify him. Was this perhaps intentional in the hope that one day someone would find them and reveal the true man behind his anonymous pseudonym?

In these manuscripts Monsieur Le Doux has sat for his portrait, and we can clearly discern him. It is a portrait of the successful secret service agent Christopher Marlowe identified by his *"coffre"*, while his library corresponds to every aspect we recognize in what the plays and his life tell us about Marlowe *alias* Shakespeare – his ardent pursuit of knowledge, his concerned involvement with philosophical and ethical problems of humanity as well as manifesting his cultural, literary tastes. These are as characteristic of the young Marlowe as they are evident in the mature Shakespeare plays. All this accords with the historical scenario presented, not vaguely as a mere hypothesis, but precisely at every point touched.

Any academic unbeliever locked in the Stratfordian straitjacket determined to deny or dispute this conclusion must first convincingly refute and answer the above twelve points with valid historic as well as literary, textual evidence. This cannot be done without ignoring and twisting Shakespeare's own words. They are the rock on which the case rests.

Thus from the evidence of these invaluable manuscripts, which have lain undiscovered for 400 years, a great historic mystery has been resolved. Combined with the clear testimony of Shakespeare's own words in his Sonnets and plays, we are able finally to come so close to proving the case, that we can now write "QED" to the vexed problem of the authorship of Shakespeare. This should produce both a sigh of relief and a thrill of excitement, for the true-life story uncovered is astonishing, of a life worthy of our greatest genius in its dramatic eventfulness, a saga stranger than any fiction we could invent. Moreover, the portrait presented of Shakespeare the man, reveals him as someone we can know as a human being and admire and love; a man who wore his genius lightly as he bestrode the Elizabethan world from the shoemaker's shop to the English court at its highest level, and doubtless of several Continental courts as well. He was a real man with an unusually wide experience of life.

Prospects for Future Research

To go forward we must first look back. The amazing documents so unexpectedly discovered open up an entirely new field of exciting research on Marlowe the intelligence agent, as well as Marlowe the dramatist. But to be absolutely sure of our case, let us judiciously weigh the evidence.

Firstly, the name. We have here a new secret agent, Monsieur Le Doux, speaking and writing fluent French, who suddenly emerges from nowhere, but is credited with particular knowledge of Italy, though not an Italian, but introduced to Essex as a "French gentleman". He is never given a Christian name, but is always referred to as Le Doux, and signs himself Le Doux, spelling it "Doulx". Is this a reference to its derivation from 'dolce', Italian for 'sweet', perhaps?

Since Le Doux is a secret agent, one must wonder whether Monsieur Le Doux is his cover-name, as Anthony Standen's was Monsieur La Faye. Regarding Standen we know that he also used the alternative *alias* Andree Sandal and letters signed with both his cover-names and with his own name Standen abound in the Bacon files. But Le Doux is always just Le Doux. Jaques Petit's and Ide du Vault's letters refer to him only as Le Doux, as do Anthony Bacon and Jean Castol. As suddenly as he emerges in October 1595 at Burley, just as suddenly he disappears. We lose track of him after his last letter dated 22nd June 1596 written to Anthony Bacon from Middelburg, in which he mentions the place names Brabant, Hulst, Axel, Ostend and "Neuport", and he is evidently accompanying Henri d'Eberbach, servant of Baron Zeirotine, the Ambassador from the Emperor, to whose court the "Memoires Instructives" direct him. It seems strange, too, that only three letters from him exist.

The huge assignment on Italy which he was charged with preparing for the Earl of Essex has not been found in these papers to date. If it was delivered to Essex it may have perished when the Countess of Essex (née Frances Walsingham and the widow of Sir Philip Sidney) went to Essex House in a panic and destroyed great quantities of her husband's papers in case they contained incriminating evidence that might be used against him at his trial. The search for this document must be continued.

Secondly, the significant evidence to weigh in the scale of probability is that this secret agent possessed a personal library of 56 books which exhibits an exact correlation of taste and interests with the taste and interests of the agent and dramatist Christopher Marlowe, and of the author of the First Folio. Not only are his books to a remarkable degree the sources of the Shakespeare plays, but the high proportion of history books (14 books on history out of 56 books is just 25%) represents an unusually high correlation with the specialist interest of Marlowe and Shakespeare in this subject. History was the main inspiration of Marlowe's plays and his lifelong passion. As a child he was steeped in the history of Canterbury, both ancient and in its living history, when stirring events left their indelible impression on his formative years. At age eight, the influx of Huguenot refugees into Canterbury telling tales of the horror of the St. Bartholomew's Eve massacre; at age nine, the visit of Queen Elizabeth who resided for a fortnight close to his home by St. George's Gate; at age fourteen, the visit of Sir Philip Sidney and

Prince John Casimir; these were boyhood highlights in a city that was the gateway to the Continent, and the seat of the Primate of England.

Of these 14 history books, four books were on Turkish history, with one on the history of Ethiopia, a country in which the dying Tamburlaine shows interest:

> I meant to cut a channel ...
> That men might quickly sail to India.
> From thence to Nubia near Borno-lake,
> And so along the Ethiopian sea,
> Cutting the tropic line of Capricorn,
> I conquered all as far as Zanzibar.
>
> *The Second Part of Tamburlaine the Great*, V, iii, 135-40

Africa held a fascination for Marlowe also, and Turkey exerted a strong influence on his imagination from his youth. Of the four books on Turkish history, two are about Scanderbeg, *alias* Prince Castrioto of Albania. Is it a mere coincidence that Le Doux and Marlowe share this rather unusual interest in a somewhat obscure fifteenth century Albanian Prince? In his library there is not just one book, but *two* devoted to this admittedly amazing character: and not one book on Turkish history, but *four*. If we include the lost play *The True History of George Scanderbeg* in the Marlowe canon, we have three plays on Turkish history out of a canon of eight plays, of which *Edward II* is English history based on Holinshed, the major source of Shakespeare's great English history cycle. If we include *Edward III*, which I have attributed outright to Marlowe, we have another English history play based on Holinshed – the play which was the inception of the vogue for English historical drama from 1588 until 1604 and produced over 200 plays in this genre. There is also a historical basis and a Turkish historical element in *The Jew of Malta*, and *Dr. Faustus* derives from a historical personage. *The Massacre at Paris* is contemporary history dramatized, and the apocryphal *Arden of Faversham*, which is in my critical assessment of the play without doubt Marlowe's work, is the dramatization of local domestic history also recorded by Holinshed, and known first-hand from Marlowe's father who may have witnessed the burning of Alice Arden at Canterbury in his boyhood. She hailed from John Marlowe's native town, for his village of Ospringe is no more than a suburb of Faversham where this notorious lady murdered her husband. *Dido Queen of Carthage* is historical legend. The interest in history is demonstrably exceptionally strong in both the plays of Marlowe and Shakespeare and in the choice of reading matter purchased by Monsieur Le Doux. Can this be dismissed as merely an interesting coincidence?

If we turn to the plays of Shakespeare this same historical bias is apparent, though balanced by the development of romantic comedy and tragedy based largely on the tales of the Northern Italian writers, Bandello, Boccaccio, Cinthio and Fiorento, as well as the Latin and Greek sources already cited. Shakespeare's English history cycle yields ten plays based on Holinshed's *Chronicles* of the reigns of the English kings, of which the *Henry VI Trilogy* on the Wars of the Roses, now attributed to Marlowe, must surely have only found its way into the First Folio by way of later revision, whereby the playscripts came into the hands of the Lord Chamberlain's Company *via* their playbroker, William Shakespeare. In addition, we have *Macbeth*, based on Scottish history; *King Lear*, based on ancient British history; three plays based on Roman history, and six plays based on Roman and Greek historical legend. Altogether, 21 plays out of 37 great dramatic works inspired by history demonstrates keen interest and avid reading of historical matter, such as is evidenced in the library of Monsieur Le Doux.

Somewhere in his exile Marlowe must have got hold of or brought with him a copy of Holinshed, and I suggest that the marvellous Holinshed collection in the Folger Shakespeare Library and in other archives should be re-investigated in case marginal annotations, however slight, might lead to a clue. Such marginal annotations in faded brown ink do exist in the copy in the British Library of John Shute's *Two Very Notable Commentaries* of 1562, which includes the history of Scanderbeg that Marlowe might have used while at Cambridge. Though only single words, these annotations bear a distinct resemblance to Marlowe's hand as in *The Massacre* 'Leaf'.

Harvey's significant apostrophizing of Marlowe as "Scanderbeg" and the "Scanderbegging wight" in his weird, cryptic poem, *Gorgon, or the wonderfull yeare*, (the year being 1593, the year when wonders were performed!) published in September 1593, has been largely ignored by scholars because they could not make head or tail of it. Only Virginia Stern in her critical biography, *Gabriel Harvey: A Study of His Life, Marginalia and Library* (1979) has elucidated the meaning of Harvey's references to the contemporary political events and persons, and has thrown significant light on Harvey's use of the archaic words with which he deliberately obfuscates his readers. However, in the light of the evidence of Marlowe's true identity as the pseudonymous Shake-speare of the Sonnets, and hence of the entire Shakespearean canon, reinforced by the present evidence of his after-life in exile as Monsieur Le Doux, we can now take our understanding of Harvey's poem a step further; particularly with reference to Marlowe, about whose mysterious death this mysterious poem is obscurely telling us great "News" – news which he dares not disclose openly.[56] Harvey's strange "Sonet", as he calls it, is an unique and very important item of contemporary, literary evidence. Only now, by the piecing together of all the known facts, duly weighed and carefully considered, does Harvey's jigsaw fit precisely and, in the end, most satisfyingly into the picture of Deptford in 1593, where a "wonderfull" event was enacted – a death that was not a death.

Confirmation of Harvey's "Sonet" is presented in another important collection of sonnets, equally misunderstood unless related to the Deptford "wonderfull" event. Not until sixteen years after Deptford, in 1609, did Marlowe dare to publish his autobiographical sonnet-sequence, which tells us about his exile and escape from imminent persecution and almost certain death as a heretic. Two sonnets placed at the heart of the sequence are highly relevant. They look back on his life and his miraculous escape from death in 1593, when his pseudonymous identity as William Shakespeare was launched with his purchase of the name from the man who became the playbroker and posthumous custodian of his dramatic works in the First Folio. These poems are imbued with the sense of his inevitably approaching, impending, actual 'second' death. This probably overtook him after failing health some four years later at about the time that John Fletcher undertook the completion of the last play of the English history cycle, *Henry VIII* or *All Is True*, and the Globe theatre caught fire during its performance on 29th June 1613, going up in flames like a funeral pyre.

---

[56] See Wraight: *The Story That the Sonnets Tell*, pp.130-8.

The two self-identifying sonnets, *Nos. 73* and *74*, are pervaded by a philosophical sadness, as of parting from life and from a very dear friend. In *Sonnet 73*, looking back in his old age upon his youth, he recollects the ruins of the Abbey of St. Augustine, still to be seen today, near his home where he played as a boy, the "Bare ruin'd choirs, where late the sweet birds sang". The historic iconoclasm of Henry VIII's destruction of the once great abbey bit deep into his soul, as revealed by his double repetition in *Edward II* and *The Massacre at Paris* of words that painfully reflect this.[57] He concludes his sonnet with an English quotation of his motto, 'QUOD ME NUTRIT ME DESTRUIT', so self-assuredly presented in his *impresa* portrait painted in 1585 at the age of twenty-one, in celebration, I suggest, of his first important assignment as a secret agent. Naturally, he sat for it in his fine, new doublet, paid for no doubt from the money he had earned, and which he was now entitled to wear as a servant of the Queen. Here he has written his farewell to life.

> ....
> In me thou seest the twilight of such day
> As after sunset fadeth in the West,
> Which by and by black night doth take away,
> Death's second self that seals up all in rest.
> In me thou seest the glowing of such fire
> That on the ashes of his youth doth lie,
> As the death-bed, whereon it must expire,
> *Consum'd with that which it was nourish'd by.*
> This thou perceiv'st, which makes thy love more strong
> To love that well, which thou must leave ere long.

Sonnet 74, that follows in this undoubtedly linked sonnet-pair, continues in reflective mood giving comfort to his friend and patron at whose home he had been arrested, and was mercifully granted bail.

> But be contented: when that fell arrest
> Without all bail shall carry me away,
> My life hath in this line some interest,
> Which for memorial still with thee shall stay.
> When thou reviewest this, thou dost review
> The very part was consecrate to thee.
> The earth can have but earth, which is his due;
> My spirit is thine, the better part of me.
> So then thou has but lost the dregs of life,
> The prey of worms, my body being dead,
> The coward conquest of a wretch's knife,
> Too base of thee to be remembered.
> The worth of that, is that which it contains,
> And that is this, and this with thee remains.

Here, assuredly, we have the reason why Thorpe's edition of SHAKE-SPEARES SONNETS was suppressed, as so many scholars have concluded. There were some who

---

[57] *Edward II*, 11.392-7; *The Massacre at Paris*, 11.1212-16.

were fearful that the cat had been let out of the bag, despite the cryptic veil cleverly cast by the Poet and his Publisher, which has however fooled us for almost 385 years. They had faith in their ability to fool us and took the risk.

Shakespeare's Touchstone, a character living in exile, complained ruefully:

> "When a man's verses cannot be understood, nor a man's good wit seconded with the forward child understanding, it strikes a man more dead than a great reckoning in a little room".
>
> *As You Like It*, III, iii 9-13

How well he understood human fallibility, our propensity for turning a blind eye!

Poetry and plays are one thing; documentary evidence, until now lacking, is what impresses the intelligent critic, and rightly so. Next to the contents of his library, the most important piece of documentary evidence that commands our attention in this investigation is the amazing list of assignments endorsed *"le coffre de Monsieur Le Doux"*. Let us look at it more closely.

The list begins with eleven itemized bundles of letters revealing the people with whom Le Doux had correspondence. The "Ltres" are listed in French. The correspondence is particularly interesting in its revelation of contacts with other known top agents in Anthony Bacon's employ, and with highly placed personages in Scotland: the agents with whom he was in correspondence were Anthony Rolston, whose coded letters from Spain are in the files; Anthony Standen (*alias* La Faye and Andree Sandal), and Edward Yates. He also corresponded with Nicholas Faunt, Sir Francis Walsingham's secretary, and Sir Anthony Perez, from whom he also had copies of other letters and papers touching his activities both before and after his departure (presumably on 11th July 1595 as referred to on page 92). Letters from "my L. Tresorer" is an important bundle as this is Lord Burghley, to whom Marlowe would have been directly answerable, the more especially after Sir Francis Walsingham's death in 1590.

These papers seem to go back for several years, probably covering the whole of Le Doux's career as an agent. His contacts with Scotland are of special significance. He was in correspondence with Thomas Moresin, a physician and diplomat in Scotland who was also in correspondence with Anthony Bacon from 1593; and with a "Mr. Bruz" who is most likely to have been Robert Bruce, minister of Edinburgh, rather than Edmund Bruce, an agent in Italy, for there is no other evidence in Le Doux's assignments papers that he was employed in intelligence work in Italy prior to 1595, when the last dated bundle of papers is listed; this being the date when his *"coffre"* was presumably left with Anthony Bacon for safe-keeping, as he did not want to take a chest of valuable, highly secret papers with him on his travels during this next extensive assignment for Essex. He also had letters from Sir Richard Cockburne, Secretary to James VI, King of Scotland, and from "grand seigneures" and gentlemen of Scotland. Among other bundles of papers relating to Scotland are two entitled "Secrett memories of Scotland" and "Autre livre de memories d'Ecosse"; "The general causes of the disorders mutinies in the Scotish common wealth"; "The tree of the comon wealth" (which may refer to Scotland); and a paper that must date from 1594 when this plot of an alleged assassination attempt was discovered: "Docteur Loppes confession to poison her Ma[jes]tie & les instructions pour my Lord Wimes", who was Lord Wemyss, the Scottish Ambassador. Le Doux was evidently a top secret agent who had dealings with important personages in the political scene, and especially in connection with Scotland, where the unstable situation was causing grave concern to Lord Burghley and Queen Elizabeth. The discovery of the notorious affair known as the "Spanish Blanks" in the autumn of 1592 revealed the plotting of the Scottish Catholic Earls of Angus, Errol and Huntly, secretly to give aid to a Spanish invasion. The "Blanks" were blank pieces of paper bearing the signatures of these Catholic noblemen, on which the Spanish invasion plans would be written as though authorized by the Scottish Earls. Burghley's secret negotiations with the Earl of Bothwell were also coming to a head in May 1593, and Robert Poley was sent to Scotland twice that year. All this activity lends credence to Kyd's statement concerning Marlowe:

> "He wold perswade with men of quallitie to goe vnto the K of Scotts whether I heare Royden is gone and where if he had livd he told me when I sawe him last he meant to be".[58]

Kyd had claimed under duress that he had had nothing to do with Marlowe for two years which, if to be believed, means that this was told to him in 1590 or '91. Kyd wrote this in his letter to Lord Keeper Puckering attempting to incriminate Marlowe in some way, which shows how little Kyd really understood of what Marlowe's reason for going to Scotland would have been, if he had, in fact, been so rash as to intimate his movements to Kyd, whom he had obviously regarded as a friend.

The interesting revelation of Le Doux's assignments list is that this otherwise new and unknown secret agent had had close connections with Scotland, the kind of involvement we would expect Marlowe to have had. Since Monsieur Le Doux had been in touch with Scottish "men of quallitie" as Marlowe had, one would have expected to find a bundle of correspondence in his *"coffre"* labelled "Ltres de Mr. Marlowe". It is perhaps strange that although Le Doux's list of contents of his chest includes letters from other known agents, there is nothing from the agent Christopher Marlowe. Could this be because Le Doux is the *nom-de-guerre* of Marlowe, and he would of course not write letters to himself?

The prolific correspondence of Anthony Standen in the Anthony Bacon Papers, totalling 131 separate communications, many of which cover from two to as many as three, four or five folios, indexed in many cases with the names of the correspondent to whom he is writing, does not once list Monsieur Le Doux as correspondent. Yet Le Doux owns a bundle of "Ltres de Mr. Standen". The same applies to the much less prolific correspondence of Anthony Rolston, a mere 31 letters – but not one written to our Monsieur Le Doux, although he owns a bundle entitled "Ltres de Monsr Rowleston". In the Bacon files only three letters from Le Doux, all to Anthony Bacon, are extant. Although Le Doux was evidently the recipient of letters from Standen, Rolston, and a great many other people, he seems to have written few letters himself.

A tremendous amount of research is waiting to be done deriving directly from the exciting implications of the list of assignments, which cannot fail to expand our

---

[58] Kyd's Second Letter to Lord Keeper Puckering.
See Wraight & Stern: *In Search of Christopher Marlowe*, p.316.

knowledge of the secret service, and of Marlowe's involvement in it. I hope that others will join in the quest for information that this treasure trove of documentation contained in the Anthony Bacon Papers promises. Ideally a team of researchers should work in collaboration to comb the vast amount of papers requiring the skill not only of historians expert at reading manuscripts, but having linguistic skill, for many are in Italian as well as in French and in Spanish and Latin.

Le Doux's "coffre" list represents, I believe, Marlowe's probable career in espionage, from the earliest dated item, "of the Princes & present state of Christendome 1582", which looks as if this might have been a paper given to him when he was first recruited and was being inducted into the ways and skills of the secret service. In 1582 Marlowe was aged eighteen, and he may have been required to study for his new career alongside his preparation for gaining his BA which he achieved on the Palm Sunday of 1584, when his name was entered in the University Grace Book, and thenceforth he was "Dominus" Marlowe. It was from this time that his extended absences from his college are recorded, implying that he was away on government service in Rheims.

This was probably Marlowe's first important assignment in his new career in espionage and intelligence, which had evidently brought him to the notice of the Queen, for her approval of his services is mentioned twice in the letter from the Privy Council of 29th June commending his loyal service and assuring the Cambridge authorities of his patriotism.[59] His visit to Rheims had placed him under a cloud of undeserved suspicion as a secret Catholic convert and the University accordingly threatened to withhold the granting of his Master's Degree. The testimonial from the Privy Council, signed by Archbishop Whitgift and Lord Burghley, is an invaluable record establishing Marlowe's status as a government agent as early as 1584-5.

Another direct link suggesting that the "coffre" belongs to Marlowe may be seen in the papers of Sir Francis Walsingham's service as ambassador in Paris at the time of the massacre of St. Bartholomew's Eve in 1572 (item 13 in the "coffre" list). These may have passed to him on Sir Francis's death in 1590 and would have provided him with first-hand data for his French political drama *The Massacre at Paris*, the last known play written in his own name. A tribute to Sir Francis?

Thus, gradually the portrait of Marlowe, the intelligence agent who was also the acknowledged creator of Shakespearean drama, is emerging revealing him to us as he really was, and not as he has been malignantly painted. Was he, or was he not, the pseudonymous William Shakespeare? The answer must be unequivocal, based firmly on evidence, not hypothesis or wishful thinking.

The entrenched Stratfordian orthodox case for the *prima facie* and unquestioning acceptance of the authorship of the works by William Shakespeare of Stratford is justified by the same fears that assailed the theologians and doctrinaire ecclesiastics of Galileo's day, who viewed Copernicanism as dangerous to scriptural authority. Galileo himself was concerned in "trying to offer reassurance to people who were understandably worried that scripture might be left undefended from bizarre and subversive private

---

[59]   *MS. Acts of the Privy Council, VI,* 29 June 1587
        See Wraight & Stern: *op. cit.* p.88

opinions".[60]   Today the often perverse and conflicting theories that surround the Shakespearean authorship question, entailing personal attacks on William Shakespeare of Stratford, are countered by a stoic orthodox refusal to examine anything critical of the Stratfordian case. Understandably, where the alternative is either a Babel of voices in contending, unproven theories or loyalty to orthodox dogma, a stone-wall defence that admits no doubts is judiciously maintained to protect the Stratfordian idol.

Predictably and ironically, it will be the zealous promoters of Bacon or de Vere and other anti-Stratfordian theories who will prove most adamantly averse to considering the new evidence here presented, because only their own candidate is of interest to them. Disregard of contrary evidence is inherent in these theories. Ironically the die-hard orthodox Shakespeareans, whose vested interest is in Stratford, and the anti-Stratfordian zealots make common cause, each locked in impenetrable self-delusion.

Wise counsel persuaded me to wait for over thirty years before bringing the overwhelming evidence of SHAKE-SPEARES SONNETS to the open forum, first making certain that every aspect bearing on the case – including every *contrary* piece of evidence – had been tested and passed as totally valid. In the labyrinth of Elizabethan history and literature only a rigorous scientific approach can bring certainty to the revelations it so richly, and sometimes misleadingly, affords. My aim is not to unseat the revered figure of William Shakespeare, but to show him in *his* true light. He will remain inevitably forever linked with the man whom Ben Jonson apostrophized in the First Folio as "my beloved the AUTHOR, Mr. William Shakespeare". When the remarkable evidence that this great book was a Masonic publication is finally evaluated, all that was so puzzling and misunderstood will be made clear. William Shakespeare of Stratford is revealed as the man chosen to fill the empty niche of the true Author, who had to remain concealed for his own safety and that of his advanced-thinking friends. The playbroker William Shakespeare played his part to full satisfaction and was well remunerated, retiring a wealthy and solid citizen to be posthumously transformed into the "Divine William" who is the embodiment of the myth. As a myth-figure he deserves to remain secure at Stratford-upon-Avon, the home of the myth where the great works are worshipped irrespective of who wrote them. His task was to act as protector of the works, enabling them to be published for posterity without endangering their concealed Author and his loyal and devoted friends. The history of literature affords no stranger story. Why should anyone wish to destroy or deny it, or belittle its unique place in our cultural heritage? It was an extraordinary partnership of necessity.

The most important of the documents discovered is undoubtedly the List, written in the Italic hand as used in his letters, of the working library of **Monsieur Le Doux**, the cultured, literary, intelligence agent, whose books are the sources of the Shakespeare plays *and* strongly reflect Marlowe's personal interst in Turkish history. In Le Doux's library we find Marlowe *linked with* Shakespeare. The true relationship between Marlowe and Shakespeare is established in a coherent, seamless scenario revealing the truth about this troubled genius in his exile. These twin playwrights emerge as, not two, but one and the same incomparable English poet-dramatist, the **pseudonymous William Shakespeare**, who was launched with *Venus and Adonis* in 1593 upon the 'death' of Christopher Marlowe, who had been hailed only six months before as "Thou famous

---

[60]   Michael Sharratt: *Galileo, Decisive Innovator* (1994) Blackwell Science Biographies, p.124.

gracer of Tragedians". There was no hint of any William Shakespeare as his rival then. Marlowe reigned supreme.

The scholars of the nineteenth and early twentieth century who were 'disintegrating' the First Folio with comparisons between Marlowe's known works and the Shakespeare plays were more attuned to the truth than they knew; whereas Peter Alexander's 'new orthodoxy' has for decades held Shakespearean scholarship in thrall in a fossilized misconception. Sooner or later the Alexandrian error that led us so badly astray must give way to re-evaluation. The excitement of fresh fields of research promising unknown possibilities beckons enticingly and it will not be possible to order the tide of progress bearing new evidence to recede. This is the voice of reaction, which tried to stifle the great free-thinker, Christopher Marlowe, that reaction which would have destroyed our Shakespeare but for the swift help of his patron and free-thinking friends.

Here the investigation of the authorship of the works of the First Folio and of the Sonnets has been presented from many angles, with hitherto unknown documentary evidence to confirm that they are from the hand of Christopher Marlowe, the pseudonymous Shakespeare many have long suspected, whose early work was but the preparation for his glorious maturity. This newly discovered documentary evidence, which is fully supported by the internal, literary evidence of the plays and the Sonnets, and by the historical context, merits, at the very least, that the case for Monsieur Le Doux *alias* Marlowe as the pseudonymous Shakespeare in exile be considered seriously and presented to the academic jury and all intelligent readers and lovers of Shakespeare for a verdict.

We may not deny the Muse's Darling a fair hearing.

APPENDICES

APPENDIX 1(a) - Coded message from Anthony Rolston, 10 April 1596
L.P.L. MS 656 f.202

01   Right worshipfull, since my last of the 27 of marche heare ys not
02   any news but that The King ys stil at Aramiues and in hel-
03   th and the prince (54?, usually means 'hath') going to Lisbon ys agayn by
04   letters from this court confirmed and that he ys to
05   depart within 15 dayes but the olde King of France staeth stil
06   at home also we have that 3 ships are to comme from
07   Lisbon to Passage,[1] before the end of may, and do
08   bring in them 210 brasse peces artillery to put
09   in the 10 new ships lately made in Renterya[2]
10   which now finished and 2 more wilbe ready
11   within a month and this general of Fontarabie[3] hath order
12   to send for a 1000 quintales of pouldre to
13   Burgus and Pamplona which must be at Passage
14   with spede so that the ships wil depart about the end
15   of iune for Lisbon yf other ordre do not come
16   from this King to the contrary. All mariners upon this
17   coast are arrested to go in the ships and allso
18   those that are gon from Passage to Sevil did
19   before they went give bond to retorn
20   within 3 monthes to go in the sayd ships to Lisbon.
21   we heare no more of Sir Francis Drake since his being at
22   Puerto Rico but that he ofted to put men on lande
23   at a place called Buacharra neare to
24   Cartagena and he was repelled thence and this
25   was in Decembre as they write from Lisbon. You
26   shall receyve herwith a declaracion in
27   print of that which passed in Puerto Rico
28   and thus not hauing else to troble you longer
29   most humblie take my leave praynge thalmightie longe to
30   preserve you. Fontarabie the 10 of Aprill 1596. Anthony Rolston[4]

---

[1] Passage (Pasajes or Passaia) is some 15kms east of San Sebastian on the northern coast of Spain. It comprised three villages around a sheltered bay connected with the open sea by only a narrow channel. It provided a perfect natural harbour for commissioning the galleons.

[2] Renteria (Errenteria) was a close neighbour to Pasajes, but nearer the coast itself, and seems to have been where the ships were actually built.

[3] Fontarabie (Fuenterrabia) was about 17km to the east of these. It was a fortress situated at the mouth of the Bidassoa river, which formed the Franco-Spanish border in the heart of the *Pays Basques*.

[4] Most of the frequently named people had three-digit code numbers. '129' was Sir Francis Drake, as used in line 21 above. Rolston's own code was '110'. (So presumably not licensed to kill!)

Santé cent ans, & accomplissement
de voz tres nobles desirs.. 251

Monseigneur, Mr. le baron vous baise les
mains & desire de sçauoir sy on a descouuert
la flotte des Espaignols coma le bruit est
de 150 voiles.

Je croy que Jaques se vengera aujourd'huy
mais ie suis marry qu'il ne le fait de soy mesme
sans y employer aultres moyenneurs. Contre mo
opinion il va trouuer Mr. Castol pour l'y employer & au—iour—d'huy y mettre vne fin.
Je Cela me console q' Mr. Castol
vous est seruiteur & prudens
Commandez moy

Vre treshumble
seruiteur

Le Doulx

136

Santé, cent ans & accomplissement
de voz tres nobles desirs

Monseigneur, Mr le baron vous baise les
mains & desire de scavoir sj on a descouvert
la flotte des Espagnols comme le bruit est
de 150 voiles.

Je croy que Jaques se vengera aujourd'huy
mais ie suis marry qu'il ne le fait de soy mesme
sans y employer aultres moyenneurs. Contre mó [mon]
opinion il va trouver Mr Castol pour l'y employer & au-iour-d'huy y mettre une fin.
Cela me console q [que] Mr Castol
vous est serviteur & prudent

Commandez moy

Vre [votre] tres humble serviteur

Le Doulx

Health [for a] hundred years and fulfilment
of your most noble desires

My Lord, Monsieur le Baron kisses your hands
and wishes to know whether the Spanish fleet
has been discovered as it is rumoured of about
150 sails.

I believe Jaques will avenge himself today but
I am sorry that he does not do it himself without
using other mediators [helpers]. Against my advice
[opinion] he is going to seek out Mr Castol for
this purpose and put an end to it today.

It comforts me that Mr Castol is devoted to you
and is prudent.

Command me

Your very humble servant
Le Doulx

Monsieur hier au soir ie trouuay vn Espagnol nõme Cyprian
& repute' hõme de bien & de scauoir, duquel le filz a servy feu
Mr Welsighan : Iceluy Cyprian m'a dit qu'il est venu de Heübüry
en ceste ville tout expres pour veoir si quelcun des
amys du Sr Anthoine Perez vouldroit faire imprimer sa
version latine de l'histoire dud Sr, Et qu'il se contentera
d'vne mediocre recõpense de son labeur soit en argent
soit en certain nombre d'exemplaires. Ie scay l'affection
que vous portez aud Sr & combien vous estimez
tout ce q est de luy, Et pour le seruice q ie
vous doibs, ie luy desire aussi tout cõtentement. C'est
pourquoy ie vous ay voulu aduertir de cecy, Et vous
prier me faire entendre vre aduis & volonte' cy dessus
Et ne vous eschauffer trop en despense Vn petit
sera beaucoup. Noz francois ne sont pas beaucoup contents de l'hõme
q est en vre librairie. Voz amys en iugent diuersement. Tous vous plaignét
Les aultres pafiet plus oultre

Monsieur, hier au soir ie trouvay vn Espagnol nome [nommé] Cyprian
& reputé home [homme] de bien & de scavoir, le fils duquel a seruy [servi] feu
Mr Welsighan : Jceluy Cyprian m'a dit qu'il est venu de Neübüry
en ceste [cette] ville tout expres pour veoir si quelcun des
amys du Sr Anthoine Perez vouldroit faire imprimer sa
version latine de l'histoire du/ [dudit] Sr, Et qu'il se contentera
d'une mediocre recopense [recompense] de son labeur soit en argent
soit en certain nombre d'exemplaires. Je scay l'affection
que vous portez aud/ [audit] Sr & combien vous estimez
tout ce q [qu'] est de luy, Et pour le service q [que] je
vous doibs [dois], ie luy desire aussi tout cotentement Cest
pourquoy ie vous ay voulu aduertir de cecy, Et vous
prier me faire entendre vre [votre] aduis & volonté cy dessus
Et ne vous eschauffer trop en despense Vn petit
sera beaucoup. Noz francois ne sont pas beaucoup contents de l'home
q'est en vre [votre] librairie. Voz amys en iugent [jugent] diuversement.
Tous vous plaignet. Les aultres passet [passent] plus oultye.

There is no signature as the bottom of the page is torn off.

Sir,   Yesterday evening I met a Spaniard named Cyprian and reputed a man
of virtue and learning, whose son had done service with the late Mr.
Walsingham. This Cyprian told me that he had come from *"Neübüry"* to this
town expressly for the purpose of finding out if any friend of Sir Anthony Perez
would be interested to have his Latin version of the history of the aforesaid Sir
printed, and told me that he would be content with a modest reward for his
labours, either in money or in the form of a certain number of copies. I know
your affection for the said Sir, and how much you value anything concerning him.
And for the duty I owe you, I also wish him every satisfaction. This is why I
wanted to advise you about this and beg you to let me know your opinion and
wishes regarding the above. And do not trouble yourself too much. A little will
be plenty. Our Frenchmen are not very happy with the man who is in your
library. Your friends are of various opinions. They all sympathize with you.
The others pass this by [take no notice?].

Cyprian was a Bishop of Carthage who, persecuted by the Emperors Decius and
Valerian for his religious beliefs, fled first into hiding in his own country, and later into
exile in Spain. This analogy would have been clear to Bacon, but whether it is relevant
in the context of this letter is questionable. This is the most personal of the letters and
is incomplete; the torn off page may therefore have contained very confidential
information.

APPENDIX 2(c) - Letter from Monsieur Le Doux, 22 June 1596.
L.P.L. MS 657 f.227

150
227

Monsieur, mon Seigneur & maistre vous escripuant
i'ay fay ce petit mot pour seruir de couuerture,
a ses lettres, attendant que soyons arriuez en Brabãt
dont nous vous escrirons amplement Cependant
Mons.r le Conte Maurice s'appreste pour obuier aux
dessems de L'Archiduc Albert sur Hulst, Axel,
& Oostende, ses soldats partent ce soir, on
pense q. led S.r Conte partira aussi d'icy ceste
nuict, Le Cardinal estoit à Nieuport il n'y a que 4
iours, Mons.r Eberbach & pour son bon
naturel & pour L'amour de vous me monstre
tresgrande amitie, il est tout oure, &
vous escrira auec meilleure occasion & quãd
il se presentera quelque subiect digne de
vous En attendant luy & moy prions
Dieu de vous donner

Mons.r accomplissement de voz tresnobles
desirs De Mittelburg ce 22 de Juin 1596

Vre tres affectione &
humble seruiteur

Le Doulx

140

Monsieur, mon seigneur & maistre vous escrivant
i'ay fay ce petit mot pour servir de couuerture
a ses lettres, attendant que soyons arriuez en Brabat [Brabant]
dont nous vous escrirons amplement Cependant
Monsr. le Conte Maurice s'appreste pour obuier [obvier] aux
desseings de L'Archiduc Albert sur Hulst, Axel,
& Oostende; ses soldats partent ce soir/ on
pense q [que] led/ [ledit] Sr Conte partira aussi d'icy ceste
nuict, Le Cardinal estoit [était] à Neuport il n'a que 4
iours [jours] Monsr. Eberbach & pour son bon
naturel & pour L'amour de vous me monstre [montre]
tres grande amitie/ il est tout vre [votre], &
vous escrira auec meillure occasion & quad [quand]
il se presentera quelque subiect digne de
vous En attendant Luy et moy prions
Dieu de vous donner
Mr accomplissement de vos tres nobles
desirs De Mittelburg ce 22 de Juin 1596

Vre [votre] tres affectioné &
humble serviteur

Le Doulx

Sir, my lord & master writing to you I have done this short note
to serve as a cover to his letters, while waiting for us to arrive in
Brabant, of which we will write amply to you. However Monsr
the Count Maurice is getting ready to forestall the designs that
Archduke Albert has on Hulst, Axel & Ostend. His soldiers are
leaving this evening. I think that their lord the Count will also
depart from here tonight. The Cardinal was at Neuport only
four days ago. Monsr Eberbach, both by his own humanity and
for love of you, has shown me very great friendship. He is
completely yours and will write to you at the right moment and
when he will present some subjects worthy of you. Meanwhile
he and I pray that God will give you, Sir, fulfilment of your
most noble desires.

From Mittelburg the 22nd of June 1596

Your very affectionate
humble servant
Le Doulx

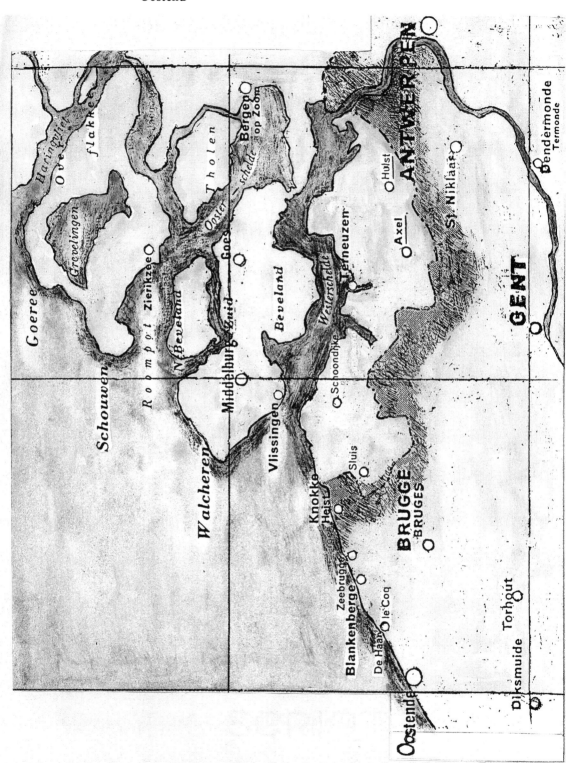

APPENDIX 3(a) - "Cathologue des liures de Mr le Douz", 15 February 1596
L.P.L. MS 655 f.185r

Librorų latinorų index   135
                                           /8   185

Medicina Weckerj in f.°——————— 12
De Origine Turcarų & Scanderseg histo. in f.° 12
Mussulmannica historia Leuenclauij in f.° 10
Paralipomena hist. Turcicæ Leuencla. in 4. 6
Opera succisiuæ Camerarij in 4.————— 8
Dialogj Castalionis ———————— 2
pædagogus freigj ——————————— 2.6
Nomenclator Junij ————————— 3.6
Constantia Lipsij ————————— 1.
                              —————————
                                   2 tt. 17/8

Italicorų.

La Bibbia ———————————————— 11
Le vite de gli Imperatorj ———————— 12
La fabrica del mondo ——————————— 11
Lettere del Tasso in 4.° ——————————— 7
Hecatonmithi ———————————————— 8.6
Gierusalemme liberata ———————— 6.
Gierusalemme conquistata ———————— 6.6
Lhore dj recreatione ———————— 2.6
Dittionario volgare e francese ——— 3.
Sleidano ————————————————— 7
Il Corteggiano in 3. lingue. ——————— 4
Trattemmentj del Bargagļ ——————— 3.
                                   —————
                                   4 tt. 1/8 6

Hispanicorp

· Historia Imperial ——————— 10

· Cromica del prīcipe Castrioto ———— 7

· Auenturas de Antonio Perez ———— 2 · 6

· Las epistolas de Gueuara ———— 6

· Vocabulario de las dos lenguas Tos. y Castellana — 3 · 6

· Historia Ethiopica ————— 3

· Euangelios y actos de los Apostoles cō coment. 2 · 6

· psalmos de Dauid ————— 1 · 6

· Reglas Grammaticales —————— 1 ·

                                 1 ₶ · 17

₶ fioretti della lingua volgare e latina — 1 /8

   the french Alphabet ———— 1

Dos tratados del papa y de la missa — 2 · 6

Bible doree en Anglois ———— 6 ·

Terence en petit volume ————— 1

      Summa summarp 14 ₶ 9 — /8 ·

Gallicor

186

- La deliurance de Hierusalem in 4º — 8
- Hierusalem en rime francoise ——— 3 · 6
- Cornelius Tacitus ——————— 4
- Les harangues militaires ——— 13
- Essays de Montaigne ——— 6
- Les sepmaines du Bartas ——— 6 ·
- Les fables d'Esope en taille doulce — 3 ·
- Sleidan des 4 empires ——— 2   Heny l'a

2 tt s · 18 6 s

Soomma summarp   11 tt 1 /8 ·

- Il nuouo testamento latino
  e volgare ——— 3 ·
- Le coffre de bonne esperance — 12
- Monsr petit vn angelot — 10   Some 12 tt 6/8
- Onomasticon 7. linguar[um] Junij ——— 4
- Sallustio volgare ——— 2 · 6
- Commentarij Cæsaris ——— 2 6
- Sallustius latine ——— 2
- Terentius latine & Italice in 4º ——— 6
- Hercolano del varchi ——— 2 · 6
- Giambularj della lingua fiorentina ——— 3
- Commentaires de Cæsar de Vigenere in fº — 5
- Comedie di plauto ——— 2
- Nomenclator quatrilinguis ——— 2   #

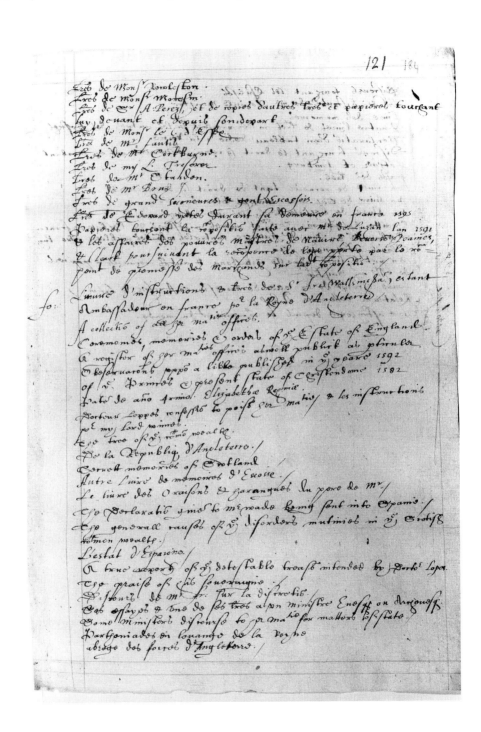

Ltres de Monsr Rowleston [Anthony Rolston, agent of Anthony Bacon]
Ltres de Monsr Moresin [Thomas Moresin, physician and diplomat in Scotland]
Ltres de S^r A: Perez, et de copies d'autres ltres et papières touchant
  luy devant et depuis son depart [Antonio Perez - see text]
Ltres de Monsr le C. d'Este
Ltres de M^r fantis [Sir Francis Walsingham's secretary, Nicholas Faunt?]
Ltres de Mr Cockburne [Sir Richard Cockburn, Secretary to James VI, King of Scotland]
Ltres de my L. Tresorer [William Cecil, Lord Burghley]
Ltres de Mr Standen [Anthony Standen, agent of Anthony Bacon]
Ltres de Mr Bruz [Robert Bruce, minister in Edinburgh, or Edmund Bruce, agent in Italy]
Ltres de grand seigneures & gent Escossois
Ltres de Edward yates durant sa demeure en france 1595 [servant of Anthony Bacon]
Papières touchant la co(m)positio(n) faite avec Mr de Luzan l'an 1591 [de Lussan, Governor
  of Blaye] & les affaires des pauvres Mastres de Navire, Berecson, Jeames(?)
    & Cleart poursuivant la reco(m)pence de --------(?) par le ro-
    pemt de promesse des Marchands sur lad(t) co(m)positio(n)
Livre d'instructions & ltres de Sr fr Wallsingham, estant
  Ambassadeur en france pour la Roy(au)me d'Angleterre [i.e. before 1573, when he returned]
A collection of all her ma(jes)ties offices.
Ceremonies, memories & orders of the Estate of England
A register of her ma(jes)ties offices aswell publick as pticuler
Obeservacons uppo(n) a lible published in the yeare 1592 [by Francis Bacon?]
of the Princes & present state of Christendome 1582
Pate(r?) de an(n)o 4rcino Elizabethae Regniae [quatercentenary was in 1583]
Docteur Loppes confessio(n) to poiso(n) her Ma(jes)tie & les instructions
  pour my Lord Wimes [James Colville, Lord of Wemyss, Scottish Ambassador]
The tree of the como(n) wealth
De la Republiq d'Angleterre
Secrett memories of Scotland
Autre livre de memoires d'Escosse
Le livre des Oraisons & harangues du père de M^r[Possibly Anthony Bacon's father, Nicholas]
The Declaratio(n) given to M^r wade being sent into Spaine [William Waad, agent of Sir F.W.]
The generall causes of the disorders mutinies in the Scotish
  comon wealth
L'estat d'Espaigne
A true report of the detestable treaso(n) intended by Docto^r Lopes (Roderigo Lopez - see text]
The praise of his soveraigne
Discours de M^r fr: sur la discretio(n) [by Francis Bacon?]
Ses essayes & une de ses ltres a un Ministre Evesq ou Archevesq (i.e. Francis Bacon's *Essays*]
Some Ministers discourse to her ma(jes)tie for matters of state
Partheniades en louange de la Reyne
abrege des forces d'Angleterre

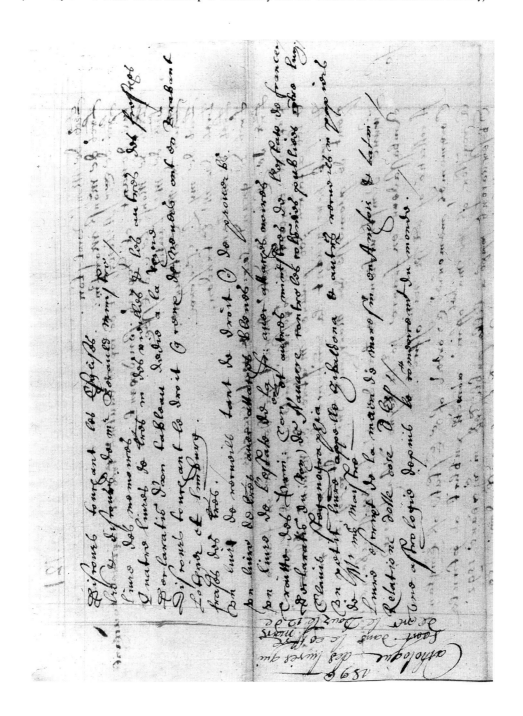

Cathologue des livres qui sont dans le coffre de Mr Le Douz le 12 de mars 1596

Discours touchant les Esglises
Ltrs & discours de Mʳ Berauld Ministre [a contact of Anthony Bacon's in Montauban]
Livre des memoires
Quatre livres de ltres .. des vieilles & les autres des fresches (?)
Declaration d'un tableau dedie a la Reyne
Discours touchant le droit que ceux de Nevers ont en Brabant
  Lothier et Limburg
frases des ltres
Un livre de recueils tant de droit & de proverbs
Un livre de ltres avec attaches bleues
Un livre de l'estate de la fr. avec attaches noires
Traitte des Princes(?) Canons et autres ministres de l'estate de france
Declaration du Roy de Navarre contre les colo(m)nies publies contre luy
Clavis steganographia [cryptographic key, i.e. a code book]
Un petit livre appelle Zibaldona & autres recueils ou papiers
  de Mʳ mon Maistre [Anthony Bacon's commonplace book?]
Livre escript de la main de moresin en Anglois & Latin
Relatione delle dose d'Esp
Une astrologie depuis le co(m)mencem(en)t du monde.

Endorsed: Des vers que Jaques Petit pensait presenter a Sr Antonio Perez
le ijme de Juillet 1595
Le Jour de son depart

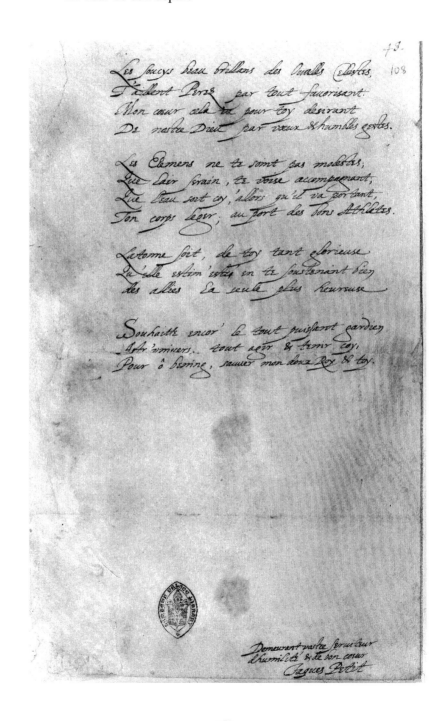

APPENDIX 5(b) - Jaques Petit's Poem L.P.L. MS 653, f.108
translation

This poem is extraordinarily difficult to present in a translation as much of it is not written in sentences. Petit seems content to use words that sound beautiful, are poetic and evocative, and is not concerned whether his poem makes complete sense. Other poems of his in the Bacon Papers are far more straightforward. Below is an attempt at a translation which more or less reflects what he wrote.

> The lovely, radiant solicitude of the celestial flocks
> Go with you, Perez, favouring you everywhere,
> My heart moves desiring this for you
> Of our God by votive offerings and humble deeds.
>
> That the elements may not trouble you,
> That serene air may accompany you,
> That the waters are calm whilst bearing
> Your light body; to the haven of good athletes.
>
> *Latorme [?] be of you so glorious
> That her esteem pleads to sustain you well
> Of the kindred the only most happy.
>
> Wishing again that the all powerful guardian
> Keep astronomers all in stillness
> For O blessed, to save my sweet King and you.

It is signed:

> Demeurant vostre serviteur d'humilite
> & de bon coeur
>
>   Jaques Petit
>
> Remaining your humble servant and of good heart

*   This word I have been unable to trace.

INDEX

156

157